ADVANCE PRAISE
FOR FRANCES WOOD'S
AENEAS ANDERSON IN CHINA

By all accounts the first British Embassy to China under the leadership of Lord Macartney during 1792-4 was part failure, part success, and part circus depending on who was doing the writing. The leading historian of China, Frances Wood has done a great service by producing a republication of the diary of the least prestigious member of the delegation, Aeneas Anderson. Anderson was then valet to Lord Macartney and accompanied the Embassy and its delegation throughout. This account is notable for its observations of Chinese society at the base, free of all the necessary over-intellectualised or over-politicised world views that shaped those of the delegation members served by Aeneas Anderson. China then was certainly different to China now, but there are very clear echoes of the present in Anderson's account, just as one can read into the leadership's misunderstandings at that time echoes of similar over-simplistic views of the Chinese difference in the minds of the contemporary British elite. Essential reading for anyone interested in the foreign intervention in China at the end of its imperial era.

Professor David S. G. Goodman
Professor of China Studies, Xi'an Jiaotong-Liverpool
University and the University of Sydney.

AENEAS ANDERSON
IN CHINA

A narrative of the ill-fated
Macartney Embassy 1792-94

Edited & Introduced
by
Frances Wood

Aeneas Anderson in China

Edited by Frances Wood

ISBN-13: 978-988-8552-45-0

HISTORY / Asia / China

EB119

Published by Earnshaw Books Ltd. (Hong Kong)

FOREWORD

When Lord Macartney set off at the head of Britain's first Embassy to get to China in September 1792, he took an entourage of ninety-five, including his secretary (and deputy ambassador) Sir George Leonard Staunton and two under-secretaries, a surgeon and a physician, several 'mechanics' or technical experts, two artists, two Chinese Jesuit interpreters, a watch-maker and a mathematical instrument maker, two botanists and five German musicians, all protected by ten dragoons, twenty artillerymen and twenty infantry. Staunton brought along his eleven-year-old son and his German tutor, and Macartney took his valet, Aeneas Anderson, who turned out to be a surprisingly enthusiastic tourist and diarist.

Macartney's was not the first Embassy to be sent to China. In 1788, the East India Company had despatched Colonel Charles Cathcart to try and negotiate with the Chinese, but he had died of tuberculosis off Sumatra and, as no deputy ambassador had been appointed to lead negotiations, the Embassy had to turn back. The East India Company persisted because, whilst trade with China was profitable, raising £1,527,775 in 1793, trading conditions imposed by the Chinese government were very restrictive. Lord Macartney's instructions were to negotiate a treaty of trade and friendship, to remove restrictions at Canton (the only port where the British were permitted to trade) and open other ports to British merchants with the cession of an island base, and to establish an ambassador in Peking. None of these were achieved, so his Embassy is generally considered a failure. However, one achievement of the Embassy was that it resulted in no less than eight substantial books.

Of all of these, that written by Macartney's valet, Aeneas Anderson, is the liveliest and most straightforwardly informative. In his immediate reactions and keen interest in everything he saw, he could be a contemporary tourist. Arriving at Tongzhou, where the Embassy had to abandon boat travel and take to the road for last part of the journey to Peking, the Embassy was lodged for four days in an old temple. Anderson lost no time in exploring his first Chinese town. He was 'very much harassed by the curiosity of the people. I was sometimes surrounded by twenty or thirty of them who pressed so much upon me, that I was frequently under the necessity of taking shelter in shops...' where he purchased souvenirs, 'fans and tobacco pipes which were formed with curious neatness and ingenuity'.

He described the town walls and the 'very pleasing' houses, the shops, 'gilt and painted...decorated with streamers which serve as signs to denote the commodities of the particular shops.' He noted that 'glass is not used anywhere in China for windows and the most common substitute for it is a thin glazed paper...'

He also writes of how he tried to find out about how the town was governed and how the law was enforced, finding the people 'happy and contented' and enjoying 'as much liberty as is consistent with the best arrangements of civilised society'. In contrast with Anderson's curiosity, the official account of the Embassy by Sir George Leonard Staunton describes at length the temple in Tongzhou (Tong-chew in Anderson's spelling) where the Embassy was to stay, with an account of Buddhism and Buddhist temples in general, but says almost nothing of the town that Anderson explored so eagerly. Similarly, Sir John Barrow, comptroller of the Embassy, recorded virtually nothing of Tongzhou in his *Travels in China*, 1804, apart from a brief description of the temple.

Anderson had a keen eye and a fine sense of hearing: his rendering of Chinese terms is much closer to reality than that of the more erudite writers such as Staunton and Barrow who entangled themselves in the variety of romanisations then current. Anderson writes, 'Pekin, or as the natives pronounce it, Pitchin' and at the back of his book he includes a glossary of seventy-one useful words and phrases, indicative of careful listening. 'Meeoulaa - have not or cannot (*meiyoule* in today's pinyin); chee-fanna - to eat meats, kowaa - to broil; tchau-wanna - a tea-cup; swee- water; man-toa – bread; loa-boo – turnips; yien – tobacco; tchee-danna (in the northern provinces)- eggs...' None of the other authors showed such a practical interest in the Chinese language: Sir John Barrow instead offers some thirty pages on the Chinese language culled from European literary sources (mainly Jesuit): theoretical, speculative and largely inaccurate.

On place names, however, Anderson's ear, or his informants, were infinitely less accurate. Sadly, it is impossible now to determine the current names of many of the places he mentions on the journey to Rehe/Jehol and on the trip south along the Grand Canal and beyond, to Canton.

Anderson was also the only member of the Embassy to leave quite a few references to Chinese food and its preparation. He describes their 'manner of dressing meat', preferring meat that was broiled rather than fried, notes the use of soy and vinegar as condiments and gives a detailed account of the method of preparing rice (washing, draining, boiling, draining again, then steaming) which he found 'a most excellent substitute for bread'. The British were not keen on steamed bread (Anderson's 'man-toa'), 'the loaves...composed of nothing more than flour and water, and ranged on bars which are laid across an iron hollow pan, containing a certain quantity of water, which is then placed on an earthen stove: when the water boils, the vessel or pan is covered over with something like a shallow tub, and the steam of the water, for a few minutes is all the baking, if it may be so called, which the bread receives.' Anderson found that it was more acceptable when toasted. He was interested in how people ate, too, noting the low tables around which the eaters squatted, wielding their chopsticks ('quoitzau', today rendered in pinyin as *kuaizi*). His description is reflected in some of William Alexander's sketches of the trackers who hauled their boats, squatting to eat with elbows raised high. Alexander was the junior of the two artists who accompanied the Embassy and his hundreds of sketches form a graphic equivalent of Anderson's descriptions of daily life in China.[1]

Anderson's interest in food was of considerable assistance to the Embassy. William Alexander wrote in his diary in November 1793 that Anderson was '...an intelligent man who kept a journal and who was appointed to cook our dinner. His stewed ducks served in an earthenware dish were excellent.'[2] On another occasion, Anderson mentions that he personally organised the heating up of the unpalatably cold food that had been provided for the ambassador and his suite.

Aside from improving the food, caring for Lord Macartney's spotted velvet suit and preparing his garter robes for the imperial audience, Anderson showed himself to be useful to the Embassy in other ways. When they were in Tongzhou, Harry Eades, described by Staunton as 'an ingenious and skilled artist in brass and other metals' from Birmingham, who had volunteered to join the Embassy in order to improve his skills as he had heard that

---

1 See Frances Wood, 'Closely Observed China: from William Alexander's sketches to his published work' in *British Library Journal*, vol. 24, no. 1, Spring, 1998, pp.98-121.
2 Quoted in Aubrey Singer, *The Lion and the Dragon: the story of the first British Embassy to the Court of the Emperor Qianlong in Peking 1792-4*, London, 1992, p. 134.

'many improvements in the arts were practised in Pekin, amongst others, that of making a kind of tinsel that did not tarnish'. Staunton described his burial 'in the midst of several Chinese tombs, interspersed with cypress trees' after a ceremony 'with much gravity and decency' in which 'every form was observed' which he felt was particularly important since a great crowd of Chinese had gathered to watch. What neither Staunton nor Barrow mention is that it was Aeneas Anderson who conducted the funeral: 'As no clergyman accompanied the Embassy, I was appointed to read the funeral service of the Church of England on this melancholy occasion.'

Conscious of the importance of form and, as a valet, conscious of the importance of appropriate clothing, Anderson was shocked when the Embassy left Peking to travel to Rehe to meet the Qianlong emperor. Carts and a carriage were prepared and the musicians and servants were provided with clothing of 'green cloth, laced with gold'. Unfortunately, the state of the clothes 'awakened a suspicion that they had already been frequently worn, and on tickets, sewed to their linings, were written the names of their former wearers; and as many of the tickets appeared, on examining them, to be the visiting cards of Monsieur de Luzerne, the late French Ambassador, that they had been made up for some gala or fête, given by that minister. But whether they were of diplomatic origin, or had belonged to theatres... they were never intended for actual service, being made for only a few temporary occasions...The Chinese may not be supposed to be capable of distinguishing on the propriety of our figures in those ill-fitting uniforms, but we certainly appeared in a very strong point of ridicule to each other...'

Anderson reported the final form of the entry of the Embassy into Rehe headed by the light-horse and infantry with Sir George Staunton in a palanquin and Lord Macartney and his page, young Staunton, in an open carriage 'with a black boy, dressed in a turban, behind it'. The rest of the procession was chaotic and offensive to the valet. 'Some wore round hats, some cocked hats, and others straw hats, some were in whole boots, some in half boots, and others in shoes with coloured stockings. In short, unless it was in second-hand coats and waistcoats, which did not even fit them, the inferior part of the suite did not enjoy even the appearance of shabby uniformity.' This sartorial shambles was, of course, not recorded by either Staunton or Barrow who maintained the dignity of the Embassy throughout.

The 'black boy' who rode postilion had been bought by Sir George Staunton in Batavia, on his way to China. Anderson mentions him in a very surprising passage which, once again, reveals much about his curiosity and his willingness and ability to communicate with the Chinese that he met. After dismissing the widely-held view of 'the rigid confinement of women' in China as 'void of truth', for he had seen great numbers of women in the streets as he pursued his explorations, Anderson turned to the question of slavery as discussed by learned China specialist such as the Abbe Grosier and asserted that they was 'no such class of people as slaves in the Chinese empire.'[3] Anderson describes how, '…the boy, being in a shop with me in the suburbs of Canton, some people who had never before seen a black, were very curious in making inquiries concerning him; when the merchant, to whom the warehouse belonged, expressed his surprise, in broken English, that the British nation should suffer a traffic so disgraceful to that humanity which they were so ready to profess, and on my informing him that our parliament intended to abolish it, he surprised me with the following extraordinary answer…"Aye, in England, the black

---

3   Grosier (1743-1823) edited *De la Chine ou description generale de cet empire*, Paris, 1777-84 based upon reports from Peking by fellow Jesuits.

men have got an advocate and friend (Mr. Wilberforce) who has, for a considerable time, been doing them service; and all good people, as well as the blacks, adore the character of a gentleman, whose thoughts have been to meliorate the condition of those men; and not like our West India planters or merchants who, for the love of gain, would prolong the misery of so large portion of his fellow-creatures as the African slaves."'

This conversation took place fourteen years before slavery was officially abolished by Parliament and it reveals not only the informed and cosmopolitan nature of Canton (today usually rendered as Guangzhou), but also Anderson's friendly relations with the small 'black boy' and his direct communication with local people.

No similar insights can be gleaned from the official account of the Embassy or from Sir John Barrow. Anderson is the only writer to convey directly what it felt like to be in China in 1792-4, what people in the streets thought and ate. Staunton and Barrow were concerned with the diplomatic aspects of the Embassy and wanted to demonstrate that they had prepared well by extensive reading of (mainly Jesuit) descriptions of China. Digressions on Tibetan wars, the nature of the Chinese language culled from second-hand sources, dismissive accounts of Chinese gardens as 'an offence to nature' and Chinese painting — 'miserable daubers, unable to pencil out a correct outline of many objects...' — fill the texts and convey a generally disapproving tone, perhaps influenced by the failure of the Embassy.

Despite his general approval of how the Chinese authorities treated the populace, Anderson was not unaware of the considerable changes in the attitude of the Manchu officials to the Embassy. After the official audience with the Qianlong emperor in Jehol, they were keen for the British Embassy to leave immediately. Macartney wanted to stay a while in Peking and demonstrate the wonders of British science, and take his time in returning to Guangzhou but, as Anderson notes, there was a sudden deterioration in the quantity and quality of the food supplied to the Embassy and the Manchu officials hustled the Embassy to leave as soon as possible.

We know sadly little about Anderson himself. William Alexander mentioned his keeping a diary and taking charge of feeding the Embassy at times. A couple of sheets of Anderson's diary survive in the Yenching Library at Harvard which show clearly that the diary was neatly kept.[4] It appears that he had support in publication from a William Coombe (1742-1823), a journalist and writer, author of *The Three Tours of Dr. Syntax - a comic poem*, the text for Boydell's *History of the Thames* and of articles for *The Times*, despite the fact that he spent much of his time in prison for debt. From the surviving fragments, it would seem that Coombe had little work to do on the text, and Anderson's book was remarkably successful, running quickly to a second edition, with two editions published in Dublin and translations into French and German. It was, perhaps, with some jealousy that Sir John Barrow dismissed it as 'a work vamped up by a London bookseller as a speculation that could not fail.'[5]

Anderson's book and the other works represented a whole new series of insights into China. Previous accounts had been almost exclusively written by Jesuit missionaries from the beginning of the seventeenth century, whilst the Macartney mission provided Britain's first eye-witness accounts of late eighteenth century China. Since the main aim of the Embassy was the opening of trade, there was much concentration on produce, products, engineering and technology, and on the prospects for

---

4   Patrick Hanan, *Treasures of the Yenching: 75th anniversary of the Harvard-Yenching library*, Hong Kong, 2003
5   Singer, p. 175.

British traders. Not only did eighteenth century China produce luxury goods such as tea and silks which were in huge demand in Europe, creating a trade imbalance that the British were keen to diminish by creating markets for British goods, but it was also enjoying a period of admirable prosperity. There were, however, signs of trouble ahead. In his diary (not published until 1957-8) Lord Macartney noted the difference between the Chinese and their Manchu rulers who occupied almost all the positions of power and sensed the growing potential for rebellion. 'A slight collision might elicit fire from the flint, and spread the flames of revolt from one extremity of China to another'. He took a fairly positive view of the possibilities of improving trade conditions at Canton, despite imperial resistance. 'We no doubt labour under many disadvantages here at present, but some of them we have it in our own power to remove... we keep aloof from them [the Chinese] as much as possible. We wear a dress as different from theirs as can be fashioned. We are quite ignorant of their language (which, I suppose, cannot be a very difficult one for little George Staunton has long since learned to speak it and write it with great readiness and from that circumstance has been of infinite use to us on many occasions)...Now I am very much mistaken if, by a proper management, we might not gradually and in some years be able to mould the China trade... to the shape that will best suit us. But it would certainly require in us great skill, caution, temper and perseverance...'[6]

Sadly, Macartney's sensible recommendations of caution and patience were not to be followed. And his cautious optimism did not extend to his prescient view of the future state of China, 'The Empire of China is an old, crazy, first-rate man-of-war, which a fortunate succession of able and vigilant officers has contrived

---

6   *An Embassy to China: being the journal kept by Lord Macartney during his embassy to the emperor Ch'ien-lung 1793-4*, London, Folio Society, 2004, p. 162.

to keep afloat for these one hundred and fifty years past, and to overawe her neighbours merely by her bulk and appearance, but whenever an insufficient man happens to have the command upon her deck, adieu to the discipline and safety of the ship. She may perhaps not sink outright; she may drift some time as a wreck, and will then be dashed to pieces on the shore; but she can never be rebuilt on the same bottom.'[7]

As an experienced diplomat, Macartney was taking the long view. Anderson's account of China was, in contrast, more immediate and much more widely welcomed by readers keen to learn about that distant and fabled country. Such was the financial success of his book that even before the publication of the second London edition, Anderson was able to purchase a lieutenant's commission in the Second Royal Manx Fencibles. He served in Malta and in the campaign against the French in Egypt which formed the basis of his second book, *the Journal of the forces which sailed from the Downs in April 1800 on a secret expedition under the command of Lieutenant-General Pigot till their arrival in Minorca and all the subsequent transactions of the army under the command of the Right Honourable General Sir Ralph Abercromby in the Mediterranean and Egypt...to the surrender of Alexandria with a particular account of Malta during the time it was subject to the British Government,* London, 1801. But readers hoping for the same insights and interest as found in his description of the Macartney Embassy to China may be disappointed.

Frances Wood

---

7   *An Embassy*, p. 165.

A

NARRATIVE

OF THE

BRITISH EMBASSY

TO

CHINA,

IN THE YEARS 1792, 1793, AND 1794.

CONTAINING THE

VARIOUS CIRCUMSTANCES OF THE EMBASSY;

WITH ACCOUNTS OF THE

CUSTOMS AND MANNERS OF THE CHINESE;

AND A DESCRIPTION OF THE

COUNTRY TOWNS, CITIES, etc. etc.

THE THIRD EDITION.

BY ÆNEAS ANDERSON,

Then in the Service of his Excellency Earl Macartney, K. B. Ambassador
from the King of Great Britain to the Emperor of China, and now
Lieutenant of the 2d Royal Manx Fencibles.

London:

PRINTED FOR J. DEBRETT, OPPOSITE BURLINGTON
HOUSE, PICCADILLY.

1795

MY LORD,

WHEN I first published this volume, it had neither friend nor patron; nor was it assisted by any of those factitious decorations which are so generally employed to seduce attention to literary productions. I relied altogether upon the importance of the work, and the fidelity with which it was executed, for its favourable acceptance in the world; and it is with pride I acknowledge that my most sanguine expectations have not been disappointed. But still, my Lord, a wish remained, that to the general patronage of the public I might add that of some eminent character, distinguished not only by birth and talents, but every private and public virtue; and I have been so fortunate as to have that wish completely gratified by your Lordship's favour and protection. For the personal kindness, my Lord, I have received from you, and the added importance which your name will stamp on this work, I beg leave to offer the warm effusions of a grateful heart, and to subscribe myself with the warmest respect,

MY LORD,

Your LORDSHIP'S most faithful
And obliged humble servant,
AENEAS ANDERSON,
Lieutenant 2d Royal Manx Fencibles.
Douglas, Isle of Man
Dec 21, 1795

PREFACE
TO THE
FIRST EDITION

AN embassy to China was a new event in the diplomatic history
of this country, and very naturally excited a general curiosity
concerning it: for, without considering the great commercial
objects it had in view, the universal ignorance which prevailed
respecting the interior parts of that empire, and the consequent
novelty which must be produced by any authentic history of
it, would irresistibly attract the attention of our enlightened
country, to the only civilised nation in the world, whose jealous
laws forbid the intrusion of any other people.

It is not my design to examine those writers who have
preceded me on the subject of China: it is not for me to point out
their contradictions, or display their fabulous interpolations —
my only business is to relate what I saw in the course of this
embassy, in every part of which I had the honour to attend Lord
Macartney, who was appointed to be the representative of his
Britannic Majesty at the court of Pekin.

The disadvantages which oppress the trade of European
countries with China are well known, and to remove them in behalf
of our own, was an object well worthy the attentive wisdom or
our government. It was not, however, a mere speculative project;
as a sufficient intimation had been made to the Court of London,
that an Ambassador from thence would be graciously received
by the Emperor of China: ministers, therefore, acted with a strict
political attention to the commercial interests of this country, by
preparing an embassy, suited to the dignity of the court of Great
Britain, and fitted out in a manner to attract the attention of the
Chinese people, as well as to command the respect, and secure

the regard of the Court of Pekin.

The Honourable Colonel Cathcart was, accordingly, invested in the year 1788, with the important character of minister from this country to the Empire of China; a man whose superior talents, amiable manners, shrewd sagacity, and active perseverance, qualified him, in a pre-eminent degree, to forward the important objects of his mission: but the premature death of that able, excellent, and accomplished man, which happened on his voyage, thwarted the progress of the embassy he was appointed to conduct; and as no person had been named in the King's commission, to succeed to his diplomatic office, if he should not reach the place of his destination, that embassy died with him; and may be said to have been buried on the distant shore where his ashes repose.

The wise attentions of government were not, however, to be turned aside from such an important national object as a commercial alliance between the Courts of London and Pekin: the character of Ambassador to China was accordingly revived, with additional splendor, in the person of Earl Macartney; and an embassy was re-appointed in such a manner as became the empire it was to represent—and the empire before which it was to appear.

It is impossible to speak in higher terms of the anxious care and liberal attention of government to this diplomatic mission than it deserves. The superior talents which direct the board of controul, and the commercial spirit which animates the direction of the East India Company, combined to form those arrangements which certainly deserved success, if they did not obtain it. No narrow, or sordid views, mingled with the preparations of it: the means of exterior figure, and the allurements of national productions in every branch of art, science, and manufacture, were amply supplied; and though the embassy has failed in its object, its failure cannot be attributed to those who framed and fashioned it in this country, and set it forward to its distant destination.

I have accurately related every circumstance that came under my observation, with many occurrences which I hear from those, whose authority it would be impertinence, to say no worse, in me to resist. My design is to attempt no more than I am qualified to fulfil; and this volume will be more particularly found to contain a faithful account of the British embassy, with its progress through China, from the time that the Lion man of war, and the Hindostan East-India Company's ship, anchored before Mettow, in the Yellow Sea, to its arrival at Canton. This Narrative is faithfully given according to the best of my abilities, and from the most accurate observations in my power to make, during the journey of the embassy by land, or its voyages by water, or its temporary residence in Pekin and Tartary.

Others who possess a brilliant fancy, or a glowing imagination, might enliven their description of the scenes through which this volume will conduct the reader, with those bright colours which we see on the Chinese manufactures that are imported into this country, try to decorate the apartments of elegant opulence; but my principal object is to give a strong and accurate out-line of the picture and I would rather be accused of the dulness and tautology of truth, than risque a suspicion that I had sacrificed to a creative imagination. Indeed in a journey, or a voyage, or by whatever name it may be distinguished, of upwards of two thousand miles, some repetition must be expected and forgiven, not only from a similitude of objects, but from the impossibility of displaying, by literal description, those differences between them, which, though evident to the eye, cannot be transferred, to the page. Cities, towns, and villages, mountains and rocks, rivers, canals, and lakes, etc. etc. will oftentimes admit of nothing more than general denominations. The regularity, also, with which the British embassy was conducted in its progress through China, will give an occasional uniformity to the narration, that may sometimes check the interest which, I trust, it will be generally found to excite: but I beg leave to assure the reader that, if unfortunately he should not always be amused by this work, he will never be intentionally deceived; and the praise due to faithful representation is all I have to claim, and all I wish to receive.

I have preceded the history of the journey through China with an account of the voyage to it; and have consequently mentioned places which have already been described by others, and are to be found in the volumes of modern geography; but I was advised by those, on whose judgment I could very much rely, to give this introductory part of it, according to my own knowledge, and from the result of my own observation.

I have also added the journal of the Lion and the Hindostan from Chusan to Canton, as it contains much curious and useful information relative to the navigation of a long range of the coasts of China not generally known, and, may be, therefore, important to the future voyager of the seas that wash them. The river of Canton is so well known, that I have compressed my account of it into a very small compass. The homeward-bound voyage, also, which was accompanied with no circumstance worthy of particular attention, is contained in a few pages. To these I have added a short glossary of such Chinese words and expressions, as I had myself acquired, and no more.

As to the names of cities, villages, etc. I have given the orthography according to their sounds, and as I was instructed by those natives, whose knowledge of the English language was sufficient to assist me.

I shall offer no apology to my country for publishing the

journal of a voyage, which had excited such universal attention. If this volume contains a faithful narrative of the public transactions of the late embassy to China, with such an account of the country and its inhabitants, as the circumstances of it, and mode of travelling through it, would allow; an apology must be considered as insulting the public, to whom the work is presented: and, if it should be found to contain nothing that can interest or amuse the public, the book itself will be an insult, and beyond the reach of apology.

But I indulge myself in better expectations; nor am I without a flattering hope, that this volume contains information which will gratify reasonable curiosity, and enlarge the knowledge of a country so little known to the other nations of the globe.

ÆNEAS ANDERSON.

Westminster, Marsham-Street
April 2, 1795.

PREFACE
TO THE
SECOND EDITION.

THE rapidity with which a very large impression in quarto of this work has been sold, determined me to publish a new edition, in a less expensive form, that the gratification of curiosity on a subject so full of novelty as an embassy to China may be more extended. I have reason to be vain of the success of my Narrative, which has been honoured with an ample share of public approbation; and still maintains its character in spite of the various efforts of malice and misrepresentation, both against the book and its author:—but while the former remains free from any specific charge of falshood or exaggeration, the latter may be perfectly at ease as to any attacks which an interested resentment may make upon him.

I have only to add, that this edition differs from the former in little more than a correction of literal errors.

Æ. A.

May 21, 1795

PREFACE
TO THE
THIRD EDITION.

TWO large impressions in quarto and octavo of this Narrative having experienced a very rapid sale, I am called upon to publish a third edition: nor can I refrain from expressing, as I trust, a justifiable satisfaction in having obtained a complete triumph over many illiberal but fruitless attempts to depreciate my work. When the spirit of rivalry exceeds the bounds of liberality and of truth, it deserves the mortification which it seldom fails to experience; and my rivals, while they have taken every opportunity to misrepresent me, and have condescended to implore, if not to purchase, the severity of venal criticism on my Narrative, have not, however, been able to shake its authenticity, nor to lessen the distinguished favour which it has received, and is still receiving, from the patronage of the public.

But while I express my sense of the general favour of my country at large, it would betray a criminal insensibility, if I did not avail myself of this occasion to make my most particular acknowledgments to the inhabitants of the Isle of Man, not only for a very large portion of personal kindness, but for their zealous encouragement of this work, which I now make a record of my regard and gratitude.

LIST

OF THE

GENTLEMEN

WHO COMPOSED THE RETINUE OF

EARL MACARTNEY.

SIR George Staunton, Bart. Secretary to the Embassy;

Lieutenant Colonel Benson, Commandant of the Ambassador's Guard;

Lieutenant H. W. Parish, of the Royal Artillery;

Lieutenant J. Crewe;

Mr. Acheson Maxwell, Joint Secretaries to the Ambassador;

Mr. Edward Winder,

Mr. Baring, Assistant Secretary, outward bound; Son of Sir Francis Baring, Bart.

Dr. Gillan, Physician and Philosopher to the Embassy;

Dr. Scott, Physician and Surgeon to the Embassy;

Mr. Barrow, Comptroller of the Household;

Dr. Dinwiddie, Mechanist, Conductor of mathematical and astronomical presents;

Master George Staunton, Son of Sir George Staunton, Bart.

Mr. Thomas Hickey, Portrait Painter;

Mr. Alexander, Draftsman;

Mr. Hutner, Preceptor to Master Staunton;

Mr. Plumb, Interpreter.

Commissioners sent by the East India Company to Canton, to notify the intended Embassy of Earl Macartney.
> Messrs. Jackson, Irwine, and Brown.

His Excellency's Servants, etc. consisted of
A Steward, and an under ditto,
2 Valets de Chambre,
A Cook,
2 Couriers,
A Footman,
A Baker,
A Band of six Musicians,
A Carpenter and Joiner,
A Saddler,
A Gardener,
A Taylor,
A Watchmaker,
A Mathematical Instrument-maker.

Belonging to Sir G. Staunton:

2 Servants   1 Gardener;
which, with Mr. Crewe's Valet de Chambre, formed the whole of the domestic establishment, except three natives of China, who went out with us from England.
The Military Establishment, or Guards, consisted of
20 Men of the Royal Artillery;
10 Ditto 11th Light Dragoons;
20 Ditto drafted from the additional Companies of Infantry, at Chatham.

The Ships which were employed to take the Embassy to China, were
The Lion, of 64 guns, Sir Erasmus Gower, Commander;
The Hindostan East Indiaman, Capt. William Mackintosh, Commander; and
The Jackall brig for a tender, manned by officers and men from

the Lion.

List of the Officers on Board his Majesty's Ship Lion,
Sir Erasmus Gower, Knight, Commander;
Mr. Campbell, 1st Lieutenant;
Mr. Whitman, 2d ditto;
Mr. Atkins, 3d ditto;
Mr. Cox, 4th ditto—died at Chusan;
Mr. Ommaney, acting Lieutenant;
Mr. Jackson, Master of the Lion;
Mr. Saunders, Master's-mate;
Mr. Tippett; ditto;
Mr. Simes, ditto (dismissed from the Ship at Batavia);
Mr. Lowe, ditto;
Mr. Roper, ditto;
Mr. Warren, ditto (son of Dr. Warren, Physician to his Majesty, and the Prince of Wales) promoted to be acting Lieutenant;
Mr. Kent;
Mr. Chapman, (appointed Gunner, vice Corke, deceased.)

Midshipmen.
Right Hon. Lord Mark Kerr, (son of the Marquis Lothian), promoted to be acting Lieutenant,
Hon. Wm. Stuart, (son of the Earl Bute),
Mr. Bromely,
Mr. Swinbourne,
Mr. Kelly,
Mr. Dilkes,
Mr. Trollope,
Mr. Heywood,
Mr. Hickey,

Mr. Thompson,

Mr. Waller, (died at Wampoa),

Mr. Beaumont, (returned home from Angara Point, for the recovery of his health),

Mr. Snipe,

Mr. Wools,

Mr. Montague,

Mr. Chambers,

Mr. Scott,

Mr. Bridgeman,

Mr. Perkins,

Mr. Sarradine.

Mr. Tothill, Purser, (died at Cochin China);

Mr. Well, Captain's Clerk;

Mr. Nutt, Surgeon;

Mr. Anderson, Chief-mate;

Mr. Cooper, 2d ditto;

Mr. Thomas, 3d ditto;

Mr. Humphries, Schoolmaster:

CONTENTS

CONTENTS

CHAP. V.

CHAP. VI.

CHAP. VII.

CONTENTS

33

CHAP. XV.

CHAP. XVI.

CHAP. XVII.

CONTENTS

CHAP. XVIII.

CHAP. XIX.

CHAP. XX.

CHAP. XXI.

CONTENTS

AENEAS ANDERSON IN CHINA

Chapter I

From England to Batavia

1792, Friday, September 21. EVERY necessary arrangement having been made, the Right Hon. Earl Macartney, with his whole suite, went from the Point at Portsmouth, in several barges, on board the Lion man of war, then lying at Spithead.

Sunday 23. Hoisted in the launch—fired the signal gun for all the officers and men on shore to repair on board.

Tuesday 25. At eleven. A.M. a signal was made for the Hindostan and Jackall to weigh: the Alfred and Orion of seventy-four guns weighed at the same time; and, at five o'clock in the afternoon, we took our final departure from Spithead.

Saturday 29. We got into Torbay, where we found the Hannibal and Niger men of war. Sir George and Mr. Staunton, with Dr. Gillan, went ashore, and penetrated into the country as far as Exeter; from whence they returned the next day.

Sunday 30. A leak was repaired that had sprung in the side of the Lion.

Wednesday, October 10. We made land at an early hour of this morning; and at eight saw the Deserter's Island at the distance of about four leagues; and the island of Porto Santo at the distance of about three leagues. These islands are subject to the crown of Portugal, and form a part of the Madeiras: the latter of them is chiefly appropriated as a place of exile for those who commit any petty depredations on the island of Madeira. It is about fifteen miles in circumference, and very mountainous: it contains no harbours; but has a large bay wherein ships may be tolerably secure, except when the wind blows from the south-west; it is frequented by Indiamen outward and homeward bound. The island produces corn, but in no great quantity; it has also pasturage for cattle; and its thickets furnish shelter for wild boars. The inhabitants are few in number, and subject to the government of Madeira. The Desart, or Deserter's Island, is an inconsiderable barren rock, and serves also as a prison for criminals, who are there obliged to pay the penance of their offences by various kinds of labour.

Thursday 11. We arrived in Funchal Bay, in the island of Madeira) and anchored in forty-four fathom waters; the town of Funchal being to the N. N. E. about a mile.

Friday 12. After breakfast, Lieutenant Campbell was sent on shore to the governor of the Madeiras, to notify the arrival of Lord Macartney: and, on the return of that officer, the Lion saluted the garrison with thirteen guns; and the compliment was immediately returned. The British Consul then came on board, attended by several English gentlemen, among whom were the most respectable merchants of the place, to pay their respects to the Ambassador, and to invite him ashore.

His Lordship having accepted of the invitation, the ship's company were ordered to get themselves clean dressed in white jackets and trowsers as preparatory for manning the yards: and, as I publish this Narrative, not merely for the use of seamen, but for the entertainment, and, as I hope, for the information of those who know nothing of maritime life, I shall endeavour to explain what is understood by manning the yards; a ceremonial never observed but on particular occasions, as well as in honour of distinguished characters, and has not only a very peculiar, but, in some degree, a very beautiful effect. The ship's company being all equipped in their best cloathing, the sailors stand upright on the yard-arms, as close to each other as the situation will admit, with their hands clasped together, and their arms extended; ropes being drawn across to prevent them from falling. In this curious manner the whole yards of the ship are filled with men up to the main-top-gallant royal. In this position the ship's company remained, till Lord Macartney had landed on the island.

On this occasion the matrosses were drawn up under arms on the larboard side of the quarter-deck, and the marines on the starboard side, lining both sides of the deck, as far as the accommodation ladder. The troops saluted his Lordship as he passed from the cabin, and the band of music continued playing till he had left the ship. Lord Macartney and Sir Erasmus Gower proceeded in one barge, and the gentlemen of the suite followed in another. The Lion then fired a salute of fifteen guns, which was answered by an equal discharge of artillery from the fort on shore. On this occasion every mark of mutual respect was paid, while the Governor of Madeira, with the British Consul and the principal inhabitants, were ready at the landing-place to welcome the Ambassador on his arrival at the island.

Saturday 13. I went on shore this morning after breakfast, with several of the midshipmen, and landed at Brazen-head rock. Opposite to this landing place stands a rock called the Loo, in which there is a pretty strong fort, surrounded with a rampart, mounted with several pieces of cannon, and garrisoned with soldiers. This rock is in the form of a pillar, being very high, perpendicular on all sides, and commands the bay; the only entrance to the fort is by a narrow flight of steps hewn out of the rock, and properly guarded. It is situated about three quarters of a mile from the shore, and in water of near forty fathom, so that there can be no communication with the land but by means of boats. The landing-place of the island is to the north-west of the Loo rock, and, from the depth of the sea, which, at the water's edge, is fifteen fathom, the violence of the surf and a rocky shore, is extremely dangerous. Steps are formed in the rock to ascend to the top, of it, which communicate with the road to Funchal, the principal town of the island.

This road is very rough and narrow, being no more than four feet and a half in breadth, with a low wall on either side. It first leads to an high ascent, on each side of which are a few unenviable dwellings of the lower class of inhabitants. On the succeeding declivity is a small church, in the front of which there is an altar and a cross, supposed to possess some healing powers of peculiar efficacy, as we saw several poor wretches afflicted with various diseases, lying naked there, and exposing their bodies covered with sores and blotches. The church has so little the appearance of any thing like a place dedicated to the worship of God, that, till I perceived the cross, which was its distinguishing decoration, it appeared to me to be a barn or stable; at the same time I was informed that the inside of it was very properly fitted up and furnished for the sacred purpose to which it is dedicated. Its situation is beautiful beyond description: it stands in a very elevated position, commands a very grand and extensive view of the sea, with Porto Santo and the Deserter's Island; overlooking, at the same time, the charming vineyards in its own immediate vicinity. Many delightful gardens are seen on either side of the road, abounding in delicious fruits; and, to the north of it, the vineyards stretch away to the extremity of the rock, which possesses a perpendicular height of several hundred feet above the sea.

About half a mile beyond the church is the entrance into the town of Funchal, through a gate, from thence a mean, dirty, narrow street leads to a public walk disposed in the form of a garden, which has a principal alley or avenue in the center, with orange and other trees on either side of it, and lamps placed between them: the whole is terminated by the cathedral church, a large Gothic building, which is fitted up in a very suitable manner for the purposes of that religion to which it is consecrated.

Monday 15. I went after breakfast to the house of the British Consul, which is in the vicinity of the cathedral; and saw Lord Macartney, attended by his whole suite, likewise accompanied by the Hon. Mr. West, brother to the Earl of De Lawarr, dressed in the uniform of the embassy, walk in procession to visit the Governor of the island; who received the Ambassador with every mark of attention and respect, and requested his company to dinner on the succeeding day. His Lordship then returned to the Consul's in the same order and formality.

As in the afternoon of this day I completed my view of this place, I shall here finish my account of it.

Madeira is extremely mountainous, and presents a most beautiful object from the bay. It lies between thirty-two and thirty-three degrees of north latitude, and between eighteen and nineteen degrees of west longitude from London. Its length is seventy-five miles, and its breadth thirty. In the center of the southern side of the island, at a small distance from the sea, and on the first rise of an amphitheatre of hills, is the town of Funchal. The population of this place is very considerable, and it contains several churches, as well as monasteries of both sexes, of the different orders of the church of Rome: the houses are built of stone, and the greater part of them are covered with white plaster, and generally roofed with tiles: the streets are very narrow, ill paved, and dirty, having no foot-path for passengers, with all the inconvenience arising from unequal ground and continual declivity. Except in the residences of the Governor, and the British Consul, and the houses of some principal merchants, glass is an article of very rare use. The houses are, in general, about three stories high, with lattice windows, and balconies in the front, where the female inhabitants are continually seen to amuse themselves in observing what happens in the streets, or conversing with those who are passing along. There arc neither courts, squares, or principal streets in this town; the whole place composing a scene of architectural deformity. The custom-house, which is on the sea side, is surrounded by a rampart mounted with cannon, and contains barracks for soldiers.

The town is about three miles in length, and one in breadth. Its inhabitants consist of Portuguese, mulattoes, negroes, and a few English, who reside there for the purpose of commerce. The wine of this island, so well known for its cordial and peculiar qualities, is the great object of its trade, and the principal source of its riches. The dress of the poorer sort of people is a kind of cap, made of cloth, which they wear instead of a hat, a short jacket, and clumsy trowsers, with a kind of boots of coarse undressed leather; though many of the lower class are seen almost naked, and manifest no common appearance of distress and misery. The religion is catholic, and the clergy possess the same power as in the mother country. The natives are of a very courteous disposition, and treat strangers with all the punctilios of politeness and respect.

No carriages are kept in this island, but by The Governor and the British Consul: the subititute for them, among the higher order of the inhabitants, is a very fine silk net, of various colours, capable of containing a person to fit in it: it is borne by two men, by means of a long pole run through the four corners, which draws the net close on each side like a purse; a silk curtain is then thrown over the pole, that entirely obsures the person who fits in this curious vehicle, which is the elegant mode of conveyance in visits of ceremony, and to the occasional entertainments of the place. These, however, are always in private houses, as there are no theatres, or any places of public entertainment, except the public garden, where there are frequent exhibitions of the most brilliant fire-works.

There are very few horses in this island; mules and oxen being principally employed both for draught and burden: nor is it easy to conceive the sagacity and agility of these animals in adapting their powers to the inequalities of this very mountainous country.

The military establishment of the Madeiras is very limited, and does not consist of more than three hundred men. The native militia, however, are numerous, but they are never embodied; except in time of danger and alarm. These soldiers are most wretchedly cloathed; the regimental consisting of a very coarse blue jacket, with a vest and breeches of the same colour; the whole bound with a coarse yellow worsted lace, and enlivened with a red facing. They wear on their heads a kind of leathern helmet; but the artillery soldiers are distinguished by hats: their arms and accoutrements are of the worst kind, and kept in the worst order: in short, such was their appearance, that when form of our matrosses and light horsemen were permitted to go on shore, the inhabitants, from the superiority of their appearance, could not be be persuaded but that they were officers in the British service.

The town is defended towards the sea, from east to west, by a strong wall, mounted with cannon, and a fort at either end. The climate of Madeira is well known for its salubrious influence, as, excepting the month of January, when there are frequent rains, accompanied with violent thunder, it seldom undergoes any change of season. Those who have money may purchase here, as in other places, all the luxuries of life; but they in general bear a very extravagant price, though the first people live in a stile of great plenty and elegance. Even the wine, which, as it is the produce of the spot, might naturally be supposed to be purchased at a reasonable rate, could not be obtained by us for less than four shillings a bottle. This island, however, notwithstanding its mountainous state, must be considered, altogether, as a very fertile colony; and, as a picturesque object, nothing can exceed the romantic and beautiful views it contains, and the delightful spots that are covered with gardens and vineyards.

Tuesday 16. Lord Macartney, with the principal people of the island, were very handsomely entertained by the British Consul, at dinner; and, in the evening, Mr. Scott, an English merchant, gave a ball and supper, in honour of his Lordship, which wanted nothing, in point of elegant hospitality, that our country can afford. The English servants also partook of the attention paid to their Lord, and were entertained with the greatest plenty, and in the most agreeable manner, beneath the same roof.

Wednesday 17. We this morning paid a visit to a convent of ladies, about three miles to the east of Funchal. It is a very handsome building, situated near the summit of an hill, and in the midst of vineyards, commanding a most beautiful, various, and extensive prospect; comprehending the adjacent country covered with gardens, the town of Funchal, and an expansive view of the ocean. Here the nuns are permitted to converse very freely with strangers, whom they compliment with toys, and other articles of their own manufacture. I saw among them several very pretty women; who, as far as I could judge by their manners, seemed to regret the loss of that society for which they were formed, and to sigh after a communication with the world, which they were qualified to adorn.

Having taken a particular view of this charming spot, we proceeded to the country residence of the Governor, where Lord Macartney and his suite had been invited to dinner. This entertainment consisted of three very splendid courses of fifty dishes: and at a certain part of it, Lord Macartney proposed to drink the health of the King and the Royal Family of England; which being notified by a signal, the Lion, at that instant, fired a royal salute of twenty-one guns; and was immediately answered by the same number of guns from the fort. The Governor then observed the same ceremony respecting the Royal Family of Portugal, which was followed by the same salutes from the Portuguese battery and English men of war. A very fine display of fire-works concluded the entertainment, which did equal honour to the distinguished persons who gave and received it.

We returned on board, where we found several friars, whore curiosity had led them to take a view of the ship; where they were received with a kindness and hospitality which called forth the most grateful expressions; and obtained from them, all they had to give, their repeated benedictions.

Thursday 18. The entire forenoon of this day was employed in making prepartions for a breakfast in the ward-room, to which Lord Macartney had invited the Governor of the island, the British Consul, and the principal inhabitants. This entertainment consisted of tea, coffee, and chocolate; cold meats of all kinds, with fruits, jellies, and variety of wines: the whole being decorated with ornamental confectionary. About noon Lord Macarney returned on board the Lion, wish the usual formalities, and was soon followed by the Governor, with his attendants, in very elegant barges. The bishop of Funchal accompanied him on the occasion. The British Consul arrived soon after them. The company then partook of the repast, during which the healths of the royal families of England and Portugal were drank with becoming ceremony; and having taken a view of the ship, they returned on shore. In the evening we weighed anchor, and quitted Madeira.

Saturday 20. At five in the afternoon we saw the extreme points of Teneriffe; at midnight we saw the east point of that island; and, early in the morning, stood in for land.

Sunday 21. We anchored in twenty-two fathom water in Santa Cruz bay; where we found a French frigate, who had called here on her homeward bound passage from the West-Indies; but, in consequence of the revolution in France, she was detained till the pleasure of his Catholic Majesty should be known, respecting the part he intended to take with the confederated powers, then at war with the national assembly. The Governor being then at the Grand Canary island, and the Commandant informing Lieutenant Campbell that there was not a sufficient quantity of powder in the magazine to admit of a salute, that ceremonial was waved on the present occasion.

The island of Teneriffe is one of the Canary islands, and subject to the King of Spain. It lies between twenty-eight and twenty-nine degrees north latitude, and between seventeen and eighteeh degrees west longitude. It is about fifty miles in length, twenty-five in breadth, and one hundred and fifty in circumference. Though it is the second in point of precedence, it is the most considerable with respect to extent, riches, and commerce. The principal place in this island is the city of Laguna, and is the residence of the Governor; but as we did not visit it, I shall confine myself to the description of Santa Cruz, before which we lay at anchor.

This town lies on the north-east side of the island, and has an haven for shipping; the best anchorage not being more than half a mile from shore, and very deep, with a rocky bottom. The shore is bold and steep, with the peak, which renders this island so famous, rising beyond it to the clouds.

Santa Cruz is about three quarters of a mile in length, and half a mile in breadth the houses are strongly built of stone, and in the same fashion as those of Madeira. It has several neat churches, two of which being decorated with large, square, and lofty towers, add much to the effect of the town from the bay. There is one pretty good street, and not inconveniently paved; but the rest answer to no other character than that of dirty lanes. There are two forts at the eastern and western end of the town which command the bay. There are but few troops in this or any of its sister islands, and they are equally deficient in cloathing, equipment, and discipline. The militia is numerous, but never embodied, or called forth, except on very particular emergencies. The town, though by no means large, is very populous: the inhabitants are chiefly Spanish, and suffer all the disadvantages that arise from the proverbial pride and indolence of their character: for, notwithstanding the abundant fertility of this island, which yields the greatest plenty to the smallest exertions, the general appearance of the people betrays their poverty and wretchedness. There is another fort to the west of Santa Cruz, on a very elevated point, which appears to be built with great strength, and commands a part of the bay.

The climate of this island is warm, and, like that of Madeira, not subject to change. During our stay here, the thermometer stood in the shade, from seventy to eighty degrees, varying a little, onboard the ship. The Governor resides chiefly at the island distinguished by the name of the Grand Canary, about twelve or fifteen leagues distant from Teneriffe.

Wednesday 24. Sir George and Mr. Staunton, with the Doctors Gillan, Dinwiddie, and Not, Messieurs. Maxwell, Barrow, and Alexander, together with Colonel Benson, having formed a plan to visit the peak; they set out at eight, o'clock the morning of this day from the hotel at Santa Cruz, with every proper aid and provision to carry the design into execution. The thermometer then stood at seventy-seven degrees. They proceeded on mules, and under the directions of guides hired for the purpose, with little or no interruption, till they had advanced about eight miles up the mountain, when the air became so cold, that every one was glad to make some addition to his cloathing; at the same time. the thermometer had fallen upwards of twenty degrees. Here the party added some very necessary refreshment to the change in their dress, and then proceeded on their journey till they arrived at the foot of the peak, which was entirely covered with snow, six feet in depth: but difficulties every moment occurred to impede their progress; Sir George Staunton had been thrown from his mule at a moment of great danger; the animal on which Doctor Gillan rode, had fallen with him, and it was at length determined, from the awful appearance of the journey before them, the exhausted condition of the party, and the late hour of the evening, to pass the night on the mountain. A kind of rude pavilion, therefore, was formed by a sail, which, being lifted with cloaks, and great coats, soon produced a comfortable apartment. A fire was then kindled near the tent; and after taking an hasty supper, every one laid himself down to repose.

Thursday 25. At six o'clock in the morning, the arduous journey was renewed; the thermometer being at that time considerably below the freezing point – but, after infinite fatigue and considerable hazard, it proved fruitless as to its principal object and three o'clock, in the afternoon, the different gentlemen of the party, who had taken different ways to ascend the peak, were, at length, happily re-assembled at the place where the mules had been stationed. It was, however, necessary, as the distance, from Santa Cruz was at least eleven or twelve miles, to pass the night of this day, as we had passed the preceding one. On the following, morning the party returned to Santa Cruz, after a most fatiguing expedition of two days and two nights, in which, curiosity, at least, had received considerable gratification.

The peak of Teneriffe is one of the highest mountains in the world, and may be seen at the distance of an hundred miles. It rises in the center of the island, and takes its ascent from Santa Cruz and Oratavia, another principal town of this island, in an oblique direction for near twenty miles; being surrounded by a great number of inferior mountains. The lower parts, towards Santa Cruz are covered with woods and vineyards; its middle is clad in snow, and the top disembogues flames from a volcano, which the natives call the Devil's Cauldron. In travelling to the peak, the best way is on the side of Oratavia, both as to the convenience of ascent, and the consequent diminution of danger. In some parts of the mountain there are hot, burning sands; in other places there are snow; and to that succeeds a strong sulphurous vapour. Though the top of the peak, from its great height, appears to finish in a point, it contains a flat surface of at least an acre of ground. We experienced three distinct changes of climate in the course of our journey. In the first stage of it the air is warm, to that succeeds intense cold, which is followed by a volcanic heat. The bottom is continual fertility, the middle is snow and frost, and the top is smoke and flames: the whole producing the successive effects of a garden, an ice-house, and a furnace,

Friday 26. Soon after our return to Santa Cruz, a signal was given for our going on board, which was obeyed with all possible expedition. On our return to the ship, we found several young ladies, inhabitants of the island, who, having been educated in England, were naturally induced to visit a ship belonging to a country to which they expressed the warmer acknowledgments. They were received with great politeness by Lord Macartney; and the band of music was ordered to play during the whole of their very agreeable visit.

The French frigate, which we have already mentioned as detained here, was, this day, released from its embargo; and set sail from the island.

About eleven o'clock at night the wind blew a very fresh gale, and the Hindostan drifted so fast towards the shore, that it was thought prudent to let go her sheet anchor. But this precaution was not sufficient to prevent the danger from becoming so imminent, that Captain Mackintosh fired a gun for assistance from the Lion; when Sir Erasmus Gower immediately ordered off three boats, by whose exertions the Hindostan was disengaged from her unpleasant situation; when she immediately put to sea, after having lost her anchors, from the rubbing of the cables against the rocky bottom.

Saturday 27. At one in the morning we weighed anchor, and took our leave of Santa Cruz.

Friday, November, 1. At three in the afternoon we saw Mayo, one of the Cape de Verd islands, bearing W.S.W. at the distance of four or five leagues. We hove to, and hoisted out the launch. At seven, we spoke to a ship from Topsham, in Devonshire, which had been out thirty-two days. At eight in the evening, Saint Jago, a town of the island of that name, bore north, half west, seven miles; and, at three quarters after eleven, we came to in Port Praya bay. The thermometer at noon stood at eighty-two degrees.

Saturday 3. After the usual salutes, several boats were employed in watering. The Seine was also hauled, and fresh fish served to the ship's company.

Monday 5. Lord Macartney went on shore in a private manner; and, after a short stay, returned to the Lion.

Tuesday 6. This day arrived three French and one American South-sea whale fishermen. A canoe came alongside the Lion, with grapes, cocoanuts, and other fruits, for sale. This is the only kind of boat used in these islands, and nothing could exceed, in the exterior appearance of wretchedness, the owner of it. The thermometer stood, this day, on shore, at ninety degrees.

Wednesday 7. Several of the men belonging to the corps

of artillery went on shore to wash and dry their linen; when they returned extremely scorched, and their legs covered with blotches, from standing in the burning sands. Having given my linen to be washed by a man of Praya, and being apprehensive that I might share the fate of others, who had not found the natives of the country perfectly correct in their returns, I went in request of my washerman; when I was obliged to be content, not only with paying an exorbitant price for what he had done very ill, but with the loss of several articles which he could not be persuaded to restore. I, however, took this opportunity of viewing the town of Praya; in which there is very little to excite curiosity, or encourage description.

Saint Jago is the largest of the Cape de Verd islands, which lie between twenty-three and twenty-six degrees of west longitude, and between fourteen and eighteen north latitude.

It is very mountainous, and has much barren land on it; nevertheless, it is the most fruitful and best inhabited of them all — and is the residence of the Viceroy, or Governor.

Praya is situated on the east side of the island, and is built on the top of a flat hill, about one hundred yards above the surface of the bay; having a miserable fort on the western side, which, however, such as it is, commands the entrance into it. The only landing place is opposite the Governor's house, which is situated in a considerable valley, formed by two large mountains. A very rugged and, ascending path, of about a quarter of a mile, and taking an easterly direction, leads to an arched gateway, which forms the entrance to the town; a mean and miserable place, consisting of nothing more than one wide street, about half a mile in length, formed of low houses built of stone and mud, and shaded with trees. The furniture of such as we could look into, was perfectly suited to the exterior appearance; consisting of nothing more than planks, which answered the double purpose of seats and tables, while the beds were as humble as solitary straw could make them. There is but one shop, and one public house in the town; and the former is as deficient in point of commodities, as the other is incapable of convenient accommodation. The church, and the Governor's house, partake of the general appearance of the place. The natives are negroes, who speak the Portuguese language, with an intermixture of exiles, banished from the Brazils and the Madeiras, for capital offences. There is one convent in the island, and the whole is subject to the spiritual jurisdiction of a Popish bishop.

There appears to be great plenty of goats here; but the scorching heat of the climate, and the consequent scarcity of every kind of herbage, is not calculated to give them a very thriving appearance.

Praya has a good port, and is seldom without ships; those outward bound to Guinea or the East Indies, from England, Holland, and France, frequently touching here for water and Refreshments.

While we were rambling about this miserable place, we heard the signal to repair on board; and, hastening to the shore, found a boat waiting to receive us, and a crowd of the naked inhabitants standing there with their fruits for sale. At noon we left Port Praya.

Sunday 18. At eleven o'clock in the forenoon, we found ourselves under the equator, where the burlesque and ridiculous ceremonies frequently allowed by the commanding officers of ships were completely observed, by permission of Sir Erasmus Gower, to the great entertainment of the ship's company.

Saturday, December, 1. At five o'clock in the afternoon, we came to anchor in the Rio Janeiro harbour, in fifteen fathom water. Passed by this afternoon into the harbour the Hero of London, a South-sea whaler, from the South Seas, bound for London. A great many ships were at this time at anchor in the river, and, among the rest, was a Portuguese East Indiaman, homeward bound; by whom it was intended to have sent letters to England, by way of Lisbon, had not the arrival of the Hero afforded a more ready, as well as more secure conveyance.

The country offers from the river a most delightful prospect, consisting of a fine range of hills covered with wood; whose intervening vallies are adorned with stately villas, and present a scene of elegance, richness, and beauty.

Sunday 2. The cutter was hoisted out, and the first lieutenant dispatched on shore, to acquaint the Viceroy with the arrival of the Ambassador, and to demand the salute; but as that officer was at his country residence, the usual formalities were necessarily suspended.

Monday 3. In the morning of this day, the deputy viceroy came, accompanied with guards and attendants, in elegant barges, to wait on Lord Macartney, to know his intentions, and to acquaint him with the regulations to which all foreigners must submit on landing at Rio Janeiro. But his Lordship having been for some time afflicted with the gout, and remaining very much indisposed, Sir George Staunton and Sir Erasmus Gower received the deputy viceroy, who after an introductory conference, partook of a cold collation, and returned on shore.

Tuesday 4. The deputy viceroy, with his attendants, paid a second visit to the ship, and accompanied the general message of congratulation front the Viceroy to the Ambassador, on his arrival at the Brazils, with an invitation to accept of an house for his residence, during the time he might find it necessary to stay there. This obliging proposition was accepted by Lord Macartney; and Sir George Staunton went on shore to make the necessary preparations for his reception, as soon as he should be sufficiently recovered to quit the ship.

Thursday 6. The Viceroy's secretary, attended by several gentlemen, came on board the Lion to inquire when the Ambassador would come on shore; who was pleased to appoint the following day at one o'clock, to make his entrance into the city of Rio Janeiro.

Friday 7. At noon, Sir Erasmus Gower having been on shore to notify to the Viceroy that Lord Macartney was ready to land, he returned to the Lion in order to conduct him; and they soon arrived with all the ceremonials suited to the occasion. The landing-place, which is immediately opposite to the Viceroy's palace, was lined on each side by a regiment of horse, and the Viceroy's body-guards. The Viceroy himself was also there with his official attendants; and the first persons of the city, to receive the Ambassador, who was conducted along the line, and distinguished by every military honour. The ceremony had altogether a very grand appearance, and a prodigious crowd of people had assembled to be spectators of it. The company then proceeded to the palace of the Viceroy, when they passed through a large hall lined with soldiers under arms, and enlivened by the sound of martial music, to the state apartments. Here they remained for some time, when Lord Macartney and Sir George Staunton were conducted to the Viceroy's state coach; Sir Erasmus Gower and Capt. Mackintosh were placed in a second; and the whole British suite being accommodated with carriages, the cavalcade set off, escorted by a troop of light cavalry, to the house appointed for Lord Macartney's reception, which is about two miles from the city: the Ambassador receiving, as he passed, every honour due to the high character with which he was invested. A captain's, guard, appointed by the Viceroy, was also drawn up in the front of the house, who received the British visitors with colours flying, and music playing, and every military distinction. Thus concluded the ceremony of the

Ambassador's reception at Rio Janeiro.

It would not only be tedious, but altogether unnecessary, to mention the common daily occurrences during our stay at the Brazils; I shall, therefore, confine myself altogether to such circumstances, as from their novelty and importance may interest the mind, and reward, in some degree, the attention of the reader.

Monday 10. Lord Macartney, with his whole suite, paid a visit of ceremony to the Viceroy, and was received with every mark of attention and respect. The gentlemen who attended on the occasion afterwards dined with his Lordship, and in the evening visited the public garden of the place. This garden is about half a mile in length, and half that space in breadth; it is surrounded by a strong high wall, and guarded at the entrance by a party of soldiers. The interior disposition consists of large grass-plots and gravel walks, agreeably shaded with trees, and perfumed with flowers. In the center is a large bason of water, and a great number of lamps are placed between the trees, on each side of the walks, for the purpose of illumination. At one end of the garden is a large building for balls and music; but, as the season of amusement at this place was passed when we were there, we must be content with giving a description of the spot, without speaking of the diversions to which, at certain seasons of the year, it is applied, as we doubt not, to the recreation of the inhabitants.

Tuesday 11. All possible preparation was made in the long gallery and great room of Lord Macartney's house to receive the Viceroy, who had given notice of his intention to return the Ambassador's visit in the morning of this day. At ten o'clock, Sir Erasmus Lowery with the officers from the Lion, dressed in their best uniforms, as well as Capt. Mackintosh, with the officer of the Hindostan, came on shore to attend the ceremony.

At eleven, the Viceroy's departure from his palace was announced by a discharge of artillery from the garrison; when the guard, appointed by the Viceroy to attend the British Ambassador, immediately paraded in front of the house; and, in about half an hour, the Viceroy arrived in grand procession, preceded and followed by a squadron of horse, and attended by all the principal officers and persons of distinction in the city. His Excellency was received at the door of the house by Lord Mcartney, and conducted to a sofa at the upper end of the best apartment. Sir George Staunton then presented all the gentlemen. attached to the embassy, according to their respective ranks, to the Viceroy; who, after partaking of a very elegant repast prepared for him and his company, returned in the same form, and with the same ceremonies, as distinguished his arrival.

The dress of the Viceroy was of scarlet cloth, very much enriched with gold, embroidery, and precious stones; his attendants, wore a splendid livery of green and gold, and he had several black running footmen, who were dressed in fancy uniforms, with large turbans on their heads, and long sabres by their sides.

Wednesday 12. This morning, at an early hour, Sir George and Mr. Staunton, accompanied by Mr. Barrow and a Portuguese gentleman, set off on a short excursion into the country. At the same time, I took an opportunity of visiting the place; of which I shall now proceed to give such a description, as my capacity for observation will enable me.

This city, which is by some called Saint Sebastian, and by others, Rio Janeiro, stands on the west side of the harbour of the latter name, in a low situation; and almost surrounded by hills, which, by retarding the circulation of the air, renders the place very unsalutary to European constitutions. Its extent is very considerable, being, from east to west, about four miles in length, and, from north to south, about two miles in breadth. The streets, for there are no squares, are very regular and uniform, intersecting each other at right angles: they are well paved, abound in shops of every kind, and are composed of houses equally well built, and adapted to the climate. In the center of the city, and opposite to the beach, stands the palace of the Viceroy: it is a large, long, and narrow building, without any attraction from its exterior appearance, but contains within a succession of spacious and noble apartments. It consists only of two stories; the lower one being appropriated to the domestics and menial officers, and the upper range, of building containing the apartments of the Viceroy: it is built of rough stone, plastered with lime, and covered with pantiles. The Viceroy's chapel is a neat edifice, near the palace, but detached from it. The streets are not only spacious and convenient, but remarkable for their cleanliness; many of them containing ranges of shops and warehouses that would do credit to the cities of Europe. There is a custom here, which appears to be worthy of imitation in all places of considerable trade and commerce; — that all persons of the same profession occupy the same street or district; and a deviation from this rule is very rarely known in this city. Of the population of this place, I could not procure any accurate information, but from its extent, and the general observations I was enabled to make, if may, I think, be considered, without exaggeration, as amounting to two hundred thousand souls. The people, who are Roman Catholics, are very much attached to the ceremonials of their religion, which they observe with extreme superstition. The churches are very numerous, and fitted up with ostentatious finery. On the festivals of their patrons these edifices are richly adorned, and beautifully illuminated. Some of them we saw lighted up with so much splendor, as to offer a very striking spectacle, and to bear the appearance rather of a public rejoicing, than a partial act of parochial devotion. Near the middle of the city, and on a commanding eminence, there is a public observatory furnished with an astronomical apparatus.

The inhabitants are very ostentatious in their dress; and every rank of people is in the habit of considering swords as essential to public appearance; even children are not considered as exempt from this ornamental weapon. The dress of the ladies bears a near resemblance to that of European women, except in the decoration of the head. Their hair is smoothed back in the front, and adorned with artificial flowers, beads; and feathers, fantastically arranged; behind, it falls down in a variety of plaited tresses, intermixed with ribands of various colours, each tress terminating in a rose made of riband. They also wear a large mantle of silk, hanging loosely behind in the form of a train which is borne by one servant, while another holds an umbrella to shade the face of his mistress from the sun. The females of Brazil are generally of a pale complexion, but have a certain delicacy of feature which renders them very pleasing objects; and the affability of their manners heightens the agreeableness of their personal attractions.

The trade of this place is very considerable, and the source of great wealth to the inhabitants, as well as to the mother country. The various articles which are exported from hence, are the same as those produced in other parts of the Portuguese settlements in Brazil. The wharfs are very large and peculiarly commodious; and we were very much amused on observing the dexterity with which the slaves loaded and unloaded the barges that lay alongside them. The rice, of which great quantities appeared to be exported from this settlement, was all contained in undressed bullock's hides.

At a small distance from the city, on the west side of it, is a large convent, but more remarkable for strength than elegance.

It is built round several quadrangular courts, paved with large flat stones, surrounded by piazzas, and kept in a state of perfect cleanliness. It is divided into two parts, containing a great number of apartments which are distinctly appropriated to a religious community of either sex.

The persons who composed Lord Macartney's suite were indulged with the permission to visit this convent, and the nuns took opportunities to throw out to them a variety of little elegant toys of their own fabric. Nor had even their confined and devoted situation prevented them from knowing the art of manufacturing another kind of article, called billets doux, which they contrived to have conveyed to some of the English visitors. They even applied to Lord Macartney, by the director of the convent, for the use of his band of music, which accordingly performed at several morning concerts, within these sacred walls. There is also a very spacious garden, where the religious ladies are allowed to enjoy such recreation as they can find in a place, surrounded with walls of at least forty feet in height; which, as if they did not form a sufficient security, are constantly guarded on the outside by a party of soldiers.

On the north-west side of the town there is a stupendous aqueduct, which is an object of uncommon curiosity. It is in the form of a bridge, contains eighty arches, and in some parts is, at least, one hundred and fifty feet in height; and is seen, in some points of view, with peculiar effect, rising gradually above the loftiest buildings of the city. This immense chain of arches stretches across a valley, and unites the hills that form it. The object for which it was erected is completely answered, as it conveys water from perennial springs, at the distance of five miles, into the town, where, by means of leaden pipes, it is conducted to a large and elegant reservoir at the beach, opposite to the Viceroy's palace. This water is of the best quality, and is withal so very abundant, as not only to afford an adequate supply for all the wants of the inhabitants, but to furnish the ships that come into the harbour with this necessary element.

The military establishment at Rio Janeiro is on a very respectable footing. The soldiers are not only well cloathed and disciplined but are allowed to enjoy all the privileges of citizens. It seems to be a policy of the Portuguese government, and a very wise one it is, to render the situation of the soldiery in their American settlements, not only comfortable in itself, and respectable in its character, but, in some degree, as I should imagine, the source of pecuniary advantage. Thus the loyalty and zeal of the soldiers are happily secured in a situation so important from its value, and where vigilance and fidelity, in those who guard it, become more necessary in proportion to its remoteness from the mother country. Whether it is that their pay is proportionably advanced in the service of these settlements, or that they are allowed any distinct advantages, I cannot tell; but they certainly appear to be in a state of comparative affluence, which no other soldiery that I have either seen or heard of can be supposed to possess. The number of troops in Rio Janeiro, including cavalry and infantry, amount to twenty thousand men; and the militia are, at least, double that number. At the same time, the place is admirably fortified both by art and nature. It is situated about two miles from the mouth of the bay, and is defended by nine strong forts, well supplied with artillery, and sufficient garrisons. There are also two small islands in the middle of the bay, one at the entrance, called Santa Cruz Fort, and another at a short distance, which still add to the strength of the situation, and the difficulty of attacking it with advantage.

Saturday 15. Sir George Staunton set off with a party on an excursion to the Sugar Loaf Hill, a very high rock, situated on the left side of the entrance to the harbour; and at five o'clock in the afternoon, Lord Macartney, who was still very much indisposed, accompanied by Sir Erasmus Gower, returned, in a private manner, on board the Lion.

All the baggage being put into carts to he carried to the beach, the officers who commanded the guard at the house where Lord Macartney had resided, ordered a party of soldiers to attend each cart, till the whole of their cargoes was deposited on board the boats which were in waiting to receive them. During my attendance on this duty, I had an opportunity of seeing the Viceroy return in great state from the church, where he had been to attend some particular ceremony of his religion.

At half past ten in the morning we weighed anchor, and worked down to Santa Cruz Fort, and came to, soon after, in fifteen fathom water. The next day we ran out of the harbour, and took our leave of Rio Janeiro.

Tuesday 25. Nothing occurred for some time, which requires particular notice; not even that change a weather which, would justify a circumstantial account of it. The weather was, in general, moderate light airs, fresh breezes, with occasional haziness and drizly rain, which would include every description of it during the remainder of the year 1792. It may not, however, be thought altogether improper in me to mention, that, though so far removed from our friends and native clime, with such a waste of water around us, and so long a tract of ocean before us, the festival of Christmas-day was not forgotten, and that its social distinctions were practised and enjoyed in the little world that bore us along.

Monday 31. About ten in the morning we saw the island of Tristan de Cunha. It is barren, uninhabited, and almost an inaccessible island, situated in the heart of the southern ocean, in thirty-seven deg. seven min. and thirty sec. south latitude, and about forty-five deg. east longitude. When we first observed this mountain rising above the clouds, it appeared to be as high as the peak of Teneriffe. It is a natural place of resort to prodigious numbers of wild birds; while the surrounding sea is the habitation of whales, sealions, and other monsters of the deep. Lieutenant Whitman, who was sent on shore in the cutter, to sound for anchorage, gave a very favourable report or the beach, as well as of a run of water which issued from a cliff, and, flowing across the shore, discharged itself into the sea.

1793, January. Mr. Whitman, on this occasion shot a sea-lion and an albatross; the latter of which he brought on board. It measured nine feet from the bill to the extremity of the tail, but weighed no more than three pounds and an half.

Tuesday 1. In consequence of this information, Sir Erasmus Gower proposed to send a watering party on shore the next morning; while Sir George Staunton suggested an excursion thither at the same time, to see what this island offered to his observation in any branch of natural history. For this purpose, a certain number of artillerymen were ordered to be in readiness, by three o'clock in the morning, and to be properly equipped for the expedition against the amphibious monsters of the shore. At midnight, however, a very heavy gale came on, which caused the ship to start her anchor, and our situations became very alarming; for if the wind, which blew directly on the rock, had not changed, we must inevitably have perished. This unexpected alteration in the weather frustrated the designs which had been formed of obtaining further information relative to this curious place.

Sunday 20. The weather continued to be moderate, with fresh breezes, till this day; when there came on an heavy gale of wind, which occasioned such a rolling of the ship, as to interfere with those enjoyments that make seamen forget the inconveniencies of their situation.

Tuesday 22. The moderate weather returned, with all the comforts that usually attend it.

Friday, February, 1. About four o'clock in the morning saw land, bearing E. N. E. supposed to be ten leagues distant which, in about four hours, was discovered to be the island of Amsterdam, situate in the Indian ocean, and lying in latitude thirty deg. forty-three min. south, and seventy-seven deg. twenty min. East longitude. As we approached the island, we could plainly discover three men on the shore in consequence of which the ensign was immediately hoisted. We here saw a great number of water snakes, and a prodigious quantity of fish resembling cod, and weighing, in general, from three to eight pounds. At noon the yawl was hoisted out; and the master sent to sound for anchorage. In consequence of this information we hove to, and anchored with the best bower, in twenty eight fathom water, on the east side of the island. The master also gave an account that there were five men on the island, who had come from the Ile de France, for the purpose of killing seals, with which this place abounds.

Wednesday 6. Sir George and Mr. Staunton, with several other gentlemen, accompanied by a party of artillery soldiers, properly armed, went on shore, and made great destruction among the natives of the place; such as seals, penguins, albatrosses, Etc. Great quantities of fish were also caught here, and salted, for the service of the ship.

On the north-east end of the island, nearly opposite to where the Lion lay at anchor, there is a very commodious bason, about a mile in diameter, and surrounded by inaccessible and per- pendicular rocks; at the entrance of which, on the north-west corner, stands a lofty isulated rock, which bears the form of a sugar-loaf. This bason might, at a small expense, be made a place of safe retreat for ships of any burthen; as it contains, in many parts, thirteen fathom water, and possesses an excellent landing place. We here caught great quantities of fish which resemble our lobster, both in shape and size, but are of a very superior flavour. We also observed great numbers of sharks all round the island which is the more extraordinary, as the shark is seldom seen in these latitudes.

On our landing, we were met by the five seal-hunters, whom we have already mentioned; who, with great civility, conducted us to an hut at a small distance from the beach. They were natives of France and America, who had made commercial engagement to come and reside in this island for the space of eighteen months, in order to kill seals, whose skins are sold to very great advantage to ships which touch at the Isle of France. At this time they had only been six months in their present situation, when, according to their account, they had already killed eight thousand seals.

At a small distance from their hut, these men had, with much labour, and no small hazard, formed a path, by which they contrived to get over a mountain to kill seals on the other side of the island. On ascending this path, we came to a small spring, whose water is equal to boiling heat; and some fish which we put into it, were as perfectly dressed in six minutes, as if they had been dressed on board the ship. It should be also observed, that while we were attending to this process, we distinctly heard the same kind of bubbling sound as proceeds from water boiling in a vessel over the fire. On the top of the mountain there is a volcano, from whence a substance issues, which these men represented as bearing the appearance, and possessing the qualities of salt-petre.

This island is about eight miles in length, and six in breadth; in some parts it is altogether flat, particularly to the west, and gradually rises to the very high land in the center of it. It is a very barren spot, bearing neither tree nor shrub, and whose only produce is a kind of coarse, tufted grass, with very thick stalks, Every thing in this island bears the mark of having undergone the action of fire. The earth, and even the rocks and stones, on approaching the volcano, were so hot as to scorch our skin, to burn our shoes, and blister our feet. We were conducted about this desolate place by the five seal-hunters; whose care and kind attentions preserved us not only from inconvenience, but danger, which it would have been impossible for us to have avoided, if we had not been subject to their direction.

The volcanic mountain is about three miles in its ascent, which is very steep and rugged; and in its ascent, as well as descent, attended with continual difficulties. In short, we had met with so many obsiacles both in going up and coming down it, that two signal guns had been fired from the Lion, which, with the Hindostan were both under weigh, when we reached the shore; where, after an interval of no common alarm and apprehension, we found a boat that conveyed us on board. The night being dark, we saw the flames of the volcano bursting forth in six different places, at a considerable distance from each other, which formed a grand and affecting spectacle.

It may here be proper to remark, that the thermometer, which, on board, stood at fifty-five degrees, rose on the island to seventy-four; and, towards the top of the mountain, to seventy-seven degrees and an half: a circumstance which must be attributed to the heat of the volcano.

Friday 15. This morning, at three o'clock, a very large meteor, or fire-ball, rose from the north-north-west, and continued in view for some minutes, passing off, without any explosion, to the south-south-east. It threw a kind of blue light over the sails and deck; but the illumination was so strong, that the most trifling object could be distinguished.

Monday 18. At eight o'clock in the morning we discovered

the Trial rocks, about a league to the windward; the sea beating over them to an immense height. These rocks are not visible as they do not rise above the surface of the water, nor are they much beneath it. They are situated in the Indian ocean, in about one hundred and six degrees of east longitude, and twenty-five or twenty-six degrees of fourth latitude.

Thursday 28. In proceeding up the straits of Sunda we saw the Hindostan lying at anchor, near the north island. In the afternoon a Dutch prow came along side the Lion, laden with turtle, poultry, and fruit, for sale. The owner of the prow was a Dutchman; but those that rowed it were Malays, and some of them females.

Wednesday, March, 6. At three o'clock in the afternoon we came to in Batavia road, in five fathom water: the careening island bearing west-north-west. We were saluted by all the English ships in the road, and one French vessel. At sun rise we saluted the Dutch garrison with thirteen guns, which were returned: at seven we returned the salutes of all the ships; and at eight received the members of the Dutch council with the same honours. Those gentlemen composed a deputation from the Governor-General of Batavia, to invite Lord Macartney on shore, and to know on what day and hour he would be pleased to land. His Lordship, accordingly, fixed on Friday, the 8th inst. at nine o'clock in the morning, it being the anniversary of the birth-day of his Serene Highness the Prince of Orange.

Friday 8. At six o'clock in the morning, a salute of twenty-one lowerdeck guns was fired, in honour of his Serene Highness: and, at the time appointed, the Ambassador, attended by his whole suite, went on shore with the usual formalities.

In a short time after Lord Macartney had quitted the ship, a Dutch officer of distinction with several ladies and gentlemen, came on board the Lion, from Batavia, to take a view of her.

They were received with all possible politeness by Lieutenant Campbell, and appeared to be much satisfied with their reception. A very fine young English lady was one of the party, and enhanced the honour of the visit.

In the afternoon I went on shore in the launch, having charge of the baggage belonging to the suite, which was, with some difficulty rowed up the canal, and safely landed before the door of the royal Batavian hotel, where the packages were distributed in the apartments or the gentlemen to whom they respectively belonged. The Ambassador, with Sir George and Mr. Staunton, were received at the house of Mr. Wiggerman, one of the members of the supreme council.

Sunday 10. At six o'clock Lord Macartney went in form to an entertainment at the Governor-General's country residence, at which the principal persons of both sexes in Batavia were present. The whole concluded with a magnificent supper and ball, which lasted to a very late hour of the morning.

While I was at breakfast this morning, my ears were assailed by the most dreadful shrieks I ever heard; and, on making the inquiry which humanity suggested, I discovered that there horrid sounds proceeded from a Malay slave, whom the master of the hotel had ordered to be punished for somee omission of his duty. This poor wretch, who was upwards of seventy years of age, appeared standing in a back court, while two other slaves were scourg-ing him in the most unrelenting manner with small canes. This horrid punishment they continued for thirty-five minutes, till the back and hips of this victim to severity exhibited one lacerated surface, from whence the blood trickled down on the pavement. The master then commanded the correcting slaves to give over their tormenting office, and sent the smarting culprit, as he was, and without any application whatever to his wounds, to continue the laborious duties of his station. On remonstrating with the master of the hotel, for this cruel and barbarous treatment of his servant—he answered, that the Malays were so extremely wicked, that neither the house, nor any one in it, would be safe for a moment, if they were not kept in a state of continued terror, by the most rigid and exemplary punishment. But this was not all; for another act of necessary severity, as it was represented to me, though of a different kind, immediately succeeded. Two slaves, in carrying off the breakfast equipage from our table, contrived between them to break a plate; for which offence, as it could not be precisely fixed upon either, they were both ordered to suffer. They were, accordingly, each of them furnished with canes, and compelled to beat each other; which they did with reciprocal severity; as two other slaves stood by with bamboos, to correa any appearance of lenity in them.

Notwithstanding the extreme heat of the weather, I was impatient to take a view of the city; and the result of my observations I now present to the reader.

The city of Batavia is situated in the island of Java, and is the capital of all the Dutch settlements and colonies in the East Indies. It lies in one hundred and four degrees of east longitude, and six degrees of south latitude; and from its situation between the Equator and the Tropic of Capricorn, the climate is insupportably hot.

The city is built in a square form, and surrounded with a strong wall, about thirty feet high. There are four gates, one in each angle, with a fort, battery, and barracks for fokliers at each gate. The forts are mounted with artillery, garrisoned with troops, and surrounded with ditches, over which draw-bridges are let down during the day; but after nine o'clock at night there is no passage over them without a signed order from the Governor-General.

The streets. of the city are broad; handsomely built, and

well paved; and in the center of every principal street there is a canal of about sixty feet broad; so that there is no communication between the two sides of the same street but by bridges, of which their are great numbers thrown over the water at no great distance from each other. The houses are, in general, three stories high; and each story very lofty, on account of the excessive heat of the climate. They are all built according to one general design, and possess a certain degree of grandeur. both in their external and interior appearance. The lower story of the houses is built of stone, covered with marble; and the upper part is composed of a fine red brick; the windows, which are very large, are coped with marble; and the wooden frame-work richly gilt and ornamented. The inhabitants appear to have a very great pride in preserving the exterior beauty of their houses, and use a sort of red paint for that purpose, with which they wash, or colour the fronts of them at least once a week.

On each side of the canal there are two rows of evergreen trees, which add very much to the beauty of the streets. There are also in different parts of each street, small square buildings, with seats in them for the accommodation of passengers, as shelter or shade may be necessary, from the violence of the rain or the heat of the sun.

The only public buildings which merit particular attention, are the palace of the Governor-General, the arsenal, the stadthouse, and the high church.

The first of them forms a termination to the principal street of the place; its fore-court is handsomely railed, and the front gate is guarded by centinels. This edifice is of stone, and of an imposing appearance it consists of four stories, with a central dome crowned with a: turret; there are also large wings projecting on either side from the main body, with surrounding piazzas. A battalion of soldiers is constantly on duty here, and consists chiefly of Malays commanded by European officers. I saw also a few European soldiers, who, though they were much better cloathed and accoutred than the native troops, have such a meagre, pale, and ghastly appearance, as to be but ill-qualified for the duties of their own, or any other profession. I was informed by some of them, that not one in twenty of the military who came from Europe ever returned thither; and that even those who escape from hence, and survive all the dangers and disorders of the climate, generally go back to their own country with emaciated forms and debilitated constitutions.

This palace appears to have been built at several distinct periods, from the dates which are engrained in different parts of it. The dates 1630, 1636, and 1660, mark, as I suppose, the particular years when certain principal parts of it were erected. Before the court there is a kind of lawn, with a walk in the middle shaded with rows of trees; and to the left of this lawn, at a small distance from the palace, stands the arsenal, before which lay a great number of new brass guns, gun-carriages; shot of all kinds piled up, and fifty large cannon completely mounted. This building, as may be supposed, is more remarkable for its strength, than the beauty of its external appearance, and contains an immense quantity of all kinds of ordnance and military stores, both in its chamber, and in the deep vaults beneath the building.

Beyond this lawn or walk is a canal, over which a draw-bridge communicates with one of the forts; and near it is a very elegant stone building, with corresponding wings, built in a very pleasing stile of architecture: it is called the small armoury, and, as I was informed on the spot, contains two hundred thousand stand of arms. Around this edifice there are several large courts, which contain residences for the principal officers, as well as barracks for twenty-thousand men: but this vast range of buildings is no longer inhabited, on account of the contagious disorders that are so frequent in this city. The officers have all of them places of residence at some distance from the town; and all the European regiments are quartered in the country; the guard on the city duty being regularly relieved every morning. The regixnent appointed for duty marches every day into town, at six o'clock in the morning, to the grand parade opposite the Governor's palace; one battalion of which attends the Governor's duty, and the other is distributed among the several guards around the city.

Near the fort, which has been already mentioned, stands the custom-house, belonging to the Dutch East-India Company, with their store-houses, and other commercial erections. There is also a small dock yard, where boats and a few inconsiderable vessels were building. There is a chain thrown across the canal, every night, to prevent all communication with boats after a certain hour, and a fort has been erected near the custom-house, with a view as it appears, to protect it: but without pretending to any knowledge in the science of defence, or military tactics, I could discover that this place was in no condition to resist a well-appointed enemy; nor could I reconcile the defenceless state of this valuable settlement to the wealth and importance of it.

At the end of the street leading from the Governor's house, and in a handsome square, stands the stadthouse, where the courts of justice are held, and the supreme council meet to proceed in their deliberations: it is a very fine building, with an interior court surrounded by a piazza. At a small distance from the stadthouse is the principal church of the city, which is surrounded by a cemetery. It is a large, plain, square building, with a dome in the center, and a lofty turret springing from it. The inside is fitted up in a very beautiful manner; the tribune belonging to the Governor-General is very much enriched; the pews are very commodiously arranged; and, indeed, every part is admirably adapted to the purposes of that religion to which it is devoted. The walls of the church are entirely covered with escutcheons and painted inscriptions, sacred to the memory of the dead: these inscriptions are of different sizes, but being painted in the same form, enclosed in gilt frames, and disposed with judgment, produce a very pleasing effect.

The civil government of Batavia and the island of Java is perfectly arbitrary, and vested in the Governor and Supreme Council in all matters excepting there of trade and commerce, which are subject to an officer called a Director General, from whose decisions there is no appeal.

The severity of the laws, and the rigour with which they are executed, could find no justification in a settlement belonging to an European government; were it not for the savage and ferocious disposition of the natives of the country, whom no punishments, however frequent or severe, are able to maintain in that state of discipline and good order, which is so necessary to the well-being and comfort of civilised life.

The number of regular troops quartered in the neighbourhood of Batavia, including both the European and Malay regiments, amounts to about twelve thousand men there are also upwards of twenty thousand native militia, who are regularly cloathed. and paid; but though they are frequently mustered, by order of the Governor, they are never actually embodied, but in time of war, or in consequence of some civil commotion. The European troops are cloathed in a manner suitable to the climate, are allowed to carry on any trade or profession for which they are qualified, and are otherwise remunerated by particular privileges; if any thing can remunerate them for the dangers and inconveniences that result from this ungenial clime. The Malay troops, on the contrary, are destitute of any decent cloathing; at least, none of them are allowed shoes or stockings; and in this miserable state of equipment they do their duty.

Batavia is extremely populous; and among its inhabitants may be found the natives of every European country: the larger proportion of them, however, are Chinese, who appear to be a quiet and induttrious people. It seemed to be a general opinion among those, of whom I had an opportunity to make the inquiry, that this city contains two hundred thousand souls; one half of which are supposed to be Chinese, And the other, Europeans and native Malays: nor when I consider the extent of the city and its suburbs, do I conceive it to be an exaggerated calculation.

On my return to the hotel after the morning's exturxion, of which I have given the information it produced, I found, with great concern, that Lord Macartney had been seized with a violent fit of the gout, and was returned on board the Lion; so that all the various entertainments which were preparing to have enlivened the time of our stay at Batavia, were frustrated by this very unpleasant change in the health of the distinguished person who was the object of them.

I supped this evening at the Batavian hotel, in company with two French gentlemen, who had been so fortunate as to escape from a band of Malays. The villains had attacked them in the street; a circumstance which often happens, and particularly to strangers who pass the streets after it is dark.

Tuesday 12. I repeated my excursions through the city.

Wednesday 13. Several gentlemen of the Ambassador's suite being taken ill, they were ordered to go on board their respective ships, and large quantities of fruit were purchased for their use and refreshment.

In the evening I went to see the tragedy of Mahomet, and paid a rix-dollar for admission. The theatre is situated in the middle of a large garden, which is a place of public resort for the Batavians of every rank and denomination. It is a spacious brick building, decorated with great elegance, and fitted up with front and side boxes, and galleries: its orchestra also contained a tolerable band of music.

The play, as far as I could judge, from the attitudes of the actors, and the expression of their countenances, for the whole was in the Dutch language, was very well performed. The entertainment, to my surprize, was Barnaby Brittle, and afforded much amusement. The audience was very brilliant, but the more splendid part of it arose from the superior figure, appearance, and beauty of some English ladies who graced the boxes on the occasion.

Thursday 14. At noon there was an auction, or, as it is here termed, an outcry of certain lands and estates, belonging to some of those fortunate individuals, who, having escaped the dangers of the climate, return with the large fortunes they have acquired here, to enjoy the comforts and luxurious ease of Europe.

These sales cannot take place, but under the inspection of the Commissary General, or his deputies, who must always be present on the occasion. Notice is given of these auctions throughout the city and suburbs by a certain number of men, who beat gongs to collect the people together in the different streets; when a person, authorised by the Commissary General, reads over the articles to be sold, and the conditions of sale: in every other respect, these sales are concluded in the same manner as those in England.

Friday 15. Captain Mackintosh came on shore, and purchased a French brig, to answer the purpose of the Jackall, from whom we had been so long separated, that we despaired of seeing her again.

Saturday 16. This evening I had reason to consider as one of the most fortunate of my life, having escaped from a gang of Malays, who certainly formed a design, as they had almost irresistible temptation to destroy me.

The principal part of the baggage belonging to the Ambassador's suite having been already sent on board the respective ships, I was charged by Mr. Maxwell to see that the ref of the packages, and a chest of dollars, were put on board a prow hired for the purpose; and was ordered, at the same time, to go down with the prow to the boom, and remain there till Mr. Maxwell arrived, which he promised to do in half an hour. I accordingly set off, and arrived at the boom about eight o'clock, when I fastened the boat to the custom-house quay, and anxiously waited the arrival of Mr. Maxwell. In this unpleasant situation I remained till nine o'clock, when the boom was thrown across the water, and the bridge drawn up. My uneasiness now became of a very serious nature, as I well knew that Mr. Maxwell could not reach me but by a special order from the Governor; while I was not only in danger of losing the property under my care, from the Malays, who were continually running backwards and forwards to the prow, and examining the articles on board, but of being myself sacrificed to make the booty more secure to them. In this situation, I formed the resolution of making the best of my way to the Lion; and, accordingly, ordered the Malays to row off for the ship, which they at first refused; but after shewing them some money, they took the oars, as I expected, to comply with my wishes; but, instead of rowing towards the ship, they rowed the prow close to the shore, about a gun-shot from the mouth of the canal, and at least half a mile from any house. They then all run ashore, and, in spite of threats or entreaties, left me to myself in a much worse situation than I was before, as I was now more remote from any assistance, in case I should be in a situation to require it.

In about twenty minutes there wretches returned in greater numbers, which increased my apprehensions, as they all entered into the prow, and, putting off from the land, attempted to row into the bay; in short, a violent scuffle ensued between us, in which I at length suceeded, by means of a drawn sword that I used with some effect, in driving them all on shore, except one man, whom I compelled, by terror of the same instrument, to row the vessel to the custom-house, where I waited till past eleven; and, despairing of seeing Mr. Maxwell till the next day, I took all the articles out of the boat, and lodged them in a public house for further security. I had, however, scarce finished this necessary arrangement, when I saw Mr. Maxwell, attended by several slaves with flambeaux, arrive on the opposite side of the water. I instantly hailed him; when he came over to me, and all the packages being again put into the prow, we set sail for the Lion, and some time after midnight arrived on board.

The hotel in which the Ambassador's suite resided, during our stay at Batavia, is a very superb building of its kind, and was erected at the expense of government for the accommodation of foreigners and mercantile strangers. It is under the sole management, and controul of the Governor-General and Council, by whose regulations the business of the house is conducted.

It is called the Royal Bativian and Foreign Hotel, and this title appears in large golden letters in the front of the house, with the date of 1729, the year in which it was built. It contains three regular stories and, as each floor is very lofty, for the benefit of the air, the building rises to a considerable height.

It is constructed, like the other edifices of the place, with brick painted of a red colour, while the seams of mortar between are proportionably whitened: the windows are also very large and broad, the frames of which are gilt or curiously painted; the whole forming a very large and handsome structure.

There are three doors in the front, and a kind of terrace raised above the pavement before them, which is covered by a portico; where the company, resident in the house, usually sit after dinner and smoke their pipes: each of these doors forms an entrance into a hall about two hundred feet in length, and about sixty in breadth; at the extremity of which there is a large staircase that leads to the bedchamber apartments, and the flat roof above them.

In the center hall there are at least thirty elegant lamps and chandeliers, which are lighted up every night, and, opposite to them, on the wall, is a range of looking-glasses, the reflection of which heightens the brilliance of the illumination: the piers between them are adorned with paintings. In the center of the middle hall is a large arch, from which a silver chandelier is suspended; the other halls have each a door of the same dimensions exactly opposite, and these respectively lead to an apartment with an alcove roof, neatly ornamented with stucco, which contains a billiard table surrounded with lamps. From the center of the principal hall the coup d'œil at night is perfectly enchanting, from the great number of lights, and the regular order in which they are placed; the billiard rooms also with their lamps corresponding exactly with each other.

Behind the house there is a spacious gallery with piazzas, from whence a large shade of silk, fancifully painted with figures and grotesque characters, is occasionally lowered in the day, as the heat of the sun may require; in the evening it is entirely dropped, when the gallery is lighted up in the same manner as the apartments already described. Beyond this gallery, there is a court paved with large flat stones, and surrounded with a variety of offices for poulterers, butchers, and other domestic uses, with a spacious kitchen, and every accessory accommodation. The upper story of this range of building is divided into granaries and chambers for the principal and other slaves, of which there are altogether at least ninety, of both sexes, who belong to the master of the hotel. These menial persons are promoted according to their merits; and, if they are industrious and attentive to the duties of their several departments, they may, from the emoluments of their situation, which are very considerable, be soon in a condition to purchase their freedom.

In the great hall on the firist floor, which serves as a vestibule to the sleeping apartments that surround it, there is a chrystal lamp replenished with cocoa-nut oil, always burning on a table at the door of each room, which is ready for the person that occupies it, at whatever time he may choose to retire to his repose; it being the custorn of the hotel that every one should keep the key of his own room, as a security against the Malays, who are of such an incorrigible nature, that no punishment can ultimately deter them from indulging their disposition to pilfer.

The public regulations of the house resemble those of European hotels, and the table which was kept for the Ambassador's suite was very superb. The breakfast always consisted of tea, coffee, chocolate, and cocoa, with every kind of cold meat, broiled fish, and eggs; to which were added jellies, sweet-meats, and honey, with various kinds of wines and confectionary, all furnished in great abundance, and arranged in the handsomest manner. Both the dinner and supper consist of the most delicate dishes, and dressed in a superior stile of cookery. The servants table was also supplied with equal propriety and plenty.

The rate of living here, however; is very expensive, and the prices of liquors very exorbitant: small beer and porter were charged half a crown English per bottle. But when the prodigious rent of this hotel, amounting, as the landlord himself assured me, to sixty thousand rix-dollars per annum, and the expense of importing liquors and other commodities from Europe, with the duties on them, is considered, the high price of living, in such a situation, could no longer be regarded either with surprise or discontent.

The dress of the inhabitants of Batavia takes its rise from the custom of their respective countries. The European ladies, indeed, seem not to be altogether governed by this principle; but suit their dresses, to their own peculiar fancy, and the circumstances the climate; while the Dutch and the Malay women, in come degree, imitate their fashions. The head-dress of the latter, however, is altogether different, and of a very curious appearance. — The hair is combed backward from the forehead, and smoothed with oil and essences in such a manner as to wear the appearance of being japanned; it is then twisted hard, and, being laid in a circular form round the crown of the head, is fastened by a large comb with a number of gold and silver pins, the heads of which are formed of precious stones, according to the rank of the wearer.

Hair powder is very little used in Batavia, and by the Europeans alone. It was, however, with no small degree of exultation that I saw the decided superiority which the few English ladies who reside here, possess over every other denomination of females, not only in gracefulness of person, and sweetness of countenance, but, also, in the simplicity of their dress and the elegance of their manners.

The suburbs of Batavia, or, as it is generally called, the Chinese town, from being chiefly inhabited by those people, lie on the south and west sides of the ditch that surrounds the city wall, and are scattered about the country for several miles. The houses are, in general, of wood, and have no pretensions to elegance or beauty; though their warehouses are fitted up with a certain degree of glare and gaudiness. A great variety of manufactures are carried on here by the industrious Chinamen: indeed, all the artificers and mechanics in Batavia are from China; the Europeans, through a foolish and unpardonable pride, considering it as beneath them to perform any mechanical operations; and the Malays appear to be cursed with a natural incapacity to be instructed in any thing above the drudgery of manual labour.

The whole of these suburbs forms a scattered mass of deformity and confusion; and the horrid stenches which arise from stagnant water, and various filthy causes, cannot be described, In the surrounding country there are a great many beautiful seats and villas, with fine gardens; but the ground being every where swampy, the number of drains with which it is necessarily intersected, renders it more or less unwholesome in every part.

In passing through the fish market, I was under the necessity of retiring into a tavern, to get some Madeira and water, in order to recover myself from the overcoming effect of the putrid smells that assailed me. There appeared, however, to be a great abundance of fish in this obnoxious place; but, except turtle, they bore a very exorbitant price.

The city and suburbs of Batavia certainly form one of the most unwholesome spots in the world, and may be justly termed the grave of Europeans: but the unsalutary and infectious nature of the place might be very much alleviated by an attention to cleanliness, which seems   not to be at all considered by the government or police of the city. A company of scavengers would be of infinite use to the comfort and health of the inhabitants of Batavia; but there is no such establishment.

The heat of the sun is so great, that the canals are frequently dried up, or their waters rendered putrid: but this is not so malignant a source of pestilential disease, as the nastiness that prevails among the lower classes of the people, and the inattention to remove the receptacles of putrefaction among the higher orders of them. Nor is it easily to be reconciled, that the spirit of cleanliness, so prevalent in Holland, should totally evaporate in a voyage to the most important of its Asiatic possessions. Nay, it has been considered by political writers, that the inattention to remedy the evils which have been described, is to be attributed to the commercial policy of the Dutch, in order to discourage foreigners from settling among them, and sharing the great, but hazardous, advantages to be derived from participating in any branch of commerce in this oriental emporium: or, in case of a foreign war, to deter any enemy from invading a place, the very airs of which are more hostile to human life than the weapons of battle. I shall only add, that, within the last twenty years, no less than ninety-eight thousand deaths appear on the records of the public hospital in Batavia.

Sunday 17. At six o'clock in the morning we weighed anchor and made sail, running between the island of Onroost and the main. This island is situated in the middle of the bay, and about four miles from Batavia. Its length does not exceed three quarters of a mile, and it is no more than half a mile in breadth. It contains, nevertheless, an handsome populous town, with a strong fort. In this little spot there are several founderies and manufactures, and the whole is a scene of industry and landscape beauty. It is also surrounded with several islands of the same description, most of which are inhabited; great numbers of people wisely preferring these situations; which, though immoderately hot, are free from those contagious diseases that infect the city and suburbs of Batavia.

CHAPTER II

The Jackall brig rejoins the Lion. – Leighton, the carpenter, murdered by the Malays. – Lord Macartney views the spot where Colonel Cathcart was buried. – Came to Pulo Condore; some account of its inhabitants; their alarm. – Passed various islands. – Arrived at Turon bay, in Cochin China. – Several mandarins came on board the Lion; an account of them. – The chief minister of the King of Cochin China visits Lord Macartney. – Presents received. – Lord Macartney returns the visit on shore in form. – the master of the Lion seized by the natives, but released in a few days. – The interment of Mr. Tothill, purser of the Lion.

1793, Monday, March, 18. The owner of the French brig came on board, and was paid for her in dollars.

The weather was insupportably hot. – Lord Macartney was still so much indisposed as not to see company.

Wednesday 20. The new brig joined us, which Lord Macartney was pleased to name the Clarence, in honour of his Royal Highness the Duke of Clarence.

Boarded the Achilles, from Ostend to Batavia, who gave some account of the Jackall brig, with whom we parted company in a gale of wind in the Bay of Biscay.

Saturday 23. This morning, at six, we discovered a sail at a great distance, which, from the account given by the Ostend vessel, was supposed to be the Jackall. After a long series of doubts, conjectures, and solicitudes on the subject, Sir Erasmus Gower dispatched Lieutenant Cox, in the pinnace, to ascertain the truth. At noon, the pinnace returned with the agreeable intelligence, that the ship we had seen was the Jackall brig, whom we had long ago supposed to have been lost.

Sunday 24. Mr. Saunders, from the Jackall came on board to deliver his log-book to Sir Erasmus Gower. At four o'clock, we saw a sail, which proved to be the Concord, from China to Bengal.

Friday 29. Good Friday. William Leighton, Lord Macartney's joiner, who went ashore in order to wash his linen at the watering-place at Sumatra beach, was murdered by the Malays. His body being found covered with wounds, was brought on board the Lion, and afterwards interred, with all becoming ceremony and respect, on North Island. He was a very ingenious artisan, and honest, intelligent, and amiable man. But the melancholy which pervaded every countenance throughout the ship's company, on his death, is a more honourable and decided testimony of his merit and character, than any expressions of regard which I might employ on the occasion.

1973, April, Monday 1. At half past six, A.M. we weighed and came to sail; at eight, Mortnay Island, south by east; Stroome Rock; south-east, half a mile: at eleven, came to, in seventeen fathom water. Angara Point flag-staff, south by east. The cap, north-north-east; and button, north by east. The accommodation ladder was hoisted out after dinner, and soon after Lord

Macartney, accompanied by Sir Erasmus Gower, went ashore, and viewed the spot where the Honourable Colonel Cathcart, brother to Lord Cathcart, a former minister from the King of Great Britain to the court of China, was interred; and whose death put an end to that diplomatic expedition, which he had been appointed to conduct.

The weather continued moderate, with occasional fresh breezes and light airs, for the succeeding fortnight, which was employed in wooding, watering, receiving buffaloes on board, and making the necessary arrangements for the remaining part of the voyage. We passed, and occasionally anchored at Ninah Hand, and the Polar, Hound, and Tamarind islands.

Sunday 14. At four in the afternoun the body of Tharbuny Island bore north-north-west; and at five we came into fifteen fathom water. Found here the Sullivan homeward bound Indiaman, the Jackall, and the Clarence, with an Imperial ship. Arrived the Royal Admiral Indiaman.

Tuesday 16. The Sullivan and the Royal Admiral, Indiamen, sailed for England.

We continued coasting along, and passed by numerous islands, with moderate weather; which was only once interrupted by a squall, accompanied by rain, and followed by thunder and lightning, till we came to anchor in the south-western extremity of Pulo Condore bay.

May, Thursday 16. A party, soon after our arrival, went on shore, after having called at the Hindostan, for Sir George and Mr. Staunton, and Mr. Niaung, one of the Chinese who had accompanied us from Europe. We reached the shore in about an hour and a half; and, on our landing, some of the natives came out to meet us on the beach, with whom we proceeded towards a wood, with six men from the boats, properly armed with musquets and ammunition. We had not, however, proceeded more than an hundred yards, when we came to a few miserable huts, built of bamboo, and scattered about the place where they are situated. One of them was inhabited by a person stiled the chief, or mandarin, in whom was vested the government of the island.

This hut, like the rest, was raised about three feet from the ground, with a roof of bamboo, and supported by four posts fixed in the earth. Such is the only miserable shelter which the inhabitants possess.

In this house, if it may be thought to deserve that name, there were fderal people, all natives of Cochin China, but who spoke the Tartar language. None of them, except the chief, had any covering but a strip of linen round their waists, and a kind of black turban on their heads. The chief, to whom the rest paid great obedience, was distinguished by wearing a loose black gown, made of a stuff like crape; under which he wore a pair of wide, black silk trowsers. Over his shoulder was thrown a silver cord, to which was suspended behind a small embroidered bag of very exquisite workmanship. His head was also covered with a black turban; but he was, in common with the rest, without shoes.

At the distance of a few yards from the hut stood their temple, whose exterior form was the same as the other buildings. The inside was furnished, or, as it must have been considered by them, ornamented with some old fire-arms, a few cutlasses, and three daggers. A swivel, and some long spontoons, were laid across the roof; while several lances, and creases, (a kind of poisonous dagger, used by the Asiatic savages) were piled up against a bamboo post in the middle of the building. It was evident, from the conduct of these people, that they were not accustomed to the use of fire-arms, as they appeared to consider these warlike instruments as objects of adoration. This opinion was confirmed by the alarm and astonishment they expressed on my discharging a musquet at the trunk of a tree; and the eagerness with which they examined the place where the ball had entered. But this did not content them; for they contrived to extract the ball, which they shewed to each other with marks of extreme amazement.

We remained near two hours on shore, and entered into a treaty with the chief, to procure us as many buffaloes, with as much poultry, fruit, etc. as could be spared from the island, and for which he was to be paid his own price: to this proposition he readily agreed, and promised that the commission should be immediately executed, and the different articles be ready for delivery on the next day. After the agreement was thus amicably settled the chief offered us a regale of rice and fish, of which we all tasted. He then pointed to same cocoa-nut trees, as if to know if we should chuse to have any of them; and no sooner was it signified to him that a present of that fruit would be acceptable, than a number of his people were instantly ordered to gather them. It was surprising to see with what agility they climbed up these very lofty trees; and as they threw down the nuts, others below immediately skinned and handed them round to the company. We then took our leave of the mandarin, and, on our way to the beach, saw several canoes which were building; and one of them appeared to be of a very ingenious construction.

The island of Pulo Condore has but few inhabitants, and those it possesses are not collected together in any town, but live in bamboo huts, scattered up and down the country. It possesses nbo fruit but cocoa-nuts and water melons, and no grain but some coarse rice. It has however, plenty of buffaloes, with a kind of wild duck, and the common fowls, some of which are domesticated with them. This island, however, has a noble bay, which produces a fish that resembles our whiting, in great abundance, and has a safe anchorage, except along the shore, where for about three quarters of a mile, it is full of shoals. The island is subject to the king of Cochin China, and lies in the China ocean. Long. one hundred and seven deg. Twenty-six min. east. Lat. two deg. forty min. north.

On returning to the Ships we met with a very heavy squall,

attended with violent rain.

Friday 17. This morning I went ashore with a party, accompanied by Mr. Niaung, in order to receive the several articles for which a bargain had been made with the mandarin on the preceding day.

On our landing, and going to the hut belonging to the chief, we found, to our utter astonishment, that the people had deserted their habitations, and carried off every article with them: even the temple was stripped of all its warlike treasure. This extraordinary and unexpected circumstance was, however, explained in a letter, which we found in the chief's hut. It was written in Chinese characters, and expressed the apprehensions of the islanders at seeing our ships in their bay: a sight they had never beheld before. In short, this appearance was so formidable to them, that they concluded our designs must be hostile; and in order to avoid the destruction which they imagined us to have meditated against them, they had, during the night, conveyed away their effects, and retired to the mountains. The letter also represented their extreme poverty, and implored us with the most humble expressions, not to burn or destroy their huts, as they proposed to re-inhabit them as soon as the squadron had sailed. We, therefore, returned to the ships as we left them, without fruits, or fowls, or buffaloes.

Saturday 18. Heavy gales. At four in the afternoon squally; at eight, weighed anchor, and came to sail.

Thursday 23. Having passed in the intermediate time several islands of different forms, we, this day, saw the extremes of Polu Canton, an island off the coast of Cochin China, bearing north by west, to north-west by west.

Sunday 26. At nine in the evening we anchored in Turon Bay, in Cochin China; and found there a Portuguese brig, who saluted us with eleven guns.

Monday 27. The ship's company employed in watering. The water here is of a reddish colour. Several prows came along-side the Lion with ducks, cocoa-nuts, and joghry, for sale. Several mandarins also came on board to see the ship.

Tuesday 28. Men were sent on shore to raise tents for the sick.

Wednesday 29. The Ambassador was visited by several mandarins, with a great train of attendants. They were entertained with wines and liquors of various kinds, which, however, they were very cautious in tasting, till Lord Macartney banished all apprehensions by setting them the example: they then drank, without reserve, whatever was offered to them; but they appeared to prefer cherry and ratberry brandy to all the other liquors with which they were regaled.

The dress of these persons consisted chiefly of a black loose gown, of a kind of crape, with silk trowsers, slippers, and a black turban: a girdle of silver cordage was also tied round their waist: Sorrie of them, but whether it arose from accident, or was a badge of distinction, I cannot tell, wore dark blue gowns of the same stuff. The domestics were clad in a plaid or Tartan dress; their trowsers were tucked up to the knee, and their legs were entirely naked, nor did they wear either shoes or slippers; their turban was of plaid, like the rest of their very curious dress.

Friday 31. In the evening, the Prime Minister of the King of Cochin China came on board the Lion, accompanied by several Mandarins, and a considerable train of attendants, to request the Ambassador's company to dinner; in the name of the King, who had given his minister a special commission to make this invitation. It was, accordingly, signified to this distinguished personage, that his Excellency received the message with the utmost respect, and would, in consequence of it, go on shore on Tuesday morning, at ten o'clock.

1793, June, Saturday 1. After this conference, the Chinese minister, and his suite, returned in their barges, which were decorated in a very gaudy manner. They were saluted on their departure from the the ship with five guns.

In the forenoon, the Ambassador received a visit from two mandarins, who brought from the King of Cochin China a present consisting of

10 Buffaloes,

50Hogs,

160 Fowls,

150 Ducks,

200 Bags of rice, and

6 Large jars of samptsoo

The last is a liquor made in China, and imported from thence.

Sunday 2. I went a shore in the forenoon and saw the town, the name, of which is Fie-foo. It consists of nothing more than a crowd of wretched bamboo huts, though it contains a spacious market-place, well supplied with: ducks, fowls, eggs, cocoa-nuts, and fruits. The surrounding country is flat, and very fertile: but the natives seem to have little or no idea of cultivation, which would make it the scene of extreme abundance. Their principal traffic seems to be with their women, by consigning them, for a certain consideration, to the society peans who touch here. They have no coin, but a fort of small caxee, a white metal piece current in China, about the size of our farthing; and all their silver is in the form of long bars, or wedges. The residence of the principal mandarin consists of a large open range of bamboo huts, of a better form, and more elegant appearance than the rest; containing several rooms of a size and agreeable proportions, which are fitted up and furnished in a neat and ornamental manner.

Monday 3. In the afternoon the Ambassador's guards, with some of the marines, went on shore to praelife the ceremonial duties that had been assigned them for the following day.

Tuesday 4. This morning the Ambassador, attended by his whole suite, in full uniform, with Sir Erasmus Gower, Captain Mackintosh, and several of the officers of the Lion and Hindostan, went on shore with great ceremony; when, in honour of the birthday of our most excellent Sovereign, George the Third, he was saluted with twenty-one guns by the Lion, the Hindostan, and Portuguese brig. The British troops, with their officers and band of music, had been previously sent ashore to wait his Excellency's arrival.

On this day the rival standard of Great Britain was displayed at the main-top-gallant-royal mast; the St. George's ensign at the foretop-gallant ditto; and the union at the mizen.

The Ambassador was received on his landing by several mandarins, with every mark of attention and respect; when he proceeded, under an escort of his own troops, to the house of the Prime Minister, where a collation in the best manner of the country was prepared for him. Here his Excellency remained for some time; and, after an exchange of mutual civilities, returned to the Lion, when he was saluted by fifteen guns from all the ships lying at anchor.

Wednesday 5. I went ashore in the afternoon, and purchased some fruit and sugar of a very good quality; it is made in large cakes, and resembles fine bread, for which, at some small distance, it may be actually mistaken. I also saw six large elephants, which had been brought for the amusement of the mandarins; they appeared to be perfectly innocent, were obedient to every command, and performed many feats of unwieldy agility. These huge animals moved at the rate of eight miles an hour.

Friday 7. In the course of this morning the sick were received on board the ships from their late station on shore.

Mr. Jackson, master of the Lion, went in the cutter to take

soundings in the bay; but

having entered the mouth of the river Camp-vella, which rises about eight miles up the country, and forms a confluence with the river that discharges itself into Turon Bay, he inconsiderately began to survey, and take plans of the coast; but, in attempting to execute this design, he, with the seven men who accompanied him, were made prisoners by the natives, who seized the boat, and carried them to the capital city of the kingdom.

This very disagreeable intelligence was communicated from the shore by the mandarins, whose good offices were earnestly solicited by Lord Macartney and Sir Erasmus Gower, to obtain the return of these men to the ship. Indeed, this unreflecting conduct of the master might, as it was feared, be attended with consequences that would have interrupted the course of the embassy, as the country of Cochin China is tributary to the Chinese empire, and sends an annual arnhassador to the court of Pekin; so that all this business might have been misrepresented in such a manner to the Chinese government, as to have lessened the good dispositions we were disposed to believe it possessed towards the British embassy. In short, it appeared, that very serious apprehensions were entertained on that subject, by those who were the best qualified to form a right judgment of the policy and temper of the court, which was the object of our destination.

Tuesday 11. Mr. Niaung went on shore with some of the Ambassador's suite, to inquire concerning the British prisoners, and he was informed by the mandarins that they had been released, and were on their return.

Wednesday 12. William Tothill, Esq. purser of the Lion, died this morning, after an illness of a few days.

The King of Cochin China sent another large prescnt of rice to the Ambassador.

Thursday 13. The body of Mr. Tothill was interred on shore with every possible mark of respect and regard; Sir Erasmus Gower also ordered an inscription to be cut in wood, which was afterwards placed on his grave.

At four o'clock in the afternoon Mr. Jackson returned with the cutter and his men, from their imprisonment; during which period they had undergone the severest sufferings both in body and mind; and no circumstance, but their belonging to the British embassy, could have preserved them from being put to death.

Chapter III

1793, June, Sunday 16. AT four in the afternoon weighed and set sail from Turon Bay.

Tuesday 20. The weather was moderate and fair. At six P.M. saw the land north-north-east; at eight the body of the Grand Ladrone bore north-north-east.

Sir George and Mr. Staunton, with one of Lord Macartney's secretaries, were charged with letters and business to the commissioners, Mssrs. Brown, Irvine, and Jackson, who were sent from England to notify in China the expected embassy, and who were then at Macao. They accordingly set sail in the Jackall brig, accompanied by the Clarence, for that place, to execute their commission. Mr. Coa and Mr. Niaung, the two natives of China whom we had brought from Europe, accompanied them on the occasion, with the design to proceed over land to the place of their nativity.

These worthy and amiable men took a very affectionate leave

of their friends on board the Lion, with whom they had made so long a voyage; but with all the impatience natural to those who had been removed at such a distance, and for so great a length of time, from their relations, friends, and native land.

At half pall eight in the morning we came to anchor in eleven fathom water, on the north point of the Grand Ladrone island.

Sunday 23. The Jackall and Clarence returned from Macao. Sir George Staunton soon after came on board; and, from the intelligence communicated to him by the commissioners, the most sanguine hopes were entertained that this extraordinary and important embassy would be crowned with success.

We now entered the Yellow Sea, when nothing material happened that can justify particular description, till we arrived at the end of this branch of our voyage. In our passage we saw many islands, and occasionally met with Chinese junks, fishing boats, and other circumstances, which denoted our approach to that part of the continent to which we were destined.

There being several rocks on the Chinese coast, in the Yellow Sea, that had no denomination in any chart, Sir Erasmus Gower thought proper to name them after the three principal characters of the embassy. Thus we find our journals contain, in this part of the voyage, the names of Cape Macartney, Cape Gower, and Staunton's Island.

1793, July, Sunday 21. At six o'clock in the afternoon, the Lion came to an anchor in Jangangsoe Bay; Mettow Islands bearing from north to north-west by west, two miles off shore.

Lieut. Campbell, with Mr. Huttner, Mr. Plumb, the interpreter, and Lieut. Ommaney, went in the cutter to Mettow, to be informed if there was any tract by which the Lion could enter the river, or if there was any river on that coast, which was navigable for ships of her burthen, and by whose navigation she could make a nearer approach to Pekin. If the answers to these questions did not prove satisfactory, those gentlemen were then to concert measures with the mandarin of the place for the disembarkation of the suite there.

Monday 22. The brig Endeavour arrived from Macao and Canton with dispatches from the commissioners.

This morning a mandarin of Chusan sent a present of twelve fine small bullocks, a number of hogs, with a large quantity of fruit, garden stuff, and rice.

Tuesday 23. The cutter returned with Lieut. Campbell and his company, who gave a very favourable account of the hospitality of the Chinese at Mettow; where they were not only received with the greatest civility, but furnished with every possible accommodation, and supplied with the greatest plenty and abundance. At the same time Mr. Campbell reported the absolute impracticability of proceeding further, as the whole way to the mouth of the river forms a chain of shoals, while a bar runs across the entrance of it, which is not more than six feet deep, even at high water. In consequence of this report, Sir Erasmus Gower resolved to proceed no further.

Saturday 27. The report of the surgeon amounted to ninety-three sick men on board the Lion.

The Jackall and Clarence sailed with Mr. Huttner and Mr. Plumb to Mettow, to make arrangements with the mandarins for the landing of the embassy, and to fix the time when the Ambassador should go on shore; the result of whose commission was, that large junks would be sent for the reception of the suite and baggage, as soon as the wind served.

1793, August, Friday 2. A present of sixteen bullocks, thirty-two fine large sheep, some hogs, with vegetables, tea, sugar, etc. was sent on board the Lion. A principal mandarin also came on board from one of the junks, and dined with Lord Macartney; where he appeared in a very awkward situation, as the Chinese do not know the use of knives and forks. This officer finally settled with his Excellency, that the succceding Monday should be the day of his disembarkation; but that the heavy baggage, etc. would be previously transshipped into the junks. The mandarin expressed great surprise at our wooden palace, and could scarce believe the various arrangernents and wonderful conveniences of it. He was hoisted into one of our boats in the accommodation chair; a ceremony with which he appeared to be infinitely delighted.

Sunday 4. A mandarin came on board to dinner. The presents, baggage, etc. were all shipped into the junks; and on board the same vessels were sent the soldiers, mechanics, and great part of his Excellency's servants.

Monday 5. This morning at four o'clock several junks came along side the Lion to receive the remainder of the Ambassador's baggage. His Excellency then took his breakfast on board, and was joined by the remainder of his suite from the Hindostan.

At eight o'clock Sir Erasmus Gower gave orders for the ship's company to man ship, previous to his Excellency's disembarkation, which took place almost immediately; when he was saluted with three cheers from the seamen, and the discharge of nineteen guns from the Lion and Hindostan.

At nine o'clock the remainder of the suite took their stations on different junks; the Ambassador, Sir George Staunton and son, having gone on board the Clarence brig, the accommodations of the junks being not only very inconvenient, but extremely dirty, and otherwise very unfit to receive them.

The number of junks employed on the occasion for the reception of the suite and baggage, amounted to twenty sail, of about an hundred tons burthen.

At two o'clock in the afternoon we saw the town and fort of Mettow; and at three the junks came to anchor at the mouth of the river, where we found the Jackall, Clarence, and Endeavour arrived before us. From the several short turnings at this part of the river, we were obliged frequently to anchor and weigh, in order to avoid the shoals.

At four the whole fleet came to anchor opposite the palace of the principal mandarin.

The town, though extensive, has not the charm of elegance, or the merit of uniformity: indeed, its situation is such as to exclude any encouragement to beautify and adorn it, being situated on a swamp, occasioned by the frequent overflowing of the sea, notwithstanding the precaution of the inhabitants to make an embankment on the shore.

The houses, or huts, for they rather deserve the latter name, are built altogether of mud, with bamboo roofs: they are very low, and without either floors or pavements. At a small distance from the town there are several buildings of a very superior form and appearance, which belong to the mandarins of the place: they are constructed of stone and wood; the body of the house being of the former, and the wings and galleries, which are very pretty, and painted of various colours, of the latter material: they are of a square form, and three stories in height; each story having a surrounding range of palisadoes, which are richly gilt and fancifully painted. The lower story, or ground floor, is fronted with piazzas, which are ornamented in the same manner. The wings project on each side the body of the house, and appear to contain a considerable range of apartments.

Each mandarin is attended by a great number of guards; consisting both of infantry and cavalry, who live in tents pitched round the residence of the personage whom they serve.

Notwithstanding its unfavourable situation, the immense crowd of speelators who assembled to see the Ambassador come on shore, proves Mettow to be a place of prodigious population. Many of these curious people were on horseback and in carriages; so that the banks of the river where our junks lay at anchor were entirely covered with them.

The only fort in this place consists simply of a square tower, and seems to have been constructed for ornament rather than public utility; for, though it stands on the very margin of the sea, and commands the entrance of the river, not a single piece of ordnance appeared on the walls.

The breadth of this part of the river is about a furlong, and the colour of the water is muddy, resembling that of the Yellow Ocean with which it mingles; its depth is very unequal, being in some parts nine, and in others six feet deep; but in no part less than two. At the entrance, as has been already mentioned, there is a bar or bank of sand, which stretches across it; and, at full tide, has not more depth than six or seven feet; though, on the side towards the sea, and at a few yards only from the bar, there are upwards of six fathoms water. The environs of the town present, on both sides of the river, an expanse of flat country; which possesses a rich soil, and boasts extraordinary fertility.

In the evening, we received from the mandarin a very refreshing and acceptable present of dressed meats and fruits.

CHAPTER IV

An account of the mandarin appointed to conduct the accommodations for the embassy. – Various presents of provisions. – Gross habits of the Chinese respecting their food. – Description of the junks. – Order of those vessels fitted up for the accommodation of the British Ambassador and his suite.

1793, August, Tuesday 6. THE whole of this morning was employed in transhipping the baggage to the accommodation junks, hired for the embassy by *Van-Tadge-In*, a mandarin of the first class, who had been appointed by the Emperor to conduct the business of the embassy, in every thing that related to the residence, provisions, and journey of the suite.

This person became interesting to us, as he was appointed to attend the embassy during the time we should remain in China. He was about five feet nine inches in height, stout, well made, and of a dark complexion, but of a remarkably pleasing and open countenance: his manners and deportment were polite and unaffected; and the appointment of such a man, so admirably qualified to fulfil the peculiar duties to which he was nominated, gave us a very favourable opinion of the good sense of the Chinese government, and served to encourage our hopes of success in the important objects of this distinguished embassy.

We received at noon, from the mandarin's boat, which was accompanied by Mr. Plumb, the interpreter, a quantity of raw beef, with bread and fruit: the beef, though not fat, is of a very good quality; but the bread, though made of excellent flour, was by no means pleasant to our palate: as the Chinese do not make use of yeast, or bake it in an oven, it is, in fact, little better than common dough. The shape and size of the loaves are those of an ordinary wash-ball cut in two. They are composed of nothing more than flour and water, and ranged on bars which are laid across an iron hollow pan, containing a certain quantity of water, which is then placed on an earthen stove; when the water boils, the vessel, or pan, is covered over with something like a shallow tub, and the steam of the water, for a few minutes, is all the baking, if it may be so called, which the bread receives. In this state we found it necessary to cut it in slices and toast it, before we could reconcile it to our appetites. The fruits, which made a part of this present, consided of apples, pears, shaddocks, and oranges of a superior flavour.

In the afternoon we received another very large supply of provisions ready dressed, consisting of beef, mutton, pork, whole pigs, and poultry of all sorts, both roast and boiled.

The roast meat had a very singular appearance, as they use some preparation of oil, that gives it a gloss like that of varnish; nor was its flavour so agreeable to our palates, as the dishes produced by the clean and simple cookery of our European kitchens. Their boiled meat, being free from the oily taste of that which is roasted or baked, was far preferable.

We were, however, in some degree affected by the accounts we had heard of the indifference of the Chinese concerning their food; and that they not only eat all animal food without distinction, but do not discard even such as die of diseases from their meals. This circumstance made several of our party very cautious of what they ate; and as to their hashes and stews, many refused their allowance of these dishes, from the apprehension of their being composed of unwholesome flesh.

But it was not merely from the information of others that we felt a disgust at Chinese cookery, as we had ocular demonstration of the gross appetites of the Chinese people. The pigs on board the Lion being affected with a disorder, which is always fatal to these animals; several of them were thrown overboard; which circumstance being observed by the Chinese belonging to the junks, they instantly got out their boats and picked up these diseased carcases, which they immediately cut up, and having dressed a part of them, appeared to make a very comfortable meal, not unaccompanied with marks of derision at the English for their extravagant delicacy.

We were at first disposecl to believe that this grossness of appetite was confined to the lower classes of the people, who were generally in such a state of indigence, as to be glad to obtain meat in the accidental way which we have just mentioned: but we afterwards learned, that the more independent classes of people, and even the mandarins themselves, are not exempt from a custom, in domestic œconomy, at which the eager appetite of the starving European would revolt.

In the warm season, this part of the country swarms with mosquitos, that tormenting insect, which is so distressing to the inhabitants of the warmer climates.

Wednesday 7. This morning I went on board the accommodation junk, occupied by Captain Mackintosh, of the Hindostan, who was required to accompany the embassy to Pekin. The squadron, in the mean time, received instructions to return to Chusan harbour, and to wait there till further orders.

The junks, or Chinese vessels, are formed on a construction I never remember to have seen in any other part of the world: They are built of beach wood and bamboo, with a flat bottom: they are of different sizes from, thirty to an hundred, feet in length; the breadth of the largest are from twenty to thirty feet, and the smaller ones in proportion.

In this junk there was on the first deck a range of very neat and commodious apartments, which were clean and decorated with paintings: They consisted of three sleeping apartments, a dining parlour, with a kitchen, and two rooms for servants. The floor is made to list up by hatches all along the junk, to each of which there is a brass ring: beneath is an hold, or vacant space for containing lumber; and the quantity of goods that can be stowed away in these places is almost incredible.

On the upper or main deck, there is a range of fourteen or fifteen small chambers, allotted for the use of the men belonging to the junk, and an apartment for the captain or owner of the vessel.

In the lower deck, the windows are made of wood, with very small square holes, covered with a sort of glazed, transparent paper; the sashes are divided into four parts, and made to take out occasionally, either to admit the air for coolness, or to sweeten the apartments. On the outside there is a coloured curtain, that extends from one end of the junk to the other, which, in very hot weather, is unfurled and fixed up to shade the apartments from the heat of the sun. There are also shutters, which slide before the windows, to prevent the effects of cold weather, or any inclemency of the season.

There is a gang-way on both sides of the vessel, about thirty inches broad, by way of passage, without entering into any of the apartments; and though many of these vessels carry from two to three hundred tons, they only draw three feet water, so that they can be worked with ease and safety in the most shoaly rivers. Some of these junks have two masts, though, in general, they have but one, with a very awkward kind of rudder; but the more elegant vessels of this kind, which I have just described, are only calculated for the navigation of a river; as they are not constructed with sufficient strength to resist the violent effects of wind and weather.

It is usual for all vessels which navigate the rivers in China, to have a lamp, with a lighted candle in it, hoisted to the mast head, as soon as it is dark, to prevent those accidents which would otherwise very frequently happen from vessels running foul of each other. There lamps are made of transparent paper, with charaders painted on them, to notify what junk it is, or the rank of any passengers on board it: if they are persons of distinction, three of these lanterns are usually suspended. The vessel is also illuminated in other parts, particularly round the deck and the number of lights are generally proportioned to the rank of the persons who occupy the junk. The same service which the lamps perform by night, as far as relates to notification, is performed in the daytime by silken ensigns, whose painted characters specify in the same manner, the existing circumstances of the vessel. It may be easily conceived, that, from the prodigious number of junks which navigate this river, a very pleasing, and sometimes, indeed, a grand effect is produced, by such an assemblage of lights moving along the water.

I am not qualified to determine whether it proceeds from the domestic policy of the Chinese, from prejudice in favour of long-established habits, or an ignorance of mechanics, but they have not made any advancement in the science of naval architecture: the junks of the latt century, and those of the present day, are invariably the same.

The order in which the vessels appropriated for the purpose of conveying the British embassy to Pekin proceeded, was as follows:

The grand Mandarin, and his suite, in five junks.

Junk No.   1. His Excellency the Earl Macartney.

— — —   2. Sir George and Mr. Staunton,

— — —   3. Mr. Plumb, the Chinese interpreter.

— — —   4. Lieut. Col. Benson, Lieut, Parish, and Lieut.
Crewe.

— — —   5. Capt. Mackintosh of the Hindostan,
Mr. Maxwell, Dr. Gillan, and   Mr. Huttner.

— — —   6. Mr. Barrow, Mr. Winder, and Mr. Baring,
(son of Sir Francis Baring.)

— — —   7. Dr. Scott, Dr. Dinwiddie, Mr. Hickey, and Mr.
Alexander.

These, with the junks which contained the soldiers, mechanics, and servants, composed the naval procession.

CHAPTER V

Lord Macartney leaves Mettow, and sets sail for Pekin. – Beauty and fertility of the country. – Various circumstances of the voyage. – The soldiers of China described. – The navigation of the river. – Some account of the tea tree, with the manner of making tea as a beverage. – Prodigious population of the country. – Arrive at the city of Tyen-sing: some account of it. – A Chinese play. – Description of the mandarin's palace, etc.

1793, *August*. THIS morning the Ambassador paid a visit to the principal mandarin of Mettow, to take leave, on his departure for Pekin; and at eleven o'clock, the fleet of junks, with his Excellency and the whole suite on board, proceeded on their voyage.

Thursday 8. We received a large supply of provisions, ready dressed, together with tea, sugar, bread, vegetables of all sorts, and a large quantity of fruit, consisting of apples, pears, grapes, and oranges, which never failed to make a part of those supplies for the table with which the embassy was at all times furnished, in the greatest abundance. We also received, at this time, a provision of wood and charcoal for culinary uses. I made some inquiries after mineral coal, but it was not known at Mettow, nor could I learn whether it is found or used in any part of China.

We had proceeded but a very few miles up the river, when the country displayed prospects of such peculiar novelty and beauty as would baffle any attempts of mine to describe them. The view on all sides presents fields rich in various cultivation, with extensive meadows covered with sheep and the finest cattle. Their gardens appeared to be equally disposed for domestic use and pleasure; producing at the same time abundance of vegetables, and the finest fruits; while the eye was charmed with the beauty of their scenery, and the gaiety of their decorations. On the first glimpse of their grounds, whether applied to the more solid uses of agriculture, or the more elegant arrangement of their gardens, in raising grain and esculent plants, or cultivating fruits and flowers, I was convinced that the Chinese were no mean proficients in botanical knowledge, as well as in the science of farming, and the art of ornamental gardening. I also observed, that the fields were as well guarded by fences, in the form of hedges and stone walls, as any I had seen in the enclosed parts of my own country,

During the day, the guards belonging to the mandarin marched along the banks of the river; and at night pitched their tents opposite to the station where the junks lay at anchor; when they kept a regular watch till the hour of the morning appointed for the fleet to proceed on its voyage. The front of each tent was adorned with lamps, so that the camp on shore, and the junks on the water, formed together a considerable illumination, and produced a very uncommon and pleasing effect.

The centinels on shore have, each of them, a piece of hollow bamboo, which they strike at regular intervals, with a mallet, to announce that they are awake and vigilant in their respective stations. This custom, as I was informed by the peyings, or soldiers themselves, is universal throughout the Chinese army.

We were awakened at a very early hour by the sound of the gongs, which formed the signal for sailing.

Friday 9. The gong is an instrument of a circular form, made of brass; it resembles, in some degree, the cover of a large stewpan, and is used as bells or trumpets are in Europe, to convey notice, or make signals, from one place to another when they are struck with a large wooden mallet, which is covered with leather, a sound is produced that may be distinctly heard at the distance of a league.

We received the usual supply of provisions, with the addition, for the first time, of some wine of the country in a stone jar; its colour is nearly that of what is called Lisbon wine in England, and is equally clear; it is rather strong, but of an unpleasant flavour, being harsh and sharp, and, in short, has more the taste of vinegar than wine. The jar which contained it was equal, in measure, to three English gallons, and the mouth of it was covered with a large plantane leaf, closed in with a cap of clay, on which was fixed a red label, marked with certain Chinese characters, to denote, as I suppose, the contents of the vessel.

We passed several very populous towns on both sides of the river, but situated at some distance from it. The Ambassador, however, received military honours from the soldiers belonging to them, who were drawn up on the bank, on either side, contiguous to their respective cantonments, and surrounded by an immense crowd of spectators.

The uniform of the soldiers consists of a large pair of loose black nankeen trowsers, which they stuff into a kind of quilted cotton stockings, made in the form of boots. They always wrap their feet in a cotton rag before they draw these boots over their trowsers; they add also a pair of very clumsy shoes, made of cotton, the soles of which are, at least, an inch thick, and very broad at the points. These trowsers have no waistband, so that they lap over, and are tied with a piece of common tape, to which is generally suspended a small leathern bag, or purse, to contain money. These soldiers do not use either shirts, waificoats, or neckcloths; but wear a large mantle of black nankeen, with loose sleeves, which is edged with the same material, but of a red colour. Round their middle there is a broad girdle, ornamented in the center with what appears to be a pebble of about the size of half-a-crown, though, as I was informed, it is an hard substance or paste made of rice. From this girdle is suspended a pipe and bag to hold tobacco, on one side, and a fan on the other; which are annually allowed them by the Emperor, as well as a daily portion of tobacco, a plant that grows in the ut-moil abundance in every part of China.

The Chinese troops were always, when I saw them, drawn up in single ranks, with a great number of colours or standards, which are chiefly made of green silk, with a red border, and enriched with golden characters. They wear their swords on the left side; but the handle or hilt is backwards, and the point for-wards, so that, when they draw these weapons, they put their hands behind their backs, and unsheath them without being immediately perceived; a manoeuvre which they execute with great dexterity, and is well adapted for the purposes of attack, as a foreign antagonist, who is not accustomed to this mode of assault, would be probably wounded, at least, before he was prepared to defend himself against it. Under their left arm is slung a bow; and a quiver, generally containing twelve arrows, hangs on their backs: others are armed with match-locks of a very rusty appearance.

Their heads are shaved round the crown, ears, and neck, except a small part on the back of the head, where the hair, which is encouraged to grow to a great length, hangs down their backs in a plait, and is tied at the end with a riband. They wear a shallow draw hat very neatly made, which is necessarily tied under the chin with a string, and is decorated with a bunch of camel's hair, dyed of a red colour.

On all occasions, similar to that which brought these troops to the banks of the river to do military honour, to the British Ambassador, a temporary arch covered with silk is placed at each end of the line, in which the mandarins sit till the procession, or person to be saluted, appears, when they come forward and make their appearance. Near these arches are three small swivels about thirty inches in length, which are fixed in the ground with the muzzle pointing to the air: these are discharged as the person to be honoured with the salute passes the mandarin at the end of the line. This mode of firing salutes the Chinese very sensibly adopt to prevent accidents, observing, at the same time, in their account of it, that a loaded gun should never be levelled, but at their enemies. In the management of artillery and fire arms, it is not to be supposed that Europeans can derive any one improvement from the inhabitants of the east; but we well know that very melancholy, and sometimes fatal accidents are occasioned from the want of similar regulations, by the discharge both of great guns and small arms on our days of public rejoicing.

The houses scattered on the banks of the river were chiefly built of mud, rarely inter- mixed with some of a better form, which were constructed of stone, and finished with great neatness, producing a very pretty effect, as we passed them, from the water.

The women at these places, of whom we saw great numbers, have their feet and ancles universally bound with red tape, to prevent, as it is said, their feet from growing the natural size: so very tight is this bandage drawn round them, that they walk with great difficulty; and when we consider that this extraordinary practice commences with their infancy, it is rather a matter of surprise that they should be able to walk at all. If we except this strange management, or rather mismanagement, of their feet, and their head-dress, there is very little distinction between the dress of the males and females.

The women wear their hair combed back on the crown of the head, and smoothed with ointment; it is then neatly rolled into a sort of club, and ornamented with artificial flowers and large silver pins: the hair on the back part of the head is done up as tight as possible and inserted beneath the club. In every other respect their dress corresponds with that of the men: they differ, indeed, in nothing from that of the soldiers, which has been already described, but that they bear no arms, have no red border on their cloaths, or tuft of hair on their hats.

As far as I could judge of the length of this day's voyage, it could not have exceeded twenty-four miles; in the course of which we reckoned upwards of six hundred junks that passed us, and, I may say, without the least fear of exaggeration, that we saw twice that number lying at anchor; nor shall I hesitate to add, that, on the inost moderate computation, we beheld at least half a million of people.

The river, besided the variety and extent of its navigation, is in itself a grand and beautiful object, enriched with an equal distribution of rich and picturesque scenery: its course waves in the finest meanders; its banks on either side are adorned with elegant villas and delightful gardens; while the more distant country offers the intermingled prospect of splendid cultivation and landscape beauty.

The fleet came to. anchor close into the shore at eight o'clock in the evening.

The gongs, as usual, gave the signal for weighing anchor, and proceeding on our voyage. The weather was extremely hot and sultry, and the country continued to wear that appearance of fertility, which had hitherto distinguished it.

We for the first time saw some plantations of the tea tree, an object which was rather interesting to the natives of a country, where, though the climate will not admit of its growth, it has descended from being a luxury, into a necessity of life.

The tea tree is of a dwarf size, with a narrow leaf resembling myrtle. It was the season when these trees were in blossom, which the Chinese pluck and dry; and the younger the blossom is, when plucked, the higher the flavour of the tea is considered with which it is mixed.

It is a curious circumstance that, although this province is so abundant in its produce of tea, it appears to be a very scarce commodity among the lower class of people; as the men belonging to our junk never failed, after we had finished our breakfast, to request the boon of our tea-leaves, which they drained and spread in the sun until they were dry; they then boiled them for a certain time, and poured them with the liquor into a stone jar, and this formed their ordinary beverage. When the water is nearly drawn off, they add more boiling water; and in this manner these leaves are drawn and re-boiled for several weeks. On same particular occasions, they put a few grains of fresh tea into a cup, and, after having poured boiling water upon it, cover it up: when it has remained in this state for a few minutes, they drink it without sugar, an article which the Chinese never mix with tea.

We this day passed several populous villages, composed of very neat houses of one story, and built of brick; and from every one of them the Ambassador received those honours which have been already described. The crowds of people which assembled to see a parade of so much novelty as the fleet that conveyed the British embassy, were beyond all calculation, and gave us a complete idea of the immense population attributed to the Chinese empire. Nor was the state of the navigation that appeared on the river less astonishing; the junks which we continued to see at every moment of our passage, were sometimes so numerous, that the water was covered with them.

The fleet came to an anchor at the usual hour of eight o'clock in the evening.

Sunday 11. At four o'clock in the morning we renewed our voyage; the country still appearing in its usual state of fertility and beauty; and as far as the delighted eye could reach, an uncultivated spot was no where to be seen.

The banks of the river were now varied with fields of millet and rice. The stalks of the former are very tall, with branching leaves, and the points of them bear the seed, which is a very principal article of food in this country. The rice grows very much like our corn, and thrives best in a marshy soil: I observed, indeed, that come of the rice fields were entirely covered with water.

About six o'clock we approached the city of Tyen-sing, where we were met by crowds of spectatators, both in junks and on the shore, that defied all attempt to calculate their numbers.

As we proceeded, we saw a long range of heaps, or ricks, of salt, in ranks or columns of fifty each, from front to rear: these heaps are about eighteen or twenty feet square, and twenty-four feet in height, and are covered with matting to preserve them from the effects of the weather; each of them containing, as I was informed, about five hundred tons of salt. In this order, and without variation, or interruption, the range continued for two miles along the banks of the river. For what purpose this immense quantity of salt was deposited there, I could not learn; nor was there any appearance of a manufactory to justify the idea of its being made there.

At nine o'clock we entered the city, amid the noise and shoutings of, I doubt not, some hundred thousands of spectators. The houses of this place are built of brick, and, in general, are carried to the height of two stories, with roofs of tiles: they are all of a lead colour; and had a very neat and pretty appearance. The place, however, is not formed on any regular plan: the streets, or rather alleys, are so narrow, as to admit, with difficulty, two persons to walk abreast; and have no pavement. It is, however, of great extent, and populous beyond description.

Before the palace of the mandarin, a larger body of troops were drawn up than we had yet seen, who carried, at least, one hundred and fifty standards.

At half past ten, the Ambassador, attended by all his suite, guards, etc. in full formality, went on shore to pay a visit to the chief mandarin of the city, whose palace is at a small distance from the river, and placed in the center of a very fine garden: it is a lofty edifice, built of brick, with a range of palisadoes in the front, fancifully gilt and painted. The center building has three, and the wings two stories. The outside wall is decorated with paintings, and the roof is coloured with a yellow varnish that produces a very splendid effea. This building contains several interior courts, handsomely paved with broad, flat stones.

The Ambassador and his suite were entertained with a cold collation, consisting of dishes dressed in the fashion of the country, with tea, fruit, and a great variety of confectionary; a branch of table luxury which is well understood by the Chinese.

A play was also performed on the occasion, as a particular mark of respect and attention to the distinguished visitor. The theatre is a square building, built principally of wood, and is ereced in the front of the mandarin's palace. The stage, or platform, is surrounded with galleries; and the whole was, on this occasion, decorated with a profusion of ribands, and silken streamers of various colours. The theatrical exhibitions consisted chiefly of war-like representations: such as imaginary battles, with swords, spears, and lances; which weapons the performers managed with an astonishing activity. The scenes were beautifully gilt and painted, and the dresses of the actors were ornamented in conformity to the enrichments of the scenery. The exhibition received also an agreeable variety from several very curious deceptions by slight of hand and theatrical machinery. There was also a display of that species of agility which we call tumbling; wherein the performers executed their parts with superior address and activity. Some of the actors were dressed in female characters; but I was informed at the time, that they were eunuchs, as the Chinese never suffer their women to appear in such a state of public exhibition as the stage. The performance was also enlivened by a band of music, which consisted entirely of wind instruments: some of them were very long and resembled a trumpet; others had the appearance of French-horns, and clarinets: the sounds of the latter brought to my recollection that of a Scotch bag-pipe; and their concert, being destitute both of melody and harmony, was of course very disagreeable to our ears, which are accustomed to such perfection in those essential points of music. But we had every reason to be satisfied with the entertainment, as the circumstances of it were replete with novelty and curious amusement.

The dress of the soldiers, as well as their arms and accoutrements, was the same as those which we have already described, except in an additional colour; as it was now white and blue, though equally bound with the same broad red binding. Some of these soldiers, on the present occasion, were employed, with long whips, to keep off the crowd from pressing the procession of the Ambassador and his suite.

His Excellency was saluted, both on his arrival and at his departure, with three pieces of small ordnance: and soon after his return to the vessel the fleet set sail, amidst the greatest concourse of boats and people I ever beheld:—indeed, so great was the crowd of both, that I considered it as impossible for us to pass on without being the witnesses of considerable mischief. One very old junk that lay at anchor had such a number of people on board it, to see the extraordinary sight of the day; that the sternmost part of the deck yielded to the enormous pressure, and suddenly gave way, when about forty of these curious people fell into the river, and several of them were unfortunately drowned. Some were, indeed, saved by clinging to the ropes which were thrown out to them; though it was very evident to those who witnessed the accident, that curiosity rather than humanity prevailed on the occasion; and that the people were more anxious to get a sight of the foreigners, than to save the lives of their countrymen.

We received the usual supply of provisions of all kinds, and a large jar of wine, from the mandarin, which contained about ten English gallons: it was found to be of a much superior quality to that which had been sent on a former occasion, and had not only the flavour, but the colour of mountain.

A considerable proportion of these provisions was distributed among the crews of the junks, who received such an acceptable mark of kindness with the utmost gratitude and delight. The superfluous hospitality of their country proved, as it ought to do, a source of occasional plenty to these poor people, during the course of that voyage in which we were conduaed by their skill and labour.

It may here be mentioned, that as the quota of provisions allotted by the Chinese government for the maintenance of the embassy, was on the calculation that every individual kept a separate table, it must have been, as it really was, infinitely beyond the possibility of being consumed by those alone for whose use it was presented.

CHAPTER VI

1793, August, Monday 12. ABOUT four o'clock in the morning there was a most tremendous storm of thunder, lightning, and rain, which lasted about two hours. The mandarin of Tyen-sing having sent three parcels of coloured silk, as a present, to be distributed among the embassy, Mr. Maxwell, by Lord Macartney's order, delivered two pieces of it to each gentleman in his suite: but as the remainder did not allow of a similar division, the lots were all separated and numbered; when the mechanics, servants and musicians, took their chance in drawing them, and, except three persons, they all obtained two pieces of the manufacture. The soldiers received, each of them, half a piece: these pieces were only half a yard wide, and about seven yards and a half in length: the colours were green, mulberry, and pink; but the silk was of a very indifferent quality, and would not, in England, be worth more than eighteen pence a yard.

During the great part of this day the junks were towed along by men particularly hired for that purpose: and the mode of drawing these vessels, as may be supposed, is very different from that employed on similar occasions in any of the European rivers.

On all the rivers of China there are large bodies of men, whose business it is to drag, or tow the junks, when the wind or tide fails. The method of proceeding in this business is by fastening one rope to the mast, and another to the head of the junk, which, being properly secured, the draughtfmen take the rope on shore along with them: the length of which must depend, in a great measure, on the breadth of the river. These men have, each of them, a piece of wood, about two feet and a half in length, with a piece of stout cord at each end, by which it is fastened to the ropes attached to the junk: these pieces of wood being thrown over their heads, rest upon their breasts, and by leaning against them the towers inerease the power of their exertions: they are thus harnessed, if I may use the expression, in a strait line, at the distance of about a pace and a half from each other, and when they are all ready, the leader of them gives the signal: they then begin a particular kind of march, the regularity of whose step is essential to the draught of the vessel, and can only be maintained by a sort of chime which they chant on the occasion: this chime, or cry, is a kind of brief song; but the words, as far as I could learn, have no more meaning annexed to them, than the bawling tones employed, by our seamen, as notices to pull at the same moment: they appeared, however, to give the following distinct, articulate sounds, not altogether unlike some of those which we might hear on the Thames, or the Severn: — Hoy-alla hoya; — which word, for it is delivered as one, was regularly succeeded by the following ones — hoya, hoya, hoy — waudi-hoya. These words are sung in a regular tune; and so universal is this custom among the class of labouring Chinese, that they cannot perform the most ordinary work, where numbers are employed together, without the aid of this vocal accompaniment; which I was disposed to think, had some agreeable notes in it.

It seemed, indeed, to be necessary that these poor men should have consolation to support, or some aid to assist them in the labour of dragging these large junks, both night and day, which is frequently increased by muddy banks, and marshy shores; where I have sometimes seen them wading up to their very shoulders, and dragging one another, as well as the vessel, after them.

Tuesday 13. This morning, at seven o'clock, we received our usual supply of provisions, which we were obliged to dress ourselves; as the Chinese are so very dirty in their cookery, that it was impossible for the inhabitants of a country where cleanliness is so prevailing a circumstance of the kitchen, unless impelled by severe hunger, to submit to it. Their manner of dressing meat is by cutting it in very small pieces, which they fry in oil, with roots and herbs. They have plenty of soy and vinegar, which they add by way of sauce.

The diet which the common people provide for themselves is always the same, and they take their meals with the utmost regularity, every four hours; it consists of boiled rice, and sometimes of millet, with a few vegetables or turnips chopped small, and fried in oil; this they put into a bason, and, when they mean to make a regale, they pour some soy upon it.

The manner of boiling rice is the only circumstance of cleanliness which I have observed among them. They take a certain quantity of rice and wash it well in cold water; after which it is drained off through a sieve: they then put the rice into boiling water, and when it is quite soft, they take it out with a ladle, and drain it again through a sieve: they then put it into a clean vessel, and cover it up: there it remains till it is blanched as white as snow, and is as dry as a crust, when it becomes a most excellent substitute for bread.

The table on which they eat their meals is no more than a foot from the ground, and they sit round it on the floor; the vessel of rice is then placed near it, with which each person fills a small bason; he then with a couple of chop-sticks picks up his fried vegetables, which he eats with his rice; and this food they glut down in a most voracious manner. Except on days of sacrifice, or rejoicing, the common people of China seldom have a better diet. Their drink, which has already been described, is an infusion of tea-leaves.

We this day passed several very populous villages, though, as far as our experience qualified us to determine, there is no such thing, as a village which is not populous; and perhaps, after all, among the wonders of this country the population is the greatest.

The shores of the river were this day lined with such crowds of people to see us, as to baffle all description; and the number of junks which we passed in this day's voyage, I solemnly believe, without the least exaggeration, amounted to at least four thousand: and if the people we saw in the different villages are calculated at twenty times that number, the account, I believe, is very much below the reality. At each of these places the Ambassador was saluted in the manner which has already been described.

Although it is not a very delicate picture to present to the attention of my readers, yet, as I profess to give a relation of every thing which I saw, I shall not omit to mention, that, this evening, two of the Chinese belonging to our junk stripped themselves naked, and, picking off the vermin, which were found in great plenty on their cloaths, proceeded to eat them with as much eagerness and apparent satisfaction, as if they were a gratifying and delicate food.

Wednesday 14. The weather was extremely hot and sultry, and the mosquitos so troublesome during the night, as to prove a very painful interruption to our repose.

We continued to pass very extensive fields of millet and rice, and the country, as we proceeded, maintained its character for fertility, cultivation, and abundance; though in several parts it assumed a more varied and irregular appearance than we had yet seen.

In the forenoon we passed a large town, whose name is Cho-tung-poa. It is pleasantly situated on the banks of the river, and is a place of considerable extent. The houses are of brick, and in general do not aseend beyond one story; they were here remarkable for the walls which were erected in the front of them, over which a great number of ladies were seen, taking a view of the junks as they passed before the town, while the spectators, whom curiosity had led to the banks of the river, were, as usual, in such numbers as to renew our astonishment.

We now came to a fork of the river, and over the lateral branch of it there were two bridges of two arches, built of stone in a pleasing form, and constructed with the appearance of no common architectural knowledge. At a small distance from them were the ruins of another bridge of one arch; it had been built of hewn stone, and the part which remained bore the appearance of regular design and European masonry. At a small distance from this ruin, and on a gentle eminence, was the seat or villa of the mandarin. It is a new stone building of two stories, in a pleasing style of architecture, with a flight of steps rising to the door. The approach to it was through a neat gateway, which was not quite finished; the rnasons were then employed in completing it; and I was rather surprised on observing that their scaffolding was erected on the same principle, and their work conducted very much in the same manner, as is employed and practised by the builders of our own country.

The junks were towed during the greatest part of this day; and at six o'clock in the evening they came to anchor near the shore.

In a short time after the fleet got to its moorings, the grand mandarin of Tyen-sing, escorted by a numerous train of attendants, came to pay a visit to the British Ambassador.

The procession commenced with an advanced troop of men, who were employed in shouting aloud as they came on, in order to notify the approach of the mandarin, that the way might be cleared from passengers, and any accidental obstacle removed which might impede his progress. This party was followed at some distance by two men carrying large umbrellas of red silk, with broad pendent curtains of the same material; they are used to shelter the palankin from the burning rays of the sun. A large band of standard-bearers then succeed; the foot-soldiers follow; the palankin next appears which bears the mandarin, and a large escort of cavalry closes the procession.

Such is the manner in which persons of distinction travel in China; and their particular rank and quality is marked by the number of their attendants.

The mandarin of Tyen-sing remained with Lord Macartney about an hour; and, on his return, the procession was illuminated by a great number of people bearing lamps and torches, which produced a very splendid appearance.

Tuesday 15. The heat still continued to be extreme; the country varies not in the fertility of its appearance, and the large fields of corn which we passed to-day, appeared to be as fine, both as to crop and cultivation, as those which are the boast of England. We also passed a large plantation of tea, and a vast number of boxes ranged in order, for the purpose of packing the tea, and sending it to Canton.

In this day's voyage the banks of the river appeared in such various cloathing of art and nature, as to distract the attention; and the alternate view of extensive meadows, luxuriant fields, and the most beautiful gardens, did not suffer the gratification of the eye, or the mind,

to be for a moment suspended. In the evening I went on shore, and walked along the banks of the river for a couple of miles; and, on a nearer examination of the cornfields, I found that the grain, which was now almost ripe, was of the best quality, and the husbandry equal to that of the English farmer.

CHAPTER VII

1793, *August*, *Friday* 16. AS we proceeded on our voyage the
villages became more frequent, and the people more numerous.
We continued to receive our usual supply of meat, fowls,
vegetables, and fruit; and about five o'clock in the afternoon of
this day, we arrived at the city of Tong-tchew, which is situated
at the distance of about twenty miles from Pekin, and where our
voyage up this fine river found its termination. It may appear to
be a continual repetition of the same subject, but the circumstance
appeared to be so extraordinary that I cannot fail to repeat it, by
observing that at this place, the people who covered the banks of
the river far exceeded in number any thing that we had yet seen.

Soon after the arrival of the fleet at this place, Lord Macartney
and Sir George Staunton, accompanied by the conducting

mandarin, Van-Tadge-In, went on shore to inspect the place allotted for the landing the presents and baggage, which the Chinese had previously erected for that purpose. It contained about the space of an acre, fenced in with matting, and furnished with long sheds made of uprights of wood and matting, with a roof of the latter, in order to prevent the packages from being injured by the rain or dew. The ground was entirely covered with mats, and the place well guarded on all sides by petty mandarins and soldiers.

The grand mandarin of the place sent to inform the Ambassador, that a public breakfast would be prepared at the place allotted for the residence of the embassy, during its stay at Tong-tchew, on the following morning at seven o'clock; to which Lord Macartney and his whole suite, including mechanics, soldiers, and servants, were invited. Notice of this general message was consequently given to each junk, and orders were at the same time issued to prepare for disembarkation.

Saturday 17. At six o'clock this morning two palankins were sent for Lord Macartney and Sir George Staunton, who, in about an hour after their arrival, left the junks, and were carried to their appointed residence, escorted by a party of Chinese soldiers, and an immense concourse of spectators.

The breakfast consisted of a profusion of stews and made dishes, meat of all kinds, tea, wines, boiled eggs, with a great variety of fruits and elegant confectionary.

A certain number of coolies, or porters, in small boats, were ordered to each junk, to re move all the articles belonging to the place already mentioned as prepared for their reception. During the greater part of the fore-noon I was employed in taking care that the proportion of baggage committed to my charge was conveyed in safety to the sheds.

At the gate of this inclosure there were two Chinese officers, who inspected all cases and packages which were brought from the junks: they first took their dimensions, of which they appeared to take a written account, and then passed, as it seemed to me, a counterpart of their minute on every separate article; nor was a single box, package, or parcel, suffered to pass, till it had undergone this previous ceremony; which was especially ordered, as I was. informed, to ascertain to the Emperor the quantity of presents and baggage in possession of the embassy.

Every exertion was made both by us and the natives to complete the landing of our cargoes from the junks; and so much expedition was used on the occasion, that the whole of the private baggage, and a great part of the presents, were safely brought on shore, and placed in the depot, in the course of this day.

The house, which had been appropriated by the Chinese government for the residence of the British Ambassador at Tong-tchew, is situated about three quarters of a mile from the river, and about one mile from the city, and stands on a rising ground. It had a neat appearance, but was so very low, as to have no claim to that distinction which it might be expected to possess, when we consider the purposes to which it was applied. It rises no higher in any part of it than one story.

The entrance to this building is a common square gateway, that opens into a neat, clean court, which was occupied by the soldiers belonging to the embassy, as a kind of barracks; another court beyond it, and to which there was an ascent of three steps, contained sevaral small buildings, occupied by the Chinese who belonged to the house; immediately adjoining to it, Lord Macartney's servants occupied a similar situation. Opposite to the servants quarter was a small square building, which is used as a place of worship, and contains only one room of common dimensions: in the middle of this chamber there was an altar, with three porcelain figures as large as life placed upon it; there were also candlesticks on each side of it, which were lighted regularly every morning and evening, and at such other times as persons come there to pay their devotions. Before these images there is a small pot of dust; in which are inserted a number of long matches, that are also lighted during the times of worship. When the period of devotion is past, the candles are extinguished, and the flame of the matches blown out, but the matches are left to moulder away. When this ceremony is over, an attendant on the altar takes a soft mallet, with which he strikes a bell that is suspended to it, three times; the persons present then kneel before the images, and bow down their heads three times to the ground, with their hands clasped in each other, which they extend over their heads as they rise; a low obeisance is then seen to conclude the ceremony of the daily worship of the Chinese; which is termed by them Chin-chin-josh, or worship of God.

Such is the domestic mode of worship that prevails throughout the whole empire of China, as every inhabitant of it, from the meanest peasant to the Emperor himself, has an altar, and a deity; the most wretched habitation is equally furnished in regard to its idols, though, as may be supposed, in proportionate degrees of form and figure, with the Imperial palace. Nor are those who are confined to the occupations of the water without them; every kind of vessel that navigates the sea, or the river, being provided with its deity and its altar.

The court adjoining to this domestic chapel is occupied by the Chinese, and employed as a kitchen; from thence there is a circular entrance to that part of the building which was particularly assigned to the Ambassador and his suite.

It surrounds a very handsome and spacious court, which was used as a dining apartment on the occasion; on one side of it there was an elegant platform, raised on two steps, with a beautiful roof, supported by four gilt pillars; and an awning was stretched over the whole court to protect it from the heat of the sun. This place was furnished also with beautiful lamps, regularly disperfed all around it: they consist of frames made of box-wood, lined with transparent silk and flowered gauze of various colours, which, when the lamps are lighted, add very much to the pleasing effect of the illumination. The two principal sides of the court were occupied by the gentlemen of the suite, who slept in two equal divisions in these separate apartments. Lord Macartney and Sir George Staunton were each accommodated with a distinct and separate wing of the building.

At two o'clock dinner was served up for the Ambassador and his company; it consisted of about one hundred various dishes, dressed according to the cookery of the country: they consisted principally of stews, and were served in small basons; but there were neither table-cloths, or knives and forks; and the only method these people have of conveying their meat to the mouth is by small pointed lengths of wood, or ivory, in the form of pencils. It is absolutely necessary, therefore, that their solid food should be cut in small pieces.

During the time of dinner, a great number of Chinese, who belonged, as I suppose, to the mandarin, whole office it was to superintend the arrangements made for the accommodation of the embassy, crowded round the table when they not only expressed their surprise by peculiar actions and gestures, but frequently burst into shouts of laughter.

Sunday 18. In order to give all possible dignity and importance to the embassy, a guard of British soldiers were ordered to attend on the Ambassador's apartments; but as they were removed from public view, these centinels were placed at the outer gate, and the entrance of the inner court, that they might attract the notice of the Chinese, and elevate the consequence of the diplomatic mission in the general opinion of the people of the country; a circumstance on which the success of it was supposed, in a great measure, to depend.

In the several apartments of the building appropriated to the residence and uses of the embassy, Chinese servants were distributed, to supply those who were disposed to call for drink, with the beverage of the country: such as kie tigau, hot tea; liang tigau, cold tea; with liang swee; cold water; kie swee, hot water; pyng swee, ice water; and any of these liquors were ready to be brought whenever they should be demanded, from an early hour of the day, till night.

This morning I took the opportunity to visit the city of Tong-tchew, with its suburbs; and with no small fatigue, and some trouble, I traversed the greatest part of it.

It appears to be built in a square form, and is defended by a very strong lofty wall, with a deep ditch on the outside of it in the most accessible parts: the wall makes a circuit of about six miles, is thirty feet high, and six broad: it has three gates, which are well fortified; each being defended by ramparts mounted with cannon: there is also a strong guard within them towards the city, in a state of regular duty. These gates are always shut at ten at night, and opened at four in the morning; the keys of which are always lodged with the mandarin of the city at night, and returned to the officer of the guard in the morning; on which occasion a report is made of whatever may have occurred, and such orders are issued as circumstances may require.

The houses of this city are like the greater part of those I have seen in China, and rose no higher than one story: they differ, however, in some degree, from the common habitations of other places which we have passed, as they are here almost universally built of wood; there being very few stone or brick houses to be seen, but such as are inhabited by the mandarins of the place.

The exterior appearance of the houses is very pleasing from

the prettiness of their decorations; but they are most wretchedly furnished within, if that term can be applied where there is very little or no furniture at all. They have only one apartment behind their shops, which is without floor or pavement, and must serve them for every domestic use and employment. Before the doors of the shops, wooden pillars are erected, from which an awning is suspended during the day, to protect not only the passengers, but the shopkeepers themselves, from the rays of the sun: some of these pillars are considerably higher than the houses before which they stand; and are not only gilt and painted, but decorated with streamers, which serve as signs to denote the commodities of the particular shops; the tops of them are frequently mounted with a wooden figure, which serves as a direction to the spot.

As to variety, either in the form or dimensions of the houses or shops, there is none; for an almost universal sameness prevails in the streets of this extensive city: they differ, indeed, in breadth; and the inhabitants of those which are narrow spread matting from the tops of the houses quite across the street, which is a very agreeable circumstance in the hot seasons: there is also, for the convenience of foot passengers, a pavement of four feet in breadth on each side of every street.

Glass is not any where used in China for windows, and the common substitute for it is a thin glazed paper, which is passed on the inside of a wooden lattice: silk, however, is employed for this purpose in the houses of the higher classes of the people.

Tong-tchew is a place of great trade, as appears from the vast number of junks which we saw lying in the river before it; and the astonishing number of its inhabitants; which is very generally believed, as I was informed by some of the resident merchants, to amount, at least, to half a million of people.

During the summer and autumn months the heat here is very sultry and oppressive: the winter, however, brings inclemency along with it, as ice of thirty inches thick is preserved here, in subterranean caverns, till the summer. It is considered as an article of great luxury among the people, who mix it with their drink, to give it a refreshing coolness in the hot seasons of the year.

In the course of my excursions through the city, I endeavoured to make tnyself acquainted with the nature of its municipal government. Of this important subject it is not to be supposed that I could learn much: I was, however, in one way or other, made to understand, that all civil causes are determined by a certain number of inferior mandarins expressly appointed to the judicial office; but that their decisions are subject to the review of the chief mandarin of the place or district, who may confirm or reverse them at pleasure: this officer, and his decrees, are also subject to the Viceroy of the province, from whom, in all civil causes, there is no appeal.

In capital offences, the final determination rests with the Emperor alone; though it is very rare indeed, that a criminal is sentenced to die: but if such a circumstance should happen in the most remote corner of the empire, application must be made to the Emperor himself to annul, to mitigate, or enforce the sentence. Executions, however, are very seldom seen in China. I was very particular and curious in my inquiries on this subjeet, wherever I had an opportunity to make them, and not one person that was questioned on the occasion, and some of them were at least seventy years of age, had ever seen or known of a capital execution. Nor are the lesser crimes so frequent as might be expeted in such a populous and commercial country; as the most obnoxious classes of them, at least, are kept down by the vigour of the police, and the promptitude of punishment, which follows conviction without the delay of a moment: a regulation which might, in many cases, be adopted with the best effects by the boasted judicature of Great Britain. Nor shall I hesitate to observe, that whatever may be the defects or excellencies of the Chinese government, of which I am not altogether qualified to judge, the people of China seem to be happy and contented under it, and to enjoy as much liberty as is consistent with the best arrangement of civilized society.

The palaces of the mandarins are the only public buildings which I could discover, or was informed of, in this extensive city: they are built of brick, and appeared to be very spacious; but were more remarkable for extent, than elegance or grandeur.

I finished this curious excursion in the evening, when I was not only very much fatigued by my walk, but very much harassed by the curiosity of the people. I was sometimes surrounded by twenty or thirty of them, who pressed so much upon me, that I was frequently under the necessity of taking shelter in shops, till the crowd that persecuted me was dispersed; and, in return for the protection afforded me, I made some purchases of fans and tobacco-pipes, which were formed with curious neatness and ingenuity.

Monday 19. This morning Mr. Barrow, the comptroller, received the whole of the remaining part of the presents, which were lodged in the depot already described. Lieutenant Parish of the royal artillery, with a party of his men, attended there to examine the ordnance fibres: they also uncased the guns, and got them mounted on their carriages; they consisted of six new brass field pieces, two mortars, and one wall piece, with a complete artillery apparatus. On the report of the state of the ordnance, etc. being made to the Ambassador, he was pleased to come to the sheds, attended by Col. Benson, the officers, and other gentlemen, to see the guns exercised; when several rounds were fired with great quickness, activity, and exactness. His Excellency remained there about two hours, when he returned to his residence, where the gentlemen of the embassy dined in the same manner as on the preceding day.

In the evening the Ambassador received a visit from the attendant mandarin, accompanied by the chief mandarin of the city. The band was ordered on the occasion to play on the platforrn, and the Chinese visitors appeared to be very much delighted with the European music.

This evening, at eight o'clock Mr. Harry Eades, one of the mechanics attached to the embassy, died in consequence of a violent flux, with which he had been for some time afilicted. Mr. Plumb, the interpreter, was requested to order a coffin on the occasion; and, as these sad receptacles are always ready made in China, our departed companion was soon placed with all possible decency, in a situation to receive the last act of respect which we can pay to each other.

The coffins of this country are all of the same size, and bear a stronger resemblance to a flat-bottomed boat, than to those of Europe: they are very strong and heavy, and the lid is not nailed down, as with us, but fastened with a cord.

About eleven o'clock there began a most tremendous storm of thunder, lightning, and rain, which continued without any intermission till four o'clock.

Tuesday 10. This morning the Amaassador issued regulations for the funeral of Mr. Harry Eades, which, in order to give the Chinese a favourable impression even of our funeral solemnities, was directed to be performed with military honours.

All the servants, mechanics, and musicians, attached to the embassy, were desired to be in readiness on the occasion: Colonel Benson also issued orders to the troops to appear with their side arms, except a serjeant and six privates of the royal artillery, who were ordered to be armed and accoutered for firing over the grave. As no clergyman accompanied the embassy, I was appointed to read the funeral service of the Church of England on this melancholy occasion.

At nine o'clock the procession began in the following order:

Detachment of the royal artillery, with arms reversed.

The coffin supported on men's shoulders.

Two fifes playing a funeral dirge.

The persons appointed to officiate at the grave.

The mechanics, servants, etc. two and two.

The troops then followed, and closed the whole.

This procession was also accompanied by several of the gentlemen belonging to the embassy. Thus we proceeded, with all due solemnity, to the burying-ground, which is situated about a quarter of a mile from the Ambassador's residence; and where permission had been granted for the interment of our countryman, with a liberality that would not have been practised in some of the countries of our own enlightened quarter of the globe. Such a ceremonial, as may well be imagined, had excited the curiosity of the city, and we were attended by a concourse of spectators that the most interesting and splendid spectacles would not assemble in the cities of Europe.

On our arrival at the place of interment, the soldiery formed a circle round the grave, with the firing party standing on the side of it. The coffin being placed on two planks of wood, the funeral service was then read, when the body was committed with the usual ceremonies to the earth, and the parties discharged three vollies over the grave, which, according to a custom of the country that we cannot reconcile with the general good sense of the people, had no greater depth than was just necessary to cover the coffin.

In this burying-ground there was a great number of marble and stone monuments with inscriptions on them. Some of these memorials were gilt, and enriched with various devices of no ordinary sculpture: the funeral spot is very extensive, but without any enclosure. There are, indeed, no public places of burial, but near large towns and cities, as in the country, every one is buried on the premises where he had lived.

When the grave was closed, and this list of duty performed to the dead, the procession returned in the same order that has been already described.

The Ambassador was visited by several mandarins, a mark of respect which we were disposed to consider as a favourable prognostication of success in the great objects of this extraordinary mission. His Excellency also received notice that the following day was appointed for the departure of the embassy to Pekin, and that every necessary preparation was made for that purpose.

It is a curious circumstance that the place of residence appointed for the embassy, proved, after all, to be the house of a timber merchant, whole yard was adjoining to it; but the communication between them was, on this occasion, closed up by a temporary fixture of deals that were nailed across it. On making inquiry concerning the truth of what had been suggested to me, a Chinese soldier pointed to the timber yard; and, at the same time, made me understand, that the owner of the place sold that kind of wood which was employed in the building of junks.

CHAPTER VIII

Leave the city of Tong-tchew. — The road to Pekin described. — Arrive at a large town called Kiyeng-Foo: Halt there to breakfast. — Prodigious crowds of people to see the embassy pass. — Arrive at Pekin: Some account of that city. — Customs and manners of the Chinese. — Leave Pekin. — Arrive at the Imperial Palace named Yeumen-man-yeumen.

1793, August, Wednesday 11. This morning at two o'clock, the general was beat through all the courts of the house, as a signal for the suite to prepare for their departure. After a hasty breakfast, the whole of the embassy was ready to proceed on their journey. The soldiers were first marched off to covered wagons provided for them; the servants then followed, and were received into similar machines; the gentlemen of the suite next proceeded in light carts. Lord Macartney, Sir George Staunton, and Mr. Plumb, the interpreter, were conveyed in palankins, which were each of the borne by four men.

The carriages which carried the soldiers and servants were common hired carts, drawn by four horses, unequally coupled together, and covered with straw matting. The harness, if it may deserve that name, was made of rope and cordage. The single-horse carts were covered with blue nankeen, and had doors of lattice work lined with the same stuff: the drivers walked by the side of them.

At four o'clock this procession was in motion, which consisted of sixty carts for the soldiers and servants, and twenty for the conveyance of the gentlemen belonging to the suite, exclusive of carts for the private baggage, and the coolies, or porters, employed to carry the presents and heavy baggage, which were conveyed on their shoulders; four hundred of whom were employed on this extraordinary occasion.

About five o'clock we had quitted the city of Tong-tchew, and entered immediately into a fine level country of the most luxuriant fertility, which, as far as the eye could reach, appeared to be one immense garden.

The road along which we travelled is not only broad but elegant; and is a proof of the labour employed by the Chinese government to facilitate the communications between the capital and the principal parts of the kingdom. The middle of this road consists of a pavement of broad flag stones about twenty feet wide, and on each side of it there is a sufficient space to admit of six carriages to run abreast. The lateral parts are laid with gravel stones, and kept in continual repair by troops of labourers, who are stationed on different parts of the road for that purpose.

At seven o'clock the cavalcade stopped at a large town, whose name is Kiyeng-Foo. To call it populous, would be to employ a superfluous expression that is equally appropriate to the whole kingdom, as every village, town, and city; nay, every river, and all the banks of it, teem with people. In the country through which we have passed the population is immense and universal: every mile brought us to a village, whose inhabitants would have crowded our largest towns; and the number of villas scattered over the country, on each side of the road, while they added to its beauty, were proofs of its wealth. Those which we approached near enough to examine as we passed, were built of wood, and the fronts of many of them were painted black, and enriched with gilded ornaments.

The day of our journey from Tong-tchew to Pekin was, I doubt not, a matter of general notification, from the prodigious concourse of people who absolutely covered the road; and notwithstanding the utmost exertions of the mandarins to keep it clear, the pressure of the crowd was sometimes so great, that we were obliged to halt, for at least a quarter of an hour, to prevent the accidents which might otherwise have happened from the passage of the carts amidst this continual and innumerable throng. I cannot but add to the obstacles which we received from the curiosity of the Chinese people, same small degree of mortification at the kind of impression our appearance seemed to make on them: for they no sooner obtained a sight of any of us, than they universally burst out into loud shouts of laughter: and I must acknowledge, that we did not, at this time, wear the appearance of people, who were arrived in this country, in order to obtain, by every means of address and prepossession, those commercial privileges and political distinctions, which no other nation has had the art or power to accomplish.

At Kiyeng-Foo, which is about nine miles from Tong-tchew, the whole embassy of all ranks alighted from their respective carriages: here the inferior department found tables spread for their refreshment in an open yard, but covered, at the same time, with great plenty of cold meats, tea, fruits, etc. while the upper departments were served with their regale in some adjoining rooms of a very miserable appearance.

Before the procession re-commenced its progress, the conducting mandarin, with his usual attention, ordered some Joau, an harsh sour white wine, to be offered to the attendants of the embassy to fortify their stomachs, as a considerable time might probably elapse before they would obtain any further refreshment; we were then summoned to prepare for our departure, when a scene of confusion and disturbance took place among ourselves, which, whatever its real effects might have been, was not calculated at least to give any very favourable impression of the manners and disposition of the English nation. In short, from the crowd of people assembled to see us, the neglect of a previous arrangement, and distribution, of the carts, together with the inconsiderate eagerness to set off among ourselves, it was a matter of no inconsiderable difficulty for the mandarins to assign the people to their respective vehicles.

At eight o'clock we took our leave of the town of Kiyeng-Foo, which is a very considerable and extensive place; the streets are broad and unpaved, and the houses are built altogether of wood; at least in the part which we traversed there were none constructed of any other materials. The shops made a very pleasing appearance, and seemed to be well furnished with their respective commodities.

Of the country, which occupies the few miles from this place to Pekin, I have little to say, as the crowds of people that surrounded us, either intercepted the view, or distracted our attention.

At noon we approached the suburbs of the capital of China, and I cannot but feel some degree of regret, that no alteration was made in the ordinary travelling, and shabby appearance, of the embassy, on such an important occasion. Whatever reasons there might be to prevent that display, which it possessed such ample provisions to make, I cannot pretend to determine, but our cavalcade had nothing like the appearance of an embassy from the first nation in Europe, passing through the most populous city in the world.

On entering the suburbs, we passed beneath several very beautiful triumphal arches, elegantly painted, and enriched with various fanciful ornaments: the upper part of them was square, with a kind of pent-house, painted of a green colour, and heightened with varnish: from the inside of this roof was suspended the model of an accommodation junk, admirably executed, and adorned with ribands and silken streamers. There suburbs are very extensive a the houses are of wood, the greater part of them two stories in height, and their fronts painted in various colours. The shops are not only commodious for their respective purposes, but have a certain grandeur in their appearance, that is enlivened by the very pretty manner in which the articles of the respective magazines are displayed to the view of the public, either to distinguish the trade, or to tempt the purchaser.

We proceeded gradually through spacious streets, which are paved on either side for the convenience of foot passengers. The whole way was lined with soldiers, and, indeed, without such a regulation, it would have been impossible for the carriages to have passed through the immense crowd that attended us.

At two o'clock we arrived at the gates of the grand imperial city of Pekin, with very little semblance of diplomatic figure or importance: in short, for I cannot help repeating the sentiment, the appearance of the Ambassador's attendants, both with respect to the shabbiness of their dress, and the vehicles which conveyed them, bore a greater resemblance to the removal of paupers to their parishes in England, than the expected dignity of the representative of a great and powerful monarch.

Pekin, or as the natives pronounce it, Pitchin, the metropolis of the Chinese empire, is situated in one hundred and sixteen degrees of east longitude, and between forty and forty-one degrees of north latitude. It is defended by a wall that incloses a square space of about twelve leagues in circumference: there is a grand gate in the center of each angle, and as many lesser ones at each corner of the wall: they are strongly arched, and fortified by a square building, or tower, of seven stories, that springs from the top of the gateway; the sides of which are strengthened by a parapet wall, with port-holes for ordnance. The windows of this building are of wood, and painted to imitate the muzzle of a great gun, which is so exactly represented, that the deception is not discoverable but on a very near approach: there are nine of these windows to each story on the front towards the suburbs. These gates are double; the first arch of which is very strongly built of a kind of freestone, and not of marble, as has been related by some writers: the depth of it is about thirty feet, and in the middle of the entrance is a very strong door of six inches thick, and fortified with iron bolts: this archway leads to a large square which contains the barracks for soldiers, consisting of mean wooden houses of two stories: on turning to the left, the second gateway is seen, whose arch is of the same dimensions and appearance as that already described, but without the tower.

At each of the principal gates there is a strong guard of soldiers, with several pieces of ordnance placed on each side of the inner entrance. These gates are opened at the dawn of day, and shut at ten o'clock at night, after which hour all communication with the city from the suburbs is impracticable; nor will they be opened on any pretence, or occasion whatever, without a special order from the principal mandarin of the city.

The four lesser gates are defended by a small fort built on the wall, which is always guarded by a body of troops.

The wall is about thirty feet high, and ten in breadth on the top: the foundation is of stone, and appears about two feet from the surface of the earth: the upper part is of brick, and gradually diminishes from the bottom to the top. Whether it is a solid structure, or only filled up with mortar or rubbish, is a circumstance concerning which I could not procure any authentic information.

This wall is defended by outworks and batteries at short distances from each other; each of them being strengthened by a small fort; but none of the fortifications are garrisoned except those which are attached to the gates; and though there is a breast-work of three feet high, with port-holes for cannon, which crowns the whole length of the wall, there is not a single gun mounted upon it. On the side towards the city, it is, in some places, quite perpendicular; and in others forms a gentle declivity from the top to the ground. It is customary for bodies of soldiers to patrole the wall every night during the time that the Emperor resides in the city, which is from October to April, when his Imperial Majesty usually goes to a favourite palace in Tartary. From its perfect state of repair and general appearance, I should rather suppose it to be of modern erection, and that many years cannot have passed away since it underwent a complete repair, or was entirely rebuilt.

The distance from the south gate, where we entered, to the east gate through which we passed out of the city, comprehends, on the most moderate computation, a course of ten miles. The principal streets are equally spacious and convenient, being one hundred and forty feet in breadth, and of great length, but are only paved on each side for foot passengers. The police of the city, however, spares no pains to keep the middle part clean, and free from all kind of nuisance; there being large bodies of scavengers continually employed for that purpose, who are assisted, as well as controlled, in their duty by soldiers stationed in every district, to enforce a due observance of the laws that have been enacted, and the regulations that have been framed, for preserving civil order among the people, and maintaining the municipal œconomies of this immense city. I observed, as we passed along, a great number of men who were sprinkling the streets with water, in order to lay the dust, which, in dry weather, would not only be troublesome to passengers, but very obnoxious also to the shops; whose commodities could not be exposed to view without injury, were it not for this beneficial and necessary precaution.

Though the houses at Pekin are low and mean, when considered with respect to size and domestic accommodation, their exterior appearance is handsome and elegant, as the Chinese take a great pride in beautifying the fronts of their shops and dwellings: the upper part of the former is ornamented with a profusion of golden characters; and on the roofs of the latter are frequent galleries, rich in painting and other decoration; where numerous parties of women are seen to amuse themselves according to the fashion of the country. The pillars which are created before the doors of the shops, are gilded and painted, having a flag fixed at the top, whose characters specify the name and business of the owner: tables are also spread with commodities, and lines attached to these pillars are hung with them.

I observed a great number of butchers shops, where the mode of cutting up meat resembles our own; nor can the markets of London boast a better supply of flesh than is to be found in Pekin. My curiosity induced me to inquire the prices of their meat, and on my entering the shop, 1 saw on a stall before it an earthen stove, with a gridiron placed upon it; and on my employing a variety of signs to obtain the information I wanted, the butcher instantly began to cut off small thin slices of meat, about the size of a crown piece, and broiled as fast as I could eat them. I took about a dozen of these slices, which might altogether weigh seven or eight ounces; and when I paid him, which I did by giving him a string of caxee, or small coin, he pulled off, as I suppose, the amount of his demand, which was one conderon, or ten caxee, the only current money in the empire. I saw numbers of people in other butchers shops, as I passed along, regaling themselves with beef and mutton in the same manner.

The houses, appropriated to the sale of porcelain utensils and ornaments, are peculiarly attractive, having a display of broad shelves ranged above each other, in the front of their shops, on which they dispose the most beautiful specimens of their trade in a manner full of fancy and effect.

Besides the variety of trades which are stationary in this great city, there are many thousands of its inhabitants who cry their goods about, as we see in our own metropolis. They generally have a bamboo placed across their shoulders, and a basket at each end of it, in which they carry fish, vegetables, eggs, and other similar articles. There are also great numbers of hawkers and pedlars, who go about with bags strapped on their shoulders like a knapsack, which contain various kinds of stuff goods, the folds of which are exposed to view. In selling these stuffs, they use the cubit measure of sixteen inches. Barbers are also seen running about the streets in great plenty, with every instrument known in this country for shaving the head and cleansing the ears: they carry with them for this purpose a portable chair, a portable stove, and a small vessel of water, and whoever wishes to undergo either of these operations, sits down in the street, when the operator performs his office. To distinguish their profession, they carry a pair of large steel tweezers, which they open with their fingers; and let them close again with some degree of violence, which produces a shrill sound that is heard at a considerable distance; and such is their mode of Peeking employment. That this trade is very profitable in China no one can doubt; because every man must be shaved on a part of the head where it is impossible to shave himself.

In several of the streets I saw persons engaged in selling off goods by auction: the auctioneer stood on a platform surrounded with the various articles he had to sell: he delivered himself in a loud and bawling manner; while the smiling countenances of the audience, which was the only language I could interpret, seemed to express the entertainment they received from his harangue.

At each end of the principal streets, for there are no squares in Pekin, there is a large gateway fancifully painted, with an handsome roof coloured and varnished; beneath which the name of the street is written in golden characters: these arches terminate the nominal street, or otherwise there would be streets in some parts of the city of at least five miles in length, which are formed into several divisions by these gateways. They are very handsome, as well as central objects, and are railed in on each side from the foot pavement. The narrow streets are enclosed at each end with small lattice gates, which are always shut during the night; but all the considerable streets are guarded both night and day by soldiers, who wear swords by their sides, and carry long whips in their hands, to clear the streets of any inconvenient throng of people, and to chastise such as are refractory into decorum or good behaviour.

Notwithstanding the vast extent of this place; there is little or no variety in their houses, as I have before observed, but in the colours with which they are painted: they are, in reality, nothing better than temporary booths, erected for exterior shew, and without any view to strength or durability. It is very rare, indeed, to see an house of more than one story, except such as belong to mandarins; and even those are covered, as it were, by the walls which rise above every house or building in Pekin, except a lofty pagoda, and an imperial palace.

There are no carriages standing in the streets for the convenience of its inhabitants, like our hackney coaches in London: the higher classes of people keep palankins; and others of less distinction have covered carts drawn by a horse or mule.

The opinion, that the Chinese women are excluded from the view of strangers, has very little, if any foundation, as among the immense crowd assembled to see the cavalcade of the English embassy, one fourth of the whole at least were women; a far greater proportion of that sex than is to be seen in any concourse of people whom curiosity assembles in our own country: and if the idea is founded in truth, that curiosity is a peculiar characteristic of the female disposition in Europe, I shall presume to say that, from the eagerness which we observed in the looks of the Chinese women as we passed by them, the quality which has just been mentioned is equally prevalent among the fair ones of Asia.

The women we saw on our passage through Pekin possessed, in general, great delicacy of feature, and fine natural complexions; with which, however, they are not content, and therefore whiten their faces with cosmetics: they likewise employ vermilion, but in a manner wholly different from the application of rouge among European ladies; they mark the middle of their lips with a stripe of its deepest colour, which, without pretending to reason upon it, certainly heightens the effect of their features. Their eyes are very small, but powerfully brilliant, and their arms extremely long and slender. The only difference between the women of Pekin, and those we had already seen, as it appeared to us, was, that the former wear a sharp peak of black velvet or silk, which is ornamented with stones, and descends from the forehead almost between the eyes; and that their feet, free from the bandages which have already been mentioned, are suffered to attain their natural growth.

When we had passed through the eastern gate of the city, some confusion having arisen among the baggage carts, the whole procession was obliged to halt; I, therefore, took the opportunity of easing my limbs, which were very much cramped by the inconvenience of the machine, and perceiving a number of women in the crowd that surrounded us, I ventured to approach them; and, addressing them with the Chinese word *Chou-au*, (or beautiful) they appeared to be extremely diverted, and gathering round me, but with an air of great modesty and politeness, they examined the make and form of my clothes, as well as the texture of the materials of which they were composed. When the carts began to move off, I took leave of these obliging females by a gentle shake of the hand which they tendered to me with the most graceful affability; nor did the men, who were present, appear to be at all dissatisfied with my conduct: on the contrary, they expressed, as far as I could judge, very great satisfaction at this public attention I paid to their ladies. It appears, therefore, that in this city, the women are not divested of a reasonable portion of their liberty, and, consequently, that the jealousy, attributed so universally to the Chinese men, is not a predominant quality, at least, in the capital of the empire.

Among other objects which we saw in our way, and did not fail to attract our notice, was a funeral procession, which proved to be a very striking and solemn spectacle: the coffin was covered by a canopy decorated with curtains of satin, enriched with gold and flowers, and hung with escutcheons: it was placed on a large bier or platform, and carried by at least fifty or sixty men, who supported it on their shoulders with long bamboos crossing each other, and marched eight abreast with slow and solemn step. A band of music immediately followed, playing a kind of dirge, which was not without a mixture of pleasing tones: the relations and friends of the deceased person then followed, arrayed in black and white dresses.

Having passed through the eastern suburbs of the city, we entered on a rich and beautiful country, when a short stage of about four miles brought us to one of the Emperor's palaces named Yeumen-manyeumen, where we arrived about five o'clock in the afternoon, oppressed with fatigue from the extreme heat of the day, and the various impediments which obstructed our passage, arising from the immense crowds of people that may be said to have filled up the whole way from Tong-tchew to this place, a journey of thirty miles.

In a short time after our arrival, we received a very scanty and indifferent refreshment; when the whole suite retired to sleep off the fatigue of the day.

CHAPTER IX

Description of the palace of Yeumen-manyeumen. – Disagreeable circumstances belonging to it. – Disputes with the natives who guarded it. – Lord Macartney applies for a change of situation. – The embassy removes to Pekin. – Description of a pagoda. – Arrive at the palace appointed for the residence of the embassy. – Description of it. – The arrangements made in it. – Several mandarins visit the Ambassador.

1793, August, Thursday 22. THE whole of this morning was employed in removing the baggage, etc. belonging to the embassy, from the outer gateway, where it had been deposited, to the different apartments appointed for the gentlemen who composed it.

The palace of Yeumen-manyeumen is in a very low situation about a quarter of a mile from a village of the same name, and is a very mean, inconvenient building of no more than one story.

The entrance to this palace, if it may be said to deserve that name, consists of a very ordinary stone gateway, guarded by soldiers; and beyond it is a kind of parade, where the baggage was placed on its being taken out of the carts that had brought it hither. In the center of this parade there is a small lodge, where several mandarins of an inferior order were in waiting; and which forms an entrance to the passage that leads to the body of the palace.

The position of this palace is not only low, but in a swampy hollow, and between two ponds of stagnant water, whose putrid exhalations cannot add to the comfort of its unwholesome situation; and some apartments which were on the banks of one of these ponds, were occupied as barracks by the British soldiers. To the west of this building there is another gate, but constructed of wood, which leads to another apartment of the palace, where I observed a considerable number of Chinese soldiers; but, on my approach to take a view of them, they suddenly retired, and locked the door against me. Indeed, the native jealousy of these people respecting strangers seemed to be awakened in a very great degree, when they thought it necessary to watch all our actions with such a minute and scrutinising attention.

The palace, for I must by way of distinction continue to give it that name, though unworthy the residence of the representative of a great monarch, is divided into two square courts, containing a quadrangular range of apartments, which were not only destitute of elegance, but in a wretched state of repair: a paved footway skirts their walls, and is covered with a wooden roof painted and varnished. Before the principal doors of the building, and in the midst of a large court, there are a few trees of no very peculiar figure or beauty; but the ground itself is covered with a kind of gravel. There are some small fields of grass belonging to the palace, which wear an appearance of neglect, that we should not have expected to find in a country where we had not yet seen an uncultivated spot.

The windows of the apartments consisted of lattice work covered with a glazed and painted paper. In the hot seasons the doors are opened during the day, and their place supplied by cooling blinds made of bamboo, fancifully coloured, and wrought as fine and close as a weaver's reed: they certainly served to refresh the rooms where they were placed, and afforded some degree of coolness to alleviate the heat of the day; but at night the doors were restored to their office, and these blinds were rolled up and fastened to the wall over them.

The whole range of apartments contained no other furniture than few very common tables and chairs; not a bed or bedstead was to be seen in the whole place; it was, therefore, a fortunate circumstance for us that we providently brought our cots and hammocks from on board the ships, or we should not have slept in a bed, at least, during our residence in China. The natives have no such comfortable article of furniture in their houses, but sleep on a kind of mattress, and cover themselves with a cushion stuffed and quilted with cotton. They pull off a very small part of their dress when they go to rest, and when the weather proves cold, they increase the number of these cushions as the circumstances of the season may require. In the place of bedsteads they use a large wooden bench, which is raised about two feet from the ground, and covered with a kind of elastic basket work made of bamboos, on which seven or eight persons may spread their bedding. I have also seen some of them formed of planks, and covered with carpets.

This habitation had a most ungracious and deserted appearance; and, from the state in which we found it, a long time must have elapsed since it was inhabited by any thing but centipes, scorpions, and mosquitos, which infested it in every part. It is surrounded by a very high and strong wall of stone, which excluded every external object; nor was any person belonging to the embassy permitted, on any pretence whatever, to pass its boundaries, mandarins and soldiers being stationed at every avenue to keep us within the precincts of this miserable abode; so that we were in reality in a state of honourable imprisonment, without any other consolation for the loss of our liberty, but that we were supplied with our daily provisions at the expense of the Emperor.

The Ambassador's apartments were guarded both night and day by British centinels; and, to support the dignity of his great diplomatic character, his Excellency required that a table should be, in future, furnished for himself and Sir George and Mr. Staunton, distinct from the gentlemen of his suite. This requisition found a ready compliance, and this day he dined in his own apartment, while the upper ranks of those who attended on the embassy, had a table prepared for them in one of the courts, and beneath the shade of a tree.

Friday 23. The place where the presents were deposited was so exposed to the sun, that it was apprehended some of them would receive considerable injury from their unfavourable situation; a temporary shed was therefore immediately erected, to which they were speedily removed.

Lord Macartney being very much dissatisfied with his situation, made a serious requisition for the appointment of a residence more suited to the character with which he was invested, as well as to the convenience and proper accommodation of the embassy. To obtain this object, Mr. Plumb, his Excellency's interpreter, made several visits to Pekin; little, therefore, occurred worthy of a recital during the remainder of our stay in this uncomfortable abode. It continued, however, till the twenty-seventh day of this month, which was appointed for the Ambassador's departure for Pekin; a more commodious residence having been allotted for the embassy, in consequence of Mr. Plumb's negociation with the Chinese government on the occasion.

This interval was not passed by any of the gentlemen of the suite, or the inferior attendants, with satisfaction or patience; and Col. Benson was so hurt and mortified at being denied the liberty of passing the walls of the palace, that he made an attempt to gratify his inclinations, which produced a very unpleasant affray; when he was not only forced back from his design, but threatened with very illiberal treatment from the Chinese who were on duty at the gates.

Several other disputes of a similar nature took place between the suite and the natives who guarded the palace. It was, without doubt, a very humiliating circumstance for Englishmen, attending also as they were upon a mission, that by the law of nations possesses the most enlarged and universal privileges, to be treated in a manner so ill-suited to their individual, as well as political character: at the same time it would, perhaps, have been more discreet to have spared those menaces which were continually expressed against persons charged with an official duty, and acting under the direction of their superiors; and to have submitted with patience to those regulations, which, however unpleasant, were such as were adopted by, and might be the usage of, that government, whose partial favour and friendship it was the interest, and, therefore, the duty of the British embassy, by insinuating address and political manoeuvre, to obtain and establish.

Saturday 24. The pleasure that was this day felt by the whole of the suite of every denomination, is not easily described, when orders were received to prepare for quitting this horrid place on the Monday following.

Sunday 25. This and the succeeding day were employed in removing the greater part of the baggage and presents, which was accomplished, as it had hitherto been, by the coolies, or porters.

The chandeliers, mathematical apparatus, together with the clocks and timepieces, were left at the palace of Yeumen-manyeumen, as such frequent removals might materially injure, if not altogether spoil those pieces of mechanism, the wonders of whose operations must depend upon the delicacy of their movements,

Monday 26. At ten o'clock in the morning single horse carts were provided for the whole train of the embassy. The soldiers, mechanics, and servants, were lodged two in a cart; and each of the gentlemen had a cart to himself; but the Ambassador, with his secretary and interpreter, were, as before, accommodated with palankins.

The business of our getting off was, as it had hitherto been, a scene of confusion and disorder; but by eleven o'clock, we had, to our extreme satisfaction, bid adieu to our late uncomfortable residence. We soon passed through the village from whence the palace appears to derive its name, amidst a vast crowd of spectators, and, at one o'clock, arrived at the north gate of the city of Pekin; which is the counterpart of that we have already described. In our progress through the streets we passed a pagoda, which is the first we had seen in China. In our voyage up the river, or in our journey from Tong-tchew to Pekin, we had not seen one of these buildings, which are, in a great measure, peculiar to this part of the east, till we arrived at this city: it is situated in the middle of a very pretty garden adjoining to a mandarin's palace.

This pagoda is a square structure, built of stone, and diminishes gradually from the bottom, till it terminates in a spire. It had only one gallery, which encircled it near the top, and was guarded by a rail; a curtain of red silk, at this time, hung from a projecting canopy, and gave this part of the building, when seen at a distance, the appearance of an umbrella. It was seven stories in height, and was without any kind of exterior ornament, but that which I have described.

As our return to Pekin was not only sudden but unexpected, our re-entry was not particularly interrupted by the public curiosity, and, at half past two in the afternoon, we arrived, without having met with any material impediments, at the princely palace which had been appointed for the future residence of the embassy. It is the property of John Tuck, a name generally given by Englishmen, but why, or wherefore, I cannot tell, to the Viceroy of Canton, who was now here as a state prisoner, for same embezzlement of the public treasures, or other misdemeanors respecting his government there.

This palace is built of a grey brick, and is extremely spacious, containing twelve large and six small courts. The bricks are cemented with such curious care, that the seams of mortar between them are as small as a thread, and placed with such peculiar uniformity, that a minute examination is necessary to convince the spectator that it is not the work of a painter, rather than that of a bricklayer, and that the pencil has not been employed to produce the effect instead of the trowel. These bricks have the smoothness of marble, are sixteen inches in length, eight inches broad, and two and a half in thickness.

The whole range of buildings, except two distinct parts, which were inhabited by the Ambassador and Sir George Staunton, occupy but one, though a very lofty story. The courts are spacious and regular squares, and paved with large flat stones. Before the building, in each of these squares, there is a railed terrace of about three feet, to which there are regular flights, of steps in the center of each angle, and, of course, corresponding with each other. Over these terraces there is a projecting roof, which extends the breadth of them, and is supported by light pillars of wood, ranged at equal distances, and conneeted by a railing of fanciful contrivance. The whole is gilt and painted with much prettiness, as to pattern and colour; and forms a most elegant piazza, that not only adds to the grandeur, but, which is a better thing, to the convenience of this superb mansion.

Here I first observed the superiority of the Chinese in the art of house painting, to which they give a gloss equal to Japan, that not only preserves the colours from fading, but never suffers any injury itself from the exposition of air, sun, or rain. I at first considered this effect to have been produced by varnish; but I afterwards discovered that it proceeded from certain ingredients with which the colours are originally mixed, and not from any second operation.

The apartments are very commodious and of large dimensions; some of them were hung with a glistening paper of a pattern, both as to colour and beauty, far superior to any I had ever seen in Europe; others were curiously painted and enriched with gilding. Those occupied by Lord Macartney were numerous and elegant, and contained a private theatre. The latter is of a square form, with a painted gallery, which runs entirely round it, for the spectators; the stage is raised from the floor about three feet, and has the appearance of a large platform; it is guarded by a wooden railing, and has a passage of eight feet wide all round it; behind the stage is a suit of rooms for the convenience of the actors, who dress in them, or retire thither to make any necessary transformation in their characters during the performance. The building is very lofty, and the roof elegantly painted. The apartments of Sir George Staunton were also very handsome and convenient. The whole suite were likewise accommodated in a manner that gave them the most entire satisfaction.

The windows are covered with glazed paper, and the doors of the principal rooms consist of gilded frame-work, which is fitted up with fine silk gauze, instead of glass. The frames, both of the doors and windows, are richly gilt: and, in the warm seasons, the former being always kept open, a curtain, if it may be so called, of painted fret-work, made of bamboo, supplies their place, as I have already observed in a former description.

In several courts of the palace there are artificial rocks and ruins of no mean contrivance, which, though not very congenial to their situation, were formed with considerable and were, in themselves, very happy imitations of those objects they were designed to represent. To these may be added the triumphal arches, which arise, with all their fanciful devices, in various parts of the building.

This noble mansion is of great extent, and calculated to afford every kind of princely accommodation; but, with all its magnificence, as to the number of the apartments, and the general display of the whole, its only furniture was some chairs and tables; and a few small platforms covered with carpets and bamboo matting.

Beneath the floor in each of the principal apartments, is a stove, or furnace of brick-work, with a circular tube that is conducted round the room where it stands, which is sufficient also to warm the apartment above it. These stoves are, in cold weather, constantly supplied with charcoal, and communicate their heat in the manner of hot-houses in England. The houses here have no chimnies that I could discover, and, of course, no other means of administering heat can be employed but those which have been mentioned.

At four o'clock in the afternoon; the whole suite sat down to dinner, which consisted, as usual, of a great variety of stews and hashes. Indeed, a joint of meat is seldom or ever seen, but on festival days; of which I shall speak more hereafter. His Excellency and Sir George Staunton dined together. But with all the superiority of accommodation we enjoyed here, we continued to be guarded with the same suspicious vigilance as in our late residence. On no pretence whatever was any one permitted to pass the gates, and every accessible part of the place was under the active care of military power.

This palace, according to the reports of the country, was

erected by the Viceroy of Canton, from the fruits of his exactions during his government there, and particularly on the shipping of the English nation at that port; for which acts of injustice and oppression he was, as I have before mentioned, at this time, a prisoner at Pekin. The money expended on this immense building amounted to ninety-seven thousand pounds sterling. A most enormous sum in a country where the materials for building, and the labour which puts them together, are to be obtained at so cheap a rate.

Tuesday 27. This day was principally occupied in arranging the various apartments for the convenience of the gentlemen, etc. to whom they were allotted, as well as in providing suitable places for the reception of the heavy baggage.

The cloths and bale goods, with that part of the more valuable presents which were of the smallest compass, were distributed between the apartments of Lord Macartney and Sir George Staunton: the remainder was removed to several large chambers, which formed a large and commodious magazine for their reception. The six pieces of small ordnance and two mortars were placed in the inner court, with all their appendages, and mounted on their carriages, in front of the Ambassador's apartments.

These arrangements being made in the most proper and convenient manner which our situation would admit, it remained for us to wait with patience, till his Imperial Majesty's pleasure should be known, whether the embassy was to proceed to Tartary, or to be cooped up in its present abode till the usual season of his Majesty's return to the capital of his empire. To obtain this intelligence so important to us, a mandarin had been dispatched, on our arrival at Tong-tchew, to the Emperor's summer residence in Tartary, and we were in continual expectation of the return of this messenger.

In the course of this day, the British Ambassador was visited by a company of mandarins, among whom were several persons, natives of France, who had been of the order of jesuits; but being prohibited from promulgating their doctrines in this country, had assumed its dress and manners, and, on account of their learning, had been elevated to the dignity of mandarins. These French gentlemen, who were, as may be very readily conceived, well acquainted with the interests of the country in which they were now naturalized, encouraged Lord Macartney to hope for the most satisfactory and beneficial issue of the embassy which he concluded.

CHAPTER X

Lord Macartney receives notice, that it is the Emperor's pleasure to receive the embassy at the imperial residence in Tartary. — The persons selected to attend the Ambassador in his progress thither. — The particular occupations assigned to those who were left at Pekin. — Arrangements for the journey into Tartary. — Leave Pekin; circumstances of the journey.

1793, August, Wednesday 28. THE Ambassador received a visit this morning from the mandarin Van-Tadge-In, who informed his Excellency, that the messenger who had been sent to know his Imperial Majesty's pleasure respecting the British embassy, was returned; and that the Emperor desired the Ambassador to proceed to Tartary, where he wished to see him, and to receive his credentials.

Thursday 29. This morning the final arrangements were made respecting that part of the suite who were to accompany the embassy into Tartary. They consisted of

Sir George Staunton,
Mr. Staunton,
Lieutenant-Colonel Benton,
Captain Mackintosh, of the Hindostan,
Lieutenant Parish,
Lieutenant Crewe,
Mr. Winder,

Doctor Gillan,

Mr. Plumb, the interpreter,

Mr. Baring, and

Mr. Huttner.

Mr. Maxwell remained at Pekin, with three servants, in order to settle the household of the Ambassador, as, on his return from Tartary, it was intended that his establishment and appearance should be, in every respect, suited to the character and dignity of the sovereign whole representative he was.

Doctor Scott was also left, in order to take care of several of the soldiers and servants, who were, at this time, very much afflicted with the bloody flux.

Mr. Hickey and Mr. Alexander were to be employed in preparing the portraits of their Britannic Majesties, which, with the state canopy, were to be the appropriate furniture of the presence chamber of the Amhassador.

Doctor Dinwiddie and Mr. Barrow were to regulate the presents that had been left at the palace of Yeumen-manyeumen, and to put them in a mate to be.presented to the Emperor, on the Ambassador's return to Pekin.

The guards, musicians, and servants received orders to hold themselves in readiness, to set out on Monday morning, with no other luggage but their bedding, and such necessaries as were indispensable on the occasion.

The gentlemen of the suite were likewise requested to content themselves with the uniform of the embassy, a common suit of cloaths, and such other articles as they might judge to be absolutely necessary for their own comfort, and the formality of the occasion.

Mr. Maxwell received orders to distribute to each of the musicians and servants, a suit of the state liveries, in order that the attendants might appear in an uniform, which would add to the dignity and splendor of the Ambassador's entrance into Jehol.

Friday 30. The carpenters were employed this morning in unpacking an old travelling chaise belonging to Sir George Staunton, in which Lord Macartney proposed to travel to Jehol. This carriage generally attracted the notice of the Chinese, who flocked about it to see the nature of its construction, and the materials of which it was formed; these they examined with a very singular curiosity; and some of them were so anxious to understand all its parts, that they made various drawings of it. But so familiar are the eyes of these people to the glare and glitter of colours and gilding, that, however they might admire the mechanism and contrivance of the carriage, they did not hesitate to express their disapprobation of its exterior appearance; which, I must own, did not possess any very uncommon degree of attraction.

At noon Mr. Plumb came to inform the suite, on the part of Van-Tadge-In, the attendant mandarin, that such as chose to travel on horseback, were to give in their names, that horses might be prepared for them; and those who chose the conveyance by carts, should be provided accordingly.

After these travelling arrangements were settled, the musicians, servants; etc. attended at Maxwell's apartment, to receive the cloaths in which they were to make their public appearance at Jehol. A large chest was produced on the occasion full of cloaths: they were of green cloth, laced with gold; but their appearance awakened a suspicion that they had already been frequently worn, and on tickets, sewed to the linings, were written the names of their former wearers; — as many of these tickets appeared, on examining them, to be the visiting cards of Monsieur de la Luzerne, the late French Ambassador, it is more than probable, that they had been made up for some gala, or fête, given by that minister. But whether they were of diplomatic origin, or had belonged to the theatres, is of no consequence, they were never intended for actual service, being made only for a few temporary occasions, whatever they might be. With these habiliments, however, such as they were, every man fitted himself, as well as he could, with coats and waist-coats; but of small-cloaths, there were not more in the whole package than were sufficient for the accommodation of six persons. The Chinese may not be supposed to be capable of distinguishing on the propriety of our figure, in these ill-suited uniforms; but we certainly appeared in a very strong point of ridicule to each other. The two couriers were furnished with beaver helmets, but not an hat was distributed to accompany these curious liveries; which, after all, the servants were ordered not to put on till the day when they were to add so much eclat to the entry of the embassy into Jehol.

When the chaise was put in complete order for the journey, a difficulty arose, for which, as it was not foreseen, no provision had been made; and this was no less than to get a couple of postillions; at length, however, a corporal of infantry, who had once been a post-boy, offered his service, and a light-horseman was ordered to assist him in conducting the carriage.

Saturday 31. This morning such of the presents and baggage as were intended to be forwarded to Tartary, were sent off: some of them were carried by mules, others in carts; but the more valuable articles, and those of delicate fabric, and curious construction, were borne by men.

This important business being dispatched, a great number of horses were brought to the palace, when each of the gentlemen, and the other persons of the suite who proposed to ride, made choice of his horse; and the animals thus selected for the service of the approaching journey, were then delivered to those persons whose office it was to take proper care of them till the time of our departure,

The postillions were permitted to exercise the horses in the chaise for an hour, through the streets of Pekin. They were guarded both by Mandarins and soldiers; and, indeed, such were the crowds which assembled to see this extraordinary spectacle, that come kind of authority and exertion was necessary to give the drivers an opportunity of showing their skill, and exhibiting the equipage and its apparatus to advantage. The corporal being also furnished on the occasion with the jacket, helmet, etc, of the light horse, the postillions not only made an uniform, but a very pretty appearance.

The Ambassador received a visit from several mandarins; when the band played on the stage of the theatre for their entertainment.

Lieut. Parish exercised his men in the ordnance evolutions, to keep them in practice, as it was thought very probable that, on presenting the artillery to the Emperor, he might desire to see an exhibition of European tactics.

September, Sunday, 1. As it was ordered that the embassy should set out tomorrow morning at two o'clock, some of the baggage, to prevent as much as possible the confusion which had been hitherto experienced, was sent forward this evening.

Monday 2. Soon after one o'clock this morning, the drums were beat through all the courts of the palace, and in half an hour the whole suite was in motion. The bedding was then sent on in carts; and the Ambassador, with his attendants, having made a slight breakfast, quitted the palace at half an hour past three o'clock, under a strong escort of Chinese cavalry; but, even at this early hour, the crowd of spectators was so great to see our departure, that the progress of the cavalcade was very much impeded; especially the carriage of the Ambassador, which, from the concourse of people and the awkwardness of the horses which had not been, properly broke into their new geer, was very much delayed.

At seven o'clock we passed through the city gate, and in about half an hour had exchanged the suburbs for a rich and finely cultivated country. The road, though very broad, bad no pavement in the center, like that which leads from Tong-tchew to Pekin. At the end of six miles we stopped at a considerable village called Chin-giho, where we stayed to take the usual refreshiments of the morning, which have been so often mentioned. Our route was then continued through a great number of villages, and near three o'clock arrived at one of the Emperor's palaces named Nanshishee, where we were appointed to remain during the first night of our journey.

The mandarin Van-Tadge-In, whom I have had such frequent occasion to mention, rather increased than diminished his activity on the present journey; which might arise, perhaps, from our being more particularly under the imperial care and protection. We were here provided with every requisite accommodation, and in a very comfortable manner. To our dinner each day was added a regale of jooaw and shamptshoo: the former is a bitter wine of the country; and the latter, a very strong spirit distilled from rice and millet, whose appearance resembles that of British gin.

In the evening the soldiers were exercised by Lieut. Colonel Benson.

We computed the journey of this day to be about twenty-five miles; and, though it may appear but dull travelling to persons accustomed to the expedition of English roads, it will be considered as no very tardy progress, when the obstacles are known which tended to impede it.

The same horses were to take us the whole journey, and the same men to carry the baggage; besides, the whole of our provisions was ordered and dressed at the several places through which we passed on the road, and conveyed in bowls, carefully covered up in trays, on men's shoulders, to every stage of our journey, for our refreshment there.

The distance from Pekin to Jehol is one hundred and sixty miles, which was divided into seven nearly equal daily journies. This arrangement was made that the embassy might be accommodated each day beneath an imperial roof; as the Emperor for his own convenience and dignity, has a certain number of palaces built at equal distances on the road from Pekin to his summer residence in Tartary. This privilege was considered to be a most flattering mark of distinction, as it is never granted even to the first mandarins of the empire.

Of this place we can say but little, as no parts were open to our inspection but those which we inhabited. It did not rise higher than one story; nor, from what we had an opportunity of seeing, did it appear that the interior apartments were superior to the external form; which had nothing either of elegance or figure to attract attention. The central part of the courts were planted with trees and flowers of various kinds, which had a very pleasing effect. An extensive garden surrounded the palace, but we could not, to our very great disappointment, obtain access to it.

Tuesday 3. We continued our journey at four o'clock this morning, with the same guard of Chinese Cavalry; and, having passed the village of Can-tim, which possesses the usual characteristic of every Chinese village we had yet seen, an overflowing population, we arrived at the town of Wheazou, a considerable place; and, after the usual refreshments, proceeded, beneath a burning sun, along dusty roads, but through a very fertile country, to the palace of Chancin, where we arrived at one o'clock. It is a very extensive building of one story throughout, and contains ten or twelve spacious courts, surrounded with piazzas, and adorned with central gardens, planted with trees and thickened shrubberies that were intersected by walks. The country around *it* boasts a continuation of that fertility which has been already mentioned. It was enclosed, and fed innumerable herds of cattle and flocks of sheep; the former are small but very fat, with white faces, and a short thick tail, which is a lump of fat, and weighs several pounds.

Wednesday 4. We set off this morning at five o'clock. The distant country appeared to be mountainous, and rose boldly in the horizon. That fertility of which so much has been said, began sensibly to diminish, and the richness of the soil was proportionably decreasing. At half past severn o'clock we arrived at a small village, called Cuaboocow, where we breakfasted, and, from some accidental circumstance, not in the usual stile of plenty in a place like a farm yard. The road, as we proceeded on our journey, became extremely rugged and disagreeable, and the heat of the weather continued without any alleviation.

At noon we saw a very large walled city, called Caungchumfoa; the walls of which were built of stone, and, though not so lofty, in the same form, as those of Pekin.

We passed at least two hundred dromedaries and camels carrying very heavy loads of wood and charcoal, as it appeared, to the city which has been just mentioned. This large drove was under the direction of one man, who seemed to manage it without the least difficulty. These animals are among the most docile of the brute creation; besides, the length of time they can fast, and their great strength as beasts of burthen, render them invaluable in the commerce of the east.

The palace where the embassy was received at the end of this day's journey, derives its name from the city of Caungchumfoa, near which it stands: it is surrounded with gardens, but has little to distinguish it from those which we have already inhabited.

This was the most fatiguing and unpleasant day of our whole route, both from the heat of the weather and the badness of the road, which was so rugged and narrow in many places, that some of the carts were overturned; but, happily, without any accident to those whom they conveyed.

Chapter XI

Arrive at the town of Waung-chauyeng. – Description of Chinese soldiers, etc. – Pass the great wall; description of it.-The different appearances of Tartary and China. – Pass an extraordinary mountain. – Arrive at the palace of Chaung-shanuve; the circumstances of it. – Example of the industry of the peasants, and the cultivation of the country. – Some account of the tenure by which lands are held in China. – Arrive at the palace of Callachot-tueng; description of it. – Arrangements settled for the manner in which the embassy was to make its entrance into Jehol.

1793, September, Thursday 5. As the country was now become very irregular and mountainous, the roads were proportionably fatiguing. At nine we arrived at the town of Waung-chauyeng. At a small distance from it, we passed an arch of great strength, which stretches across a valley to unite the opposite hills, and is guarded by a broad wall on either side of it. A little further, the road proceeds up a very steep hill, on the top of which there is a fort, with a strong wall or rampart extending on either side of it, to the distance of two or three miles. From the elevated situations which the inequality of the road frequently offered, this wall was a very visible object in its whole extent, and appeared to be in a state of decay.

Beneath the fort is a strong, thick, stone archway, through which the road conducted us down a hill, whose declivity was such, as to oblige the drivers to have but one horse in each carriage, and to secure a wheel with ropes, to prevent a too rapid descent. At the bottom of this hill, and in a most romantic valley, stands the town of Waung-chauyeng, which resembles those places of the same kind that have been already described, except in the uniformity of them; this being built with greater irregularity than any we had yet seen. It is about a mile in length, as well as I could judge from our passage through it, but I had no opportunity of ascertaining its breadth: populous it was, of course, and appeared to be a very busy place.

After breakfast we proceeded towards a spot on our journey, of which we had all heard or read with wonder and astonishment; which so few Europeans had ever seen, and which no one of our own country would probably ever see but ourselves: this was the great wall, the ancient boundary of China and Tartary, through whose portals our passage lay.

At the end of the town which has been just mentioned, there was a temporary arch erected in honour of the embassy, finely decorated with streamers and silks of various colours: — at the entrance of it the Ambassador was saluted with three guns. There we passed between a double line of soldiers, which extend on either side of the road, from the triumphal gateway towards the great wall.

These were the only soldiers we had yet seen in China, who possessed a martial appearance; and, according to my notion of such things, never saw a finer display of military parade. They were drawn up in a very regular manner, each regiment being distinguished hy a different dress, and divided into companies: these were ranked in close columns, and in their fronts stood the officers with two stands of colours. They were all arrayed in a kind of armour, which consisted of a loose coat or robe, in imitation of a coat of mail, with steel helmets that covered their heads and shoulders. Their implements of war were various, comprising matchlocks, sabres, daggers, spears, halberds, lances, bows and arrows, with some other weapons, of which I knew not the name, and cannot particularly describe. Those companies of soldiers who wore no warlike instrument but the sword, had a shield to accompany it. In short, every one of these military divisions was distinguished by their dress and arms, and arranged with the utmost propriety, not merely as to regularity of position in their general distribution, but as to the effect of contrast in the variety of external appearance. On one side of the road there were seventeen of these divisions, each consisting, as I should think, of about eighty men; and a band of musicians, placed in a building erected, as it appeared, for the occasion, continued to play, as the cavalcade of the English embassy passed between the lines.

On approaching the wall, there were cantonments for a considerable army, at the extremity of which there is a very strong gateway, built of stone, and still strengthened with the addition of three vast iron doors; on passing them, we entered Tartary. On the outside of another gateway is a strong redoubt, from whence we ascended the hill, and contrived to get on the top of the great wall which formerly separated the two empires.

This wall is, perhaps, the most stupendous work ever produced by man: the length of it is supposed to be upwards of twelve hundred miles, and its height in the place where I stood upon it, for it varies in its circumstances, according to the nature of the surface, is upwards of thirty feet, and it is about twenty-four feet broad. The foundation is formed of large square stones, and the rest is brick: the middle is of tempered earth, covered with broad stones there is also an embattled parapet or breastwork of stone, three feet thick, on each side of the wall.

When it is considered that this immense structure is not

merely carried along level ground, but passes over immense rivers, where it assumes the form of bridges, some of which contain double rows of immense arches; or stretches, in the same expansive shape, across deep vallies to connect the mountains that form them; and that it not only descends, but also ascends, the steepest declivities; the idea of its grandeur, and the active labour employed in constructing it, in the short space of a few years, is not easily grasped by the strongest imagination.

Where it climbs the heights, the ascent is aided by large flights of steps, so that the passage along it is at once easy, secure, and uninterrupted. In short, it formed a fine military way, by which the armies of China, employed to defend its frontier against the Tartars, could march from one end of the kingdom to the other. There are also, at proper distances, strong towers, from whence, by certain signals, an alarm could be communicated, in a very short space of time, across the whole empire; and wherever the wall attains the summit of an hill, or mountain, there is a strong fort designed to watch the incursions and movements of the enemy.

The part of this wall on which I stood, commanded a very extensive view of it, with all the romantic scenery connected with it. From hence I saw the amazing fabric take its course for many miles over a beautiful plain, watered by a large river, which it crossed in the form of a bridge. A little to the westward it ascends a very lofty mountain, which, on that side, completes the prospect.

But the most stupendous works of man must at length moulder away; and since Tartary and China are become one nation, and consequently subject to the same government, the wall has lost its importance: it being no longer necessary for defence or security, no attention is now paid to its preservation; so that the time is approaching when this stupendous monument of persevering labour; when this unparalleled effort of national policy, will become an enormous length of ruins, and an awful example of decay: many parts of it are already fallen down, and others threaten to encumber the plain that they were reared to defend.

One of the mandarins informed me, as we were walking together on the wall, that, according to the histories of his country, it had been finished upwards of two thousand years ago; and, consequently, several centuries before the Christian era.

I must, however, acknowledge that, after all, this renowned barrier of China did not, altogether, satisfy my expectations. The wonder of it consists in its extent, of which a small part is to be seen; and the short time in which it was erected, may equally astonish by reading an account of it. When I stood on it, I was still obliged to exercise my imagination as to the astonishing circumstances connected with it, and saw it also in a comparative view with natural objects superior, at least, to any partial appearance of it.

When we had passed the wall, there was an immediate change in the appearance of the country. Instead of a level range of various and unceasing cultivation, of the habitations of wealth, the crowd of population, and the exertion of industry, we beheld a wide and barren waste, sinking into vallies, and rising into mountains; where no harvest waved, no villages poured forth their inhabitants, or splendid mansions enriched the scene. The traveller, however, is amply compensated by the variety of natural objects which present themselves to him; and the lover of picturesque beauty finds, amidst all the increasing inconveniencies of his journey, a source of enchantment which make him forget them all.

At the distance of about seven miles from the great wall, we came to the foot of a very high mountain, which the carts could not ascend without an additional number of horses. The passage through this mountain is another proof of the genius and indefatigable spirit of the Chinese people in all works that relate to public utility. It is thirty feet in breadth, cut through a solid rock; and, which is the more extraordinary part of this undertaking, the incision made from the top of the mountain to the surface of the road, is, at least, one hundred feet: — a stupendous labour! But surmounting with this aid in the passage, the beginning of the ascent has a very fearful appearance; while on the other side the way slopes down with a gentle declivity between two large mountains towards a beautiful valley.

At two o'clock we arrived at the palace of Chaung-shanuve, which is situated on a small elevation, at the distance of a mile and an half from the bottom of the hill which has been just described. It is of large dimensions, and surrounded by an high wall, being the residence of a considerable number of the Emperor's women; many of whom I saw peeping over the partition which separated their apartments from the part of the palace assigned to the accommodation of the embassy. Though it was not permitted for any of the Ambassador's suite, as may well be supposed, to visit these ladies, the guardians of them, who were all eunuchs, came to visit us. There were, indeed, several mandarins among them, to whom was consigned the care and conduct of the female community. This palace was surrounded with very extensive gardens, but, from the particular service to which it was applied, it would have been a strong mark of folly, as well as an idle risk of danger, to have made any attempt to see them.

Friday 6. We left Chaung-shanuve this morning at half past six, and found the weather extremely cold and piercing. The road continued to take the form of the country, which was very mountainous and irregular, as well as naked, and without any other marks of cultivation but such as denoted the poverty of it. But this barren appearance does not proceed from the inactivity of the inhabitants, who seize on every spot capable of being tilled, and in situations which are accessible only to the adventurous peasant, whom necessity impels to gather a scanty and dangerous harvest. One example of this hazardous industry, which I observed this morning, will sufficiently iilustrate the barrenness of the country, and the spirit of its scattered inhabitants.

On a very high mountain I discovered several distinct patches of cultivated ground, in such a state of declivity, as appeared to be altogether inaccessible; and while I was considering the means which the owner of them must employ to plant and gather his vegetables on these alarming precipices, I beheld him actually employed in digging a small spot near the top of the hill, and in a situation where it appeared to me to be irnpossible, without some extraordinary contrivance, for any one to stand, much less to be following the business of a gardener. A more minute examination informed me, that this poor peasant had a rope fastened round his middle, which was secured at the top of the mountain, and by which this hardy cultivator lets himself down to any part of the precipice where a few square yards of ground gave him encouragement to plant his vegetables, or his corn: and in this manner he had decorated the mountain with those little cultivated spots that hung about it. Near the bottom, on an hillock, this industrious peasant had erected a wooden hut, surrounded with a small piece of ground, planted with cabbages, where he supported by this hazardous industry, a wife and family. The whole of these cultivated spots does not amount to more than half an acre; but situated, as they are, at such considerable and hazardous distances from each other, they offer a very curious example of the natural industry of the people.

It is, certainly, a wise policy in the government of China to receive the greater part of the taxes in the produce of the country:

and is a considerable spur to improvement and industry in every class of the people, who are to get their bread by the exertions of genius, or the sweat of their brow. The landlord, also, receives the greater part of his rents in the produce of his farms; and the farmer pays his servants, in a great measure, by giving than pieces of waste uncultivated land, where there are any, with occasional encouragement to excite their in-dustry. Such are the customs which prevail throughout China, and tend so much to preserve the prosperity, and promote the cultivation of every part of that extensive empire.

By ten o'clock this morning we arrived at the palace of Callachottueng, near a small village of the same name, where we remained the whole of this day, on account of the length of the next stage; and in order to make a more equal division of the rest of our journey.

This palace is situated in a plain, between two very large and lofty mountains: in form and external appearance it resembles those we have already described; but appears to be of modern erection; and its apartments are fitted up in a better style than any we had yet seen. In come of the courts there were artificial ruins, a favourite object in the ornamental gardening of this country, surrounded with plots of verdure.

As the embassy now approached the termination of its journey, and was soon to appear before the sovereign, to obtain whose favour and friendship it had traversed so large a part of the globe, the Ambassador gave orders for rehearsing the procession, with which we were to make our appearance at the Imperial court. This evening, therefore, the ceremonial was arranged, and performed, under the direction of Lieut. Col. Benson, and approved by the Ambassador. The band played the Duke of York's march during the time of our rehearsal.

Chapter XII

Arrive at the palace of Callachotreshanfu. – Stop at one of the Emperor's pagodas. – The public entry into Jehol. – Description of the palace provided for the British embassy. – A principal mandarin pays a visit of ceremony to the Ambassador. – Singular conduct respecting the provisions supplied for the suite. – The presents unpacked and displayed. – An account of them.

1793, September, Saturday 7. WE set off this morning at six o'clock, when the air was cold and piercing, and passed through a very hilly and mountainous country. After having breakfasted at a village of the name of Quanshanglin, the route was continued.

The villages we now paired were well peopled, but the difference is very great indeed between the population, as well as cultivated state of China and Tartary. On this side of the wall, the picture is extremely varied, the face and productions of the country are no longer the same; nor were there any towns of consideration in the latter part of our journey.

At two o'clock in the afternoon we arrived, very much fatigued by the badness of the roads, and the jolting faculties of our carriages, at the palace of Callachotreshangfu. It is a spacious and noble edifice, but has not been lately inhabited; as might well be supposed, from the great number of squirrels running about the courts, and haunting the apartments.

Sunday 22. The embassy continued its route at six o'clock, and, in about two hours, arrived at one of the Emperor's pagodas, about three miles from the imperial residence. There a more abundant display of refreshments was prepared than we had seen for some time, from the difficulty of procuring them in the country through which we passed. Some time was also necessary for every part of the suite to arrange their dress, and settle their appearance. At half past nine, however, we arrived at a small village, called Quoangcho, at about the distance of a mile from Jehol. Here the suite alighted from their horses and carriages, and put themselves in a state of preparation for the entry; which proceeded in the following manner, amidst a prodigious concourse of people, whom curiosity had led to see such a spectacle as they had never seen before, and will never, I believe, behold again.

The soldiers of the royal artillery, commanded by Lieut. Parish;

The light-horse and infantry, commanded by Lieut. Crewe;

The servants of the Ambassador, two and two;

The couriers;

The mechanics, two and two;

The musicians, two and two;

The gentlemen of the suite, two and two;

Sir George Staunton in a palankin;

The Ambassador and Mr. Staunton in the post-chaise, with a black-boy, dressed in a turban, behind it, closed the procession.

There was, indeed, somewhat of parade in all this business, but it was by no means calculated to impress a favourable idea of the greatness of the British nation on the minds of those who beheld it; they might be pleased with its novelty; but it did not, in any degree, possess that characteristic appearance which was so necessary on the present occasion. The military departments made a respectable figure, and the gentlemen of the suite cannot be supposed for a moment to derogate from the diplomatic character in which they were involved; but the rest of the company exhibited a very awkward appearance: some wore round hats, come cocked hats, others straw hats; some were in whole boots, some half boots, and others in shoes with coloured stockings. In short, unless it was in second-hand coats and waistcoats, which did not fit them, the inferior part of the suite did not enjoy even the appearance of shabby uniformity.

In this state and order the procession moved on with a slow pace to the city of Jehol, and soon after ten o'clock arrived at the palace provided for the accommodation of the British embassy in this city. Here the military part of the cavalcade formed a line to receive the Ambassador with the usual honours.

Thus the embassy arrived at the end of its tedious and troublecome journey: but the manner of its reception did not fill us with any extravagant expectation as to the issue of it; for not a mandarin appeared to congratulate the Ambassador on his arrival, or to usher him, with that form which his dignity demanded, to the apartments provided for him. In short, we came to this palace with more than usual ceremony; but we entered into it with as little, as any of those where we had been accommodated during our journey. This appeared to be the more extraordinary, as it was the avowed expectation of the principal persons of the suite, that the Ambassador would be met, on his entry at Jehol, by the Grand Choulaa, the imperial minister of state: but on what grounds this expectation was formed, or for what reason it received such a disappointment, is not for me to offer a conjecture.

On our arrival, Lieut. Col. Benson ordered the troops to hold themselves in readiness to fall into a line at a moment's warning; and desired the servants, mechanics, etc. to range themselves in order before the door of the Ambassador's apartments, in order to receive the Grand Choulaa, who was expected every moment to pay his visit of salutation and welcome.

In this state of suspense we remained from our arival till past four o'clock; in the course of which time we had paraded at least a dozen times, as several mandarins came to take a curious view of us, and every one of them was supposed, in his turn, to be the Grand Choulaa. The arrival of dinner, however, put an end to all expectations of seeing him on this day.

The palace, which was now become the residence of the embassy, is built on the declivity of a hill; the entrance to it is by eight large broad steps that lead to a wooden gateway, through which there is a passage to a large court, paved in the center with large flat stones. On each side of this court there is a long and broad gallery roofed with black shining tiles and supported in front by strong wooden pillars. That on the left was employed at this time as a kitchen, and enclosed by mats nailed along the pillars to the height of seven or eight feet; the other, on the opposite side, was quite open, and used as a place of parade and exercise for the soldiers. At the upper end of this court there is another neat gallery or platform laid with stones, and roofed in the same manner as the others. To this there is an ascent of three steps, and a door opens from it into another court, the wings of which afforded chambers for the military part of the embassy; and the center part, fronting the gallery, to which there is an ascent of three steps, contained the apartments of the Ambassador and Sir George Staunton: beyond this is another court of the same dimensions, the wings of which were occupied by the mechanics, musicians, and servants, and the center of it by the gentlemen of the suite; but it consisted only of two 'large rooms, where they slept in two divisions, and a lobby of communication, which was used as an eating saloon.

This building cannot be described as possessing either

grandeur or elegance: it does not rise beyond a ground floor, and is of unequal height, as the ground on which it is built is on a gradual ascent. It is surrounded by a wall, but is overlooked from the upper parts of the hill, on whose declivity it is erected.

But though we were as yet rather disappointed in the reception of honours, we had no reason to be dissatisfied with the attention paid to our more urgent necessities; and we dined in comfort and abundance.

Monday 9. This morning, at so early an hour as seven o'clock, we received a large quantity of boiled eggs, with tea and bread, for breakfast. At noon his Excellency was visited by several mandarins. Nothing, however, as yet transpired that could lead us to form a judgment as to the final issue of the business: as far as any opinion could be formed as to the general aspect of things, it did not bear the promise of that success which had been originally expected from it.

The Grand Choulaa still delayed his expected visit.

In this palace, as in our former places of residence, we experienced the jealous precaution of the Chinese government: we were also kept here in a state of absolute confinement; and, on no pretext, was it permitted to any person, attached to the embassy, to pass the gates.

Tuesday 10. This morning his Excellency was visited by a mandarin, accompanied by a numerous train of attendants. He remained with the Ambassador and Sir George Staunton about an hour, when some necessary formalities were interchanged and he then returned with the same form in which he came. During the visit of the mandarin, his attendants were very busily employed in examining the dress of the English servants; the lace of which they rubbed with a stone to certify its quality, and then looking at each other with an air of surprise, they shook their heads and smiled; a sufficient proof that the Tartars are not unacquainted with the value of metals; at least they clearly comprehended the inferior value of the trimmings that decorated the liveries of the embassy. They appeared to be a polite and pleasant people, and of an agreeable aspect.

Though it cannot be supposed that such a conference as was this morning held between the British Ambassador and the mandarin would be communicated to the general attendants on the embassy, yet we could not resist the spirit of conjecture on the occasion: the following circumstance, which took place this morning, did not serve to dissipate that disposition to forebode ill, which prevailed among us.

The Ambassador ordered Mr. Winder, one of his secretaries, to intimate to the servants, that, in case they should find, in the course the day, any deficiency in their provisions, either in quality or quantity, they should not complain to the people who supplied them, but leave them untouched, and intimate the grievance to his Excellency; who requested, for very particular and weighty reasons, that this order might be punctually observed.

It became those to whom this intimation was made, to pay the most willing obedience to it; at the same time, it excited no small degree of astonishment that we should thus be ordered to prepare ourselves for ill-usage in the article of provisions, of which we had, hitherto, so little reason to complain. Our treatment in this respect had been not only hospitable, but bounteous in the extreme. To suggest causes of complaint to those who never yet had reason to complain, was a conduct perfectly unintelligible in itself; and was, therefore, very naturally referred to the interview of the morning between the mandarin and the Ambassador.

When, however, dinner came, we were sensible, that the precautions communicated to us were, as we expected to find them, the result of some well-grounded suspicion; for, instead, of that abundance with which our tables had hitherto, been served, there was not now a sufficient quantity of provisions for half the persons who were ready to partake of them.

The emotions of every one attached to the embassy were, I believe, very unpleasant upon the occasion. We not only felt the probability that we might be starved as well as imprisoned; but that the embassy itself was treated with dis-respect; and, of course, we felt some alarm, lest the important objects of it would quickly vanish into nothing. We had also our feelings as Britons, and felt the insult, as it appeared to us, which was offered to the crown and dignity of the first nation in the world.

This meagre meal, therefore, was left untouched; and, in conformity to the orders which had been received, complaints were preferred to his Excellency on the occasion; and, on a report being made to him that the representations which had been made were founded in reality, Mr. Plumb, the interpreter, was requested to communicate the cause of discontent to the mandarin, and to insist on more hospitable usage: nor was the remonstrance without an immediate effect; for, within five minutes after it was made, each table was served with a variety of hot dishes, not only in plenty, but profusion.

Why this entertainment, when it must have been in actual state of preparation to be served, was thus withheld from, us, could not be reconciled to any principle of justice, or policy. To suppose that it proceeded from caprice, or an humorous spirit of tantalising, cannot be readily imagined; and, as for any saving of expense in the business, that could be no object to the treasury of the Emperor. It was treated, therefore, as an enigma, which, when the evil was removed, soon ceased to be a subject, of curiosity or inquiry.

Wednesday 11. The Ambassador was this morning pleased to order the presents which were brought from Pekin, to be unpacked in the great platform, or portico, facing his Excellency's apartments; where several ranges of tables were placed to receive them. They were as follows:

Two hundred pieces of narrow coarse cloth, chiefly black and blue.

Two large telescopes.

Two air guns.

Two beautiful fowling pieces; one inlaid with gold, and the other with silver.

Two pair of saddle pistols, enriched and ornamented in the same manner.

Two boxes, each containing seven pieces of Irish tabinets.

Two elegant saddles, with complete furniture: the seats of these were of fine doe skin, stitched with silver thread; the flaps were of a bright yellow superfine cloth, embroidered with silver, and enriched with silver spangles and tassels; the reins and stirrup-traps were of bright yellow leather, stitched with silver; the stirrups, buckles, etc. were of steel double plaited; and,

Two large boxes, containing the finest carpets of the British manufactory.

These were all the presents which were brought from Pekin: the rest consisting of various pieces of clock-work and machinery, with carriages, and pieces of artillery, were either too cumbersome or too delicate to venture on so long a journey; and were, therefore, intended to be presented to his Imperial Majesty, on his return, for the winter season, to the capital of his empire.

The presents were ordered to remain in their present situation till the imperial pleasure should be known concerning them. Centinels were appointed to do duty on the platform where they were placed.

CHAPTER XIII

The presents removed from the palace. – A notification received that the Emperor would give audience to the British Ambassador. – Orders issued to the suite on the occasion. – The procession to the imperial palace described. – The Ambassador's first audience of the Emperor. – Presents received on the occasion. – The Ambassador's second visit to the Emperor. – Additional presents. – Favourable opinions entertained of the success of the embassy.

1793, September, Thursday 12. THIS morning, the conducting mandarin, Van-Tadge-In, accompanied by several of his mandarin brethren, and a troop of attendants, removed the presents, as was presumed, to the palace of the Emperor.

His Excellency, at the same time, received a visit from a mandarin of the first order, who came to notify that the Emperor would, on Saturday morning, give audience to the Ambassader of the King of Great Britain at the imperial palace. This intelligence enlivened the spirits, as it animated the hopes of the whole embassy: and, though the Grand Choulaa had not visited the Ambassador, and other circumstances of an unfavourable aspect had taken place, the news of the day not only dissipated our gloom, but renewed the tide of expectation, and made it flow with an accelerated current.

His Excellency received the visits of several mandarins of distinction, who continued with him upwards of an hour.

Orders were issued, that the whole suite should be ready on the following morning, at three o'clock, to accompany the Ambassador to the imperial palace. The servants were ordered to dress in their green and gold liveries, and to wear white silk, or cotton stockings, with shoes; boots of any kind being absolutely prohibited on this occasion. It was, at the same time, intimated, that neither the soldiers, or the servants, were to remain at the palace for the return of the Ambassador; but when they had attended him there, they were requested to return immediately to Jehol, without presuming to halt at any place whatever for a single moment; as his Excellency had every reason to expect that, in a few days, the present restrictions, which were so irksome to the retinue of the embassy, would be removed, and every indulgence granted them which they could reasonably desire: and as any deviation from this order would tend to risque the loss of that meditated favour, his Excellency seriously expected it to meet with a general and willing obedience.

Saturday 14. This morning, at so early an hour as three o'clock, the Ambassador and his suite proceeded, in full uniform, to the Emperor's court.

His Excellency was dressed in a suit of spotted mulberry velvet, with a diamond star, and the red riband; over which he wore the full habit of the order of the Bath, with the hat, and plume of feathers, that form a part of it. Sir George Staunton was also in full court dress, over which he wore the robe of a doctor of laws in the English universities, with the black velvet cap belonging to that degree.

Though the morning was so dark that we could not distinguish each other, Lieutenant-Colonel Benson made an attempt to form a procession, to proceed the palankin of the Ambassador. But this manoeuvre was of very short duration, as the bearers of it moved rather too fast for the solemnity of a flow march; and, instead of proceeding it with a grave pace, we were glad to follow it with a quick one. Indeed, whether it was the attraction of our music, or any accidental circumstance, I know not, we found ourselves interminged with a cohort of pigs, asses, and dogs, which, broke our ranks, such as they were, and put us into irrecoverable confusion. All formality of procession, therefore, was at an end; and the Ambassador's palankin was so far advanced before us, as to make a little smart running necessary to overtake it.

After a confused cavalcade, if it can deserve that name, we arrived at the palace of the Emperor, in the same state of confusion in which we had proceeded — the pedestrian part of the suite being a little out of breath with running; and the gentlemen on horseback, not altogether insensible to the risk of accidents from the dark hour of the morning. In short, it appeared, to the greater part of those who were concerned in it, to be rather ridiculous to attempt to make a parade that no one could see.

At about five o'clock the Ambassador alighted from his palankin, amidst an immense concourse of people; Sir George, and Mr. Staunton bearing the train, were followed by the gentlemen attached to the embassy.

The servants, etc. returned according to order, and the soldiers marched back with fife and drum. As our return was by day-light, we had some opportunity of examining the appearance of the city where we resided.

It is a large and populous plate, built without any attention whatever to regularity of design, and lies in a hollow, formed by two large mountains. The houses are low, of a mean appearance, and built chiefly of wood: the streets are not paved in any part of the city, but in that quarter of it which is most contiguous to the Emperor's palace; the road to which is laid with large flat stones.

As this place is not watered by any river, it cannot be supposed to enjoy a large portion of commerce. Its trade, however, is not altogether inconsiderable, from the consumption occasioned by the residence of the Emperor in the immediate neighbourhood; a circumstance which not only occasions a great increase of inhabitants, but brings with it the wealth, the luxury, and the expenses of a court;

The surrounding country wears a greater appearance of fertility than any I had seen in those parts of Tartary through which the embassy had passed; but, in its best state, it is by no means comparable to that of China.

At eleven o'clock in the forenoon, the Ambassador and his suite returned from the imperial palace. It was a visit of mere form and presentation; and his Excellency, Sir George Staunton, and Mr. Staunton, with Mr. Plumb, the interpreter, were alone admitted into the presence of the Emperor.

The Emperor, it was said, received the credentials of the embassy with a most ceremonious formality. All, however, that we could learn, as matter of indubitable occurrence, was the notice his Imperial Majesty was pleased to take of Master Staunton, the son of Sir George Staunton. He appeared to be very much struck with the boy's vivacity and deportment; and expressed his admiration of the faculty which the young gentleman possessed of speaking six different languages. The Emperor, to manifest the approbation he felt on the occasion, not only presented him, with his own hand, a very beautiful fan, and several small embroidered bags and purses, but commanded the interpreter to signify, that he thought very highly of his talents and appearance.

In a very short time after the Ambassador had returned from court, a large quantity of presents were received from his Imperial Majesty.

They consisted of the richest velvets, satins, silks, and purses beautifully embroidered. To these were added large parcels of the best tea of the country, made up in solid cakes, in the size and form of a Dutch cheese. It is thus baked together, by which means it will never be affected by air or climate, nor ever lose its flavour, though kept without any covering whatever. Each of these balls weigh above five pounds.

His Excellency distributed to every gentleman of his suite his proportion of the presents. Those which were peculiarly addressed to their Britannic Majesties, were deposited in the lobby, in the boxes wherein they arrived.

Sunday 15. This morning, at one o'clock, the Ambassador, accompanied by his suite, but unattended by any of his guards or servants, proceeded to pay a second visit to the Emperor. The object of this interview was, as we understood, to make an attempt to open the negociation, for the purpose of obtaining that extension of commerce so anxiously desired by the British East India Company.

His Excellency did not return till near three o'clock; and, on his arrival, appeared to be very much exhausted. Mr. Plumb, the interpreter, gave, however, such a favourable account of the general aspect of the negociation, as to elevate the hopes of every one concerned in the issue of it. He mentioned, that the Emperor had, through the medium of the Grand Choulaa, entered upon the business of the embassy with Lord Macartney; which, as far as it went, had altogether succeeded. This favourable information appeared to be confirmed by a second cargo of presents from his Imperial Majesty. They consisted of large quantities of rich velvets, silks, and satins, with some beautiful Chinese lamps, and rare porcelain. To these were added a number of callibash boxes of exquisite workmanship, beautifully carved on the outside, and stained with a scarlet colour, of the utmost delicacy: the inside of them was black, and shone like japan.

His Excellency made the same distribution as he had before

done to the gentlemen of the suite; while the presents addressed to their Britannic Majesties were aligned to the same apartment which contained those of the preceding day.

The evening of this day was passed in great mirth and festivity by the whole suite, from the very favourable forebodings which they now entertained of the final success of their important mission.

CHAPTER XIV

The Ambassador visited by mandarins on the part of the Emperor, to invite him to court on the anniversary of his Imperial Majesty's birthday. – The whole suite attended on the occasion. – The imperial palace described. – Some account of the Emperor. – A succession of presents. – Busines transacted with the imperial court, – Particular presents of the Emperor of China to the King of Great Britain. – Description of theatrical amusements. – A British soldier tried by a court martial, and punished. – Leave Jehol.

1793, September, Monday 16. THE Ambassador received the visits of several mandarins, who came to inform him, that as the following day was the anniversary of the Emperor's birthday, his presence, and that of the whole embassy, would be expected at court.

Tuesday 17. This moming, at two o'clock, his Excellency, with the whole of the British suite, set out for his Imperial Majesty's palace, where we arrived, with much interruption, in about two hours, amidst an immense crowd of spectators without, and a great concourse of people within, the palace; the latter consisting of mandarins of all classes and distinctions.

This palace is built on an elevated situation, and commands an extensive view of the mountainous country that surrounds it. The edifice itself is neither lofty or elegant, but very extensive; and contains a very numerous range of courts, surrounded with porticos, ornamented with gilding and colours. The gardens extend for several miles, and are surrounded by a strong wall about thirty feet in height. In the front of the palace there is a large plain, with a considerable lake in the center of it.

Here we waited several hours, till, at length, the approach of the Emperor was announced, by the prostration of the mandarins as he advanced. This great personage was in a very plain palankin, borne by twenty mandarins of the first order; and were it not for that circumstance, he could not have been distinguished from a common mandarin, as he wore no mark or badge of distinction, nor any article of dress superior to the higher classes of his subjeets. The simplicity of his appearance, it seems, proceeds from that wise policy which distinguishes his reign; as it is a favourite principle of his government to check as much as possible all useless luxury, and to encourage œconomy, among his people. It is from the same paternal regard for the situation and circumstances of his subjects, that he has suppressed all public rejoicings on account of his birthday, in this less flourishing part of his dominions; from the apprehension that the loyal and affectionate spirit of the poorer classes of the people would distress themselves, in promoting the festive celebration of the day. This prohibition, however, as we understood, reached no further than the immediate vicinity of the imperial residence; the birthday of the sovereign being observed with great joy and solemnity through every other part of a grateful empire.

The emperor on this day completed the eighty-fifth year of his age, as he was, in the fifty-seventh of his reign. Though he had dark, piercing eyes, the whole of his countenance discovered the mild traits of benignant virtue, mixed with that easy dignity of exalted station, which results rather from internal consciousness than exterior grandeur.

The appearance of the suite was exactly the same as on the

first day of audience; and we returned, in an equal state of embarrassment and fatigue, at one o'clock. A very large quantity of presents soon followed us, consisting of the same kind of articles as had been already sent, but of different colours and patterns. There were, however, added, on the

present occasion, a profusion of fruits and confectionary, sufficient to have furnished a succession of fine deserts, if our stay had been prolonged to twice the period which was destined for our abode at Jehol.

The Chinese possess the art of confectionary in a very superior degree, both as to its taste, and the variety of its forms and colours. Their cakes of every kind are admirably made, and more agreeable to the palate than any I remember to have tasted in England, or any other country. Their pastry is also as light as any I have eaten in Europe, and in such a prodigious variety, as the combined efforts of our best European confectioners, I believe, would not be able to produce.

Wednesday 18. This morning the Ambassador went to the imperial palace, but not in the former style of parade, to have his audience of leave, as the time of our stay in Tartary was verging to a period.

His Excellency, at the same time, transacted certain official business at court, which was said without reserve at the time, by the gentlemen of the suite, to be as follows:

The Emperor of China refused, in the first instance, to sign, and of course, to enter into any engagement by a written treaty with the crown of Great Britain, or any other nation; as such a conduit, on his part, would be contrary to the ancient usage, and, indeed, an infringement of the ancient constitutions of the empire. At the same time he was pleased to signify his high respect for his Britannic Majesty and the British nation; and that he felt a strong disposition to grant them greater indulgencies than any other European power trading to his dominions: nor was he unwilling to make such a new arrangement of the duties payable by British ships arriving at Canton, as appeared to be a leading object of the negotiation. At the same time, however, he should be ever attentive to the real interests of his own subjects, an atom of which he would never sacrifice; and should, therefore, withdraw his favours to any foreign nation whenever it might appear to be incompatible with the interests of his own; or that the English should, by their conduct in trade, forfeit their pretensions to any advantages which might be granted them in preference to other nations trading to China. There were the declarations of the Emperor on the occasion, which did not, in his opinion, require any written instrument or signature to induce him to realize and fulfil.

At the same time, to prove the high regard and esteem the Emperor of China entertained for the King of Great Britain, his Imperial Majesty delivered, from his own hand into that of the Ambassador, a very valuable box, containing the miniature pictures of all the preceding emperors; to which is annexed, a description in verse by each emperor, of himself, and the principal features of his government, as well as rules of conduct recommended to their several successors.

The Emperor, on presenting this gift to the Ambassador, spoke to the following purport:

"Deliver this casket to the King your master, with your own hand, and tell him, though the present may appear to be small, it is, in my estimation, the most valuable that I can give, or my empire can furnish: for it has been transmitted to me through a long line of my predecessors; and is the last token of affection which I had reserved to bequeath to my son and successor, as a tablet of the virtues of his ancestors, which he had only to peruse, as I should hope, to inspire him with the noble resolution to follow such bright examples; and, as they had done, to make it the grand object of his life to exalt the honour of the imperial throne, and advance the happiness and prosperity of his people."

Such were the words delivered by the Emperor on the occasion, as communicated by Mr. Plumb, the interpreter, and which occasioned, as may be imagined, no small degree of speculation among the gentlemen of the retinue.

The Ambassador returned to dinner, and soon after repaired again to the imperial palace, with his whole suite and attendants, to see a play which was expressly performed as a particular mark of respect to the embassy.

This dramatic entertainment was represented in one of the inner courts of the palace, on a temporary stage erected for the purpose. It was decorated with a profusion of silk, ribands, and streamers, and illuminated with great splendour and elegance.

The performance consisted of a great variety of mock battles and military engagements; lofty tumbling, as it is expressed with us, and dancing both on the tight and slack ropes; and in all these exercises that agility was displayed, which would have done no discredit to the gymnastic amusements of Sadler's Wells or Astley's Amphitheatre; but the skill of the performers was more particularly astonishing in the art of balancing, in which they excelled any thing of the kind I had ever seen. By an imperceptible motion, as it appeared, of the joints of their arms and legs, they gave to basons, jugs, glasses, etc. an apparent power of locomotion, and produced a progressive equilibrium, by which there vessels changed their positions from one part to another of the bodies of the balancers, in a manner so extraordinary, that I almost, suspected the correctness of my own senses.

The succession of entertainments was concluded by a variety of curious deceptions by slight of hand, which the almost magical activity of Breslaw or Comus has never exceeded. I shall mention one of them, which, I must own, astonished me, and seemed to have an equal effect on the rest of the spectators.

The performer began by exhibiting a large bason in every possible position, when he suddenly placed it on the stage with the hollow part downwards, and instantly taking it up again, discovered a large rabbit, which escaped from the performer, who attempted to catch it, by taking refuge among the spectators. This deception was perfectly unaccountable to me, as there were no visible means whatever of communication, by which it was possible to convey so large an animal to the spot; the stage was also covered with matting, so that it could not be conveyed through the floor, which, if that had been the case, must have been discovered by those, and there were many of them, who were within three yards of the juggler; besides, the whole display of the trick occupied but a few seconds. Several other deceptions of a similar kind prolonged our amusement. The whole of the entertainment was accompanied by a band of musicians placed on the stage.

The theatre was filled with persons of distinction, and formed a very splendid appearance: The Ambassador and his suite returned about nine o'clock, having been very much gratified by the entertainment of the evening.

Thursday 19. At noon several mandarins came to visit his Excellency; when every individual belonging to the embassy received a pipe and tobacco-bag containing a quantity of that herb for smoking.

In the several visits which the mandarins of different classes paid to the Ambassador, they never varied in their exterior appearance, and changes of raiment do not seem to be an object of attention in China, as it is, more or less, in every part of Europe. Even the court dress of the mandarins differs very little from their ordinary habiliments. It consists of a robe that falls down to the middle of the leg, and is drawn round the lower part of the neck with ribands. On the part which covers the stomach, is a piece of embroidery worked on the garment about six inches square; and is finished in gold or silk of different colours, according to the rank of the wearer; this badge of distinction has its counterpart on a parallel part of the back, minutely corresponding in pattern and dimensions. In winter, it is generally made of velvet, and its prevailing colour is blue. The sash, which, on all other occasions is worn round the waist, is dispensed with at court, and the dress is left to its own ease and natural flow.

As I am now come to a period when a certain degree of authority was attempted to be assumed, altogether inconsistent with the character and privileges of Englishmen, and which, I fear, conveyed no favourable impression to the Chinese of our national character and customs, I shall previously state the orders issued by Lord Macartney, and read to the ship's companies, and all persons of every rank attached to the suite, about five o'clock in the evening of the 20th day of July, 1793.

Sealed and signed MACARTNEY.

"As the ships and brigs attendant on the embassy to China are now likely to arrive in port a few days hence, his Excellency the Ambassador thinks it his duty to make the following observations and arrangements:

"It is impossible that the various important objects of the embassy can be obtained, but through the good will of the Chinese: that good will may much depend on the ideas which they shall be induced to entertain of the disposition and conduct of the English nation, and they can judge only from the behaviour of the majority of those who come amongst them. It must be confessed, that the impressions hitherto made upon their minds, in consequence of the irregularities committed by Englishmen at Canton, are unfavourable even to the degree of considering them as the worst among Europeans; these impressions are communicated to that tribunal in the capital, which reports to, and advises the Emperor upon all concerns with foreign countries. It is therefore essential, by a conduct particularly regular and circumspect, to impress them with *new, more just and more favourable* ideas of Englishmen; and to shew that even to the lowest officer in the sea or land service, or in the civil line, they are capable of maintaining by example and by discipline, due order, sobriety, and subordination, among their respective inferiors. Though the people in China have not the smallest share in the government, yet it is a maxim invariably pursued by their superiors, to support the meanest Chinese in any difference with a stranger, and if the occasion should happen, to avenge his blood: of which, indeed, there was a fatal instance not long since at Canton, where the gunner of an English vessel, who had been very innocently the cause of the death of a native peasant, was executed for it, notwithstanding the utmost united efforts on the part of the several European factories at Canton to save him: peculiar caution and mildness must consequently be observed in every sort of intercourse or accidental meeting with any, the poorest individual of the country.

"His Excellency, who well knows that he need not recommend to Sir Erasmus Gower to make whatever regulations prudence may dictate on the occasion, for the persons under his immediate command, as he hopes Capt. Mackintosh will do for the officers and crew: of the Hindostan, trusts also that the propriety and necessity of such regulations, calculated to preserve the credit of the English name, and the interest of the mother country in these remote parts, will insure a steady and cheerful obedience.

"The same motives, he flatters himself, will operate likewise upon all the persons immediately connected with, or in the service of, the embassy.

199

"His Excellency declares that he shall be ready to encourage, and to report favourably hereupon the good conduct of those who shall be found to deserve it; so he will think it his duty, in case of misconduct or disobedience of orders, to report the same with equal exactness and to suspend or dismiss transgressors, as the occasion may require. Nor, if offence should be offered to a Chinese, or a misdemeanor of any kind be committed, which may be punishable by their laws, will he deem himself bound to interfere for the purpose of endeavouring to ward off or mitigate their severity.

"His Excellency relies on Lieutenant-Colonel Benson, commandant of his guard, that he will have a strict and watchful eye over them: vigilance, as to their personal demeanor, is as requisite in the present circumstances, as it is, though from other motives, in regard to the conduct of an enemy in time of war. The guard are to be kept constantly together, and regularly exercised in all military evolutions; nor are any of them to absent themselves from on board ship, or from whatever place may be allotted them for their dwelling on shore, without leave from his Excellency, or commanding officer. None of the mechanics, or servants, are to leave the ship, or usual dwelling on shore, without leave from himself, or from Mr. Maxwell; and his Excellency experts, that the gentlemen in his train will shew the example of subordination, by communicating their wishes to him before they go, on any occasion, from the ship, or usual dwelling place on shore.

"No boxes or packages, of any kind, are to be removed from the ship, or, afterwards, from the place where they shall be brought on shore, without the Ambassador's leave or a written order from Mr. Barrow, the comptroller; such order describing the nature, number, and dimensions of such packages.

"His Excellency, in the most earnest manner, requests that

no person whatever belonging to the ships be suffered, and he desires that none of his suite, guard, mechanics, or servants, presume to offer for sale, or propose to purchase, in the way of traffic, the smallest article of merchandize of any kind, under any pretence whatever, without leave from him previously obtained. The necessity of avoiding the least appearance of traffic accompanying an embassy to Pekin was such, as to induce the East India Company to forego the profits of a new market, and deterred them from shipping any goods for sale in the Hindostan, as being destined to attend upon the embassy, the dignity and importance of which, in the prejudiced eyes of the Chinese, would be utterly lost, and the good consequences expected from it, even on commercial points, totally prevented, if any actual transactions, though for trifles, for the purpose of gain, should be discovered amongst any of the persons concerned in conveying, or attending an Ambassador; of which the report would soon infallibly swell into a general system of trading. From this strictness his Excellency will willingly relax whenever such advances shall have been made by him in negotiation as will secure the object of his mission: and when a permission from him to an European, to dispose of any particular article of merchandize, shall be considered as a favour granted to the Chinese purchaser. His Excellency is bound to punish, as far as in him lies, any the slightest deviation from this regulation he will easily have it in his power to do so, in regard to the persons immediately in his train, or service. The discipline of the navy will render it equally easy to Sir Erasmus Gower, in respect to those under his immediate command; and the East India Company have, by their order of the 5th of September, 1792, and by their letter of the 8th of the same month and year, fully authorized his Excellency to enforce compliance, with the same regulation, among the officers of the Hindostan. A copy of the said order, and an extract from the said letter, here follow, in order that Capt. Mackintosh may communicate the same to his officers. His Excellency depends upon him to prevent any breach or evasion of the same among any of his crew."

At a Court of Directors held on Wednesday, the fifth of September, 1792,

"Resolved,

"That the Right Honourable Lord Viscount Macartney be authorized to suspend, or dismiss the commander, or any officer of the Hindostan, who shall be guilty of a breach of covenants, or disobedience of orders from the Secret Committee, or from his Excellency, during the continuation of the embassy to China.

(Signed) "W. RAMSEY, Sec."

Extract from the Chairman and Deputy Chairman's Letter to Lord Macartney, dated the 8th of September, 1792.

"The Secret Committee having given orders to Captain Mackintosh, of the Hindostan, to put himself entirely under your Excellency's direction, as long as may be necessary for the purpose of the embassy, we have inclosed a copy of his instructions, and of the covenants which he has entered into, together with an account of his private trade, and that of his officers: there is no intention whatever, on the part of the Court, to permit private trade in any other port, or place, other than Canton, to which the ship is ultimately destined, unless your Excellency is satisfied that such private trade will not prove of detriment to the dignity and importance annexed to the embassy, or to the consequences expected therefrom, in which case your consent in writing becomes necessary to authorize any commercial transaction by Captain Mackintosh, or any of his officers, as explained in the instructions from the Secret Committee. But as we cannot be too guarded with respect to trade, and the consequences which may result from any attempt for that purpose, we hereby authorize your Excellency to suspend, or dismiss the commander, or any officer of the Hindostan, who shall be guilty of a breach of covenants, or disobedience of orders from the Secret Committee, or from your Excellency, during the continuance of the present embassy."

"His Excellency takes this opportunity of declaring also, that however determined his sense of duty makes him to forward the objects of his mission, and to watch, detect, and punish, as far as in his power, any crime, disobedience of orders, or other behaviour tending to endanger, or delay the success of the present undertaking, or to bring discredit on the English character, or occasion any difficulty, or embarrassment to the embassy; so in the like manner shall he feel himself happy in being able at all times to report and reward the merit, as well as to promote the interest, and indulge the wishes, of any person who has accompanied him on this occasion, as much as may be consistent with the honour and welfare of the public.

In case of the absence or engagements of his Excellency, at any particular moment, application may be made in his room to Sir George Staunton, whom his Majesty was pleased to honour with a commission of minister plenipotentiary, to act on such occasions."

Given on board his Majesty's
ship the Lion, the 16th day
of July 1793.
By his Excellency's command.
(Signed)
ACHESON MAXWELL,   }
EDWARD WINDER,   } Secretaries.

Having thus given at large, and from the first authority, the whole of those regulations which were framed, and with great good sense and true policy, to forward the objects of the embassy, I shall now proceed to state certain circumstances, which do not altogether appear to be consistent with, if they may not be considered by some, as violations of them.

It was now hinted to all the servants of the Ambassador, that they were hereafter to consider themselves as subject to military law, and that the corporeal punishment usual in the army would be applied to them, if they should refuse to obey the commands of any of their superiors in the suite. Such an idea, as may be supposed, occasioned no small alarm, as well as an abhorrence in the minds of those who would be affected by a regulation so contrary to every principle of right or justice; and when they were at such a distance from their own happy country, that any one injured by such an act of tyranny, might never again return to the protection of that power which would avenge it.

To the honour of Sir George Staunton, I have the satisfaction to say, from the general report in the palace, that he reprobated, in very severe terms, the proposition of a measure so subversive of those privileges, which, as Englishmen, we carried with us into the heart of Tartary; and which no power of the embassy had a legal right to invade.

This strange extension of military discipline was certainly proposed to Lord Macartney by some officious persons in his suite; but the experiment, very happily for all parties, was never attempted to be made.

When Lieutenant-colonel Benson ordered a court-martial to be held on one of his soldiers, and saw the sentence of it carried into execution, he did that which he had a legal power to do, however indiscreet the exercise of it might be: but in the verge of an embassy, which, within its own circle, carries the liberties of

English subjects to the remotest regions of the globe, any attempt to infringe them, deserves the severest reprobation.

This morning, James Cootie, a private in the infantry, who composed a part of the Ambassador's guards, was reported to the commanding officer, for having procured, by the assistance of a Chinese soldier, a small quantity of samtchoo, a spirituous liquor already described: for which offence he was immediately confined, and soon after tried by a court-martial, consiting of a certain number of his comrades, and a corporal as president; and the sentence pronounced on this unfortunate man was approved by Lieutenant-colonel Benson.

In consequence of this sentence, all the British were drawn up in the outer court of the palace; and, after observing all the forms usual on such occasions, the culprit was tied up to one of the pillars of the great portico, and, in the presence of a great number of the Chinese, he received the punishment of sixty lashes, administered with no common severity.

The mandarins, as well as those natives of the inferior elasses who were present, expressed their abhorrence at this proceeding, while some of them declared, that they could not reconcile this conduct in a people, who professed a religion, which they represented to be superior to all others, in enforcing sentiments of benevolence, and blending the duties of justice and of mercy. One of the principal mandarins, who knew a little of the English language, expressed his own sentiments, and those of his brethren, by saying, "Englishman too much cruel, too much bad."

Of the nature of the soldier's offence, I do not pretend to determine; nor shall I observe on the necessity of applying the severity of military discipline on the occasion; these things are not within the scope of my information or experience: but a little common-sense alone is necessary to determine on the impolity of exhibiting a kind of punishment which is unknown in China, and abhorrent to the nature of the people, in the presence of so many of them; as from their numbers, and our general ignorance of the language, it was impossible to explain or justify it to them, by the usage and p``olicy of our laws. Whether this punishment was necessary to the discipline or good order of the troops, I do not, as I before observed, propose to consider; but of this I am sure, that it was by no means necessary to make it a public spectacle, and to risque the unfavourable impressions which it might, and, indeed, did make in the minds of the Chinese, before whom it was purposely exhibited.

This measure, as I have reason to believe, was very much canvassed at the time when it was carried into execution, and justified on the policy of convincing the Chinese of our love of order, and the rigour we employed in punishing any infringement of it. That it had, as I suspected it would have, the contrary effect, the looks, gestures, and expressions of the Chinese present on the occasion are unanswerable testimonies.

Sir Erasmus Gower, however, as I was informed on my return to the Lion, went a step further at Chusan, when she lay at anchor off that island, in the Yellow Sea. The fact to which I allude is known to every one at that time on board the ship.

A Chinese had come on board the English man of war, from Chusan, and brought with him a small bottle of samtchoo, a kind of dram, in expectation of exchanging it with the sailors for some European article. A discovery, however, being made of his design, Sir Erasmus Gower ordered him to be seized and punished by the boatswain's mate with twelve lashes; and, to add to the bad effects of such a conduct, in the pretence of a great many of the Chinese who were then on board.

This is one of those irreconcileable circumstances which occasionally happened in the progress and completion of this embassy: because an application to the mandarins would have had all the effect which could be desired in redressing the grievance, and, at the same time, have assumed the form of a proper and regular proceeding.

CHAPTER XV

Leave the city of Jehol. – Description of two rocks in its neighbourhood. – Circumstances of the journey. – Arrive at Pekin. – Arrangements made there. – The remainder of the presents prepared to be sent to the Emperor. – Sickness prevails among the soldiers. – The Ambassador attends his imperial Majesty. – Brief account of his palace. – Further arrangements respecting the household of the embassy. – Presents to the Emperor and the Grand Choulaa. – The Emperor goes to Yeumen-man-yeumen to see the presents. – His person and dress particularly described. – Presents received from court for their Britannic Majesties. – Circumstances concerning those which had been sent to the Emperor. – Report prevails that the embassy is to leave Pekin.

1793, September, Friday 20. IT was notified by orders issued this morning, that the embassy was to quit Jehol on the morrow, to proceed to Pekin, where the final issue of it would be known and settled.

In the evening the whole of the heavy baggage was sent off for Pekin. At nine there was a very heavy storm of thunder, lightning, and rain, which continued, without any intermission, till four o'clock of the following morning.

Saturday 21. This morning, at eight o'clock, the British embassy took their leave of the city of Jehol, after a strict confinement of fourteen days; as the liberty with which we had been flattered soon after our arrival had never been granted.

We passed the Emperor's pagoda at nine o'clock, where we saw an Ambassador and his suite, from the King of Cochin China, refreshing themselves. It is an annual visit to pay tribute from that Prince to the Emperor of China.

The confusion and solicitude which attended the entry into Jehol prevented me from giving a description of the two rocks, which are among the most extraordinary objects I have ever seen or read of, and must not be passed by without such a particular description, as it is in my power to give.

The first is an immense pillar, or column of solid rock, which is seen from the palace, occupied by the embassy at Jehol, at the distance, as it appeared to me, of about four miles. It is situated on the pinnacle of a large mountain, and near the verge of it; from which it rises, in an irregular manner, to the height of, at least, one hundred feet. Its base is small, but it gradually thickens towards the top; and from several of its projecting parts issue streams of the finest water.

The upper part of this enormous rock, which is rather fiat, appears to be covered with shrubs and verdure; but as it is absolutely inaccessible, there is no possibility of knowing the kind of plants which crown it. When its own individual height is considered, and added to the eminence where nature, or, perhaps, some convulsion of the elements, has placed it, the passenger in the valley below cannot look up to it without an equal degree of horror and amazement. It is esteemed, and with great propriety, by the natives, as among the first natural curiosities of their country; and is known by the name of Pansuiashaung.

The other rock, or rather clutter of rocks, is also a very stupendous object, and stands on the summit of a very grand, though not a fertile, mountain. They are also in the form of pillars, and appear, except in one particular point of view, to be a solid rock; though they are actually separated from each other by an interval of several feet. Their height rises to near two hundred feet, as I understand, from a correct mathematical admeasurement.

Opposite to the mountain which forms the base, rises another of a similar appearance, though it slopes with a more gentle declivity, down to a charming valley, that is formed by them, and is watered by a pretty rivulet, abounding in fine trout.

In the course of this afternoon we arrived at the imperial palace of Callachottueng, where we had the misfortune to lose Jeremiah Reid, one of the royal artillery, who died of the bloody flux, with which he had been afflicted but a very few days. Several men belonging to the military detachments were attacked with the same complaint.

Sunday 22. This morning, at one o'clock, the body of the deceased soldier was removed to the next village, to remain their till our arrival, to receive the interment which was due to him. This measure was suggested by the mandarin, who expressed great apprehension lest the circumstance should reach the Emperor, and awaken his alarm respecting any contagious disorder.

At six o'clock the embassy continued its route, and at the small village of Quangchim, where it stopped to breakfast, the body of our deceased companion was interred with military honours.

In the course of this morning intelligence was received by the mandarin, Van-Tadge-In, that his Imperial Majesty had left Jehol, on his return to Pekin: he, therefore, requested the

Ambassador and his train to exert themselves in making two stages without halting, that the palaces might be left to receive the attendants of the Emperor.

In consequence of this unexpected requisition, we arrived, after a very fatiguing journey, at the town of Waungchauyeng, in the vicinity of the great wall, of which stupendous object I took another and a last view; but without any novelty of impression, or the acquisition of an additional circumstance concerning it.

Monday 23. At a very early hour we continued our route; the air was cold and piercing, and we breakfasted at a place called Caungchumfau; after which we passed a prodigious number of carts, containing the Emperor's baggage. Arrived at three o'clock at Cubacouoo, as the station of the day.

Tuesday 24. We proceeded on our journey at four in the morning, by the assistance of a very bright moon, and took our first meal at the town of Chanchin;. our second regale was taken at Mecucang, and we then proceeded to Whiazow, the last stage of the day.

Wednesday 25. Breakfast was this morning provided for the embassy in the barn-yard of a small village; and the journey of the day was finished at Nanshishee. There I was surprised by the sight of several fields of turnips of an excellent quality.

Thursday 26. This day finished our returning journey from Tartary, which, as it was by the same route that conducted us thither, and offered no novelty that deserved attention, I have dispatched with little more than the names of those places where we stopped for refreshment, or repose. After a breakfast at Chingeho, which we found less plentiful than on former occasions, we ar rived early in the afternoon at Pekin, and proceeded to the palace of the British Ambassador.

Friday 27. His Excellency employed a great part of this morning in examining the several arrangements which had been made in the palace during his absence; the whole of which was favoured with his approbation. The gentlemen of the suite also received their particular baggage in their respective apartments, and the final distribution of the different parts of the palace was settled.

In the principal room of the Ambassador's apartments, the

state canopy, brought from England, was immediately put up. It was made of flowered crimson satin, with festoons and curtains, enriched with fringes of gold. On the back part of it the arms of Great Britain appeared in the richest embroidery; the floor beneath it was spread with a beautiful carpet, on which were placed five chairs of state, of the same materials as the canopy, and fringed with gold. The center chair immediately under the coat of arms was elevated on a platform above the rest, to which there was an ascent of two steps. The whole had been arranged with great taste in England, and, in its present situation, made a very superb appearance, in every respect suited to the occasion for which it was erected. At the other extremity of the apartment, opposite to the canopy, were hung the whole length portraits of their Britannic Majesties; so that this chamber wanted no decoration appropriate to the exterior of diplomatic dignity.

These dispositions being completed, and in a manner equally suited to the splendor of the embassy, as to the individual convenience of those who composed it, nothing remained to perfect the domestic establishment, but the regulation of the different tables to be provided for the several departments of the household; which it was thought proper to delay till the arrival of the Emperor in Pekin.

Captain Mackintosh proposed to set off on the Monday to join his ship, the Hindostan, which lay at Chusan, and to proceed to Canton; there to take in his cargo for England, having seen, as he conceived, a favourable commencement of this important embassy, in which his masters, the East India Company, had such a predominant interest.

Saturday 28. This day the Emperor of China returned to the imperial palace in Pekin; and his arrival was announced by a grand discharge of artillery.

The occupations of this day in the palace of the Ambassador

were entirely confined to writing letters for England, of which Capt. Mackintosh was to take the charge; it being then considered by Lord Macartney as a settled arrangement with the court of Pekin, that the

English embassy should remain there during the winter, to carry on the important negotiations with which it was entrusted.

Sunday 29. His Excellency received the visits, of several mandarins. Certain packages designed for the Emperor were prepared to be presented to his Majesty: they consisted of superfine broad, and other cloths of British manufacture.

Monday 30. In consequence of the sickness that prevailed among the soldiers belonging to the embassy, it was thought expedient to establish an hospital for their more speedy cure, as well as to separate the invalids from those who were in health and capable of duty. Dr. Gillan and Dr. Scott were accordingly desired to examine a range of buildings behind the Ambassador's apartments, with an open area beyond them, and on the report of those gentlemen, it was determined that they should he formed into an hospital. Accordingly several arrangements took place, to render it comfortable to those who were under the necessity of taking up an occasional abode in it. At this time, of the fifty men which composed the guards of the embassy, eighteen were in such a state as to require the attentive care and skill of the physician.

October, Tuesday 1. A mandarin, came from the Emperor to request that the ordnance presents might be immediately sent to the palace of Yeumen-man-yeumen, where they were to be proved and examined: but the Chinese thought themselves equal to the task of proof and examination; for the British artillery soldiers were never employed, as was expected, to display their superior skill in the sciencc of engineering and gunnery.

The chariots, etc. were also removed to the same place, and

the sadler and carpenters belonging to the embassy, with some assistant mechanics, were sent thither to unpack and hang them on their carriages: this was done, but the workmen were not permitted to adjust them fully for presentation; and came back in the evening to Pekin without receiving further orders to complete their work, and explain the mode of applying the different machines, under their direction, to the respective uses for which they were designed.

Wednesday 2. The Ambassador received a formal intimation to wait on the Emperor as tomorrow; when it was hoped and anxiously expected that the final ratifications would take place between the ministers of the two courts, and prepare the way for entering upon the projected negotiation, from which so many advantages were expected to be derived to the commerce of Great Britain.

The sick were this day removed to that part of the palace which had been fitted up as an hospital.

Another package of presents was opened and examined preparatory to their being sent to his Imperial Majesty.

Thursday 3. The Ambassador, in obedience to the requisition of yesterday, went in a private manner to the Emperor's palace, where business was transacted between his Excellency and the officers of state; and it was a report among the Engish suite, but on what foundation I cannot tell, that the requisitions of the British Minister were submitted to the consideration of the imperial council. This conference lasted two hours, but the result of it was not, as may be supposed, a matter of general communication; but there were no apparent reasons to suppose that it was not favourable to the success of the embassy.

As I had this day attended the Ambassador I shall just mention what I saw of the imperial palace, which will be comprised in a very few lines.

It is situated in the center of the city, and surrounded by a wall about twenty feet in height, which is covered with plaster painted of a red colour, and the whole crowned or capped with green varnished tiles. It is said to occupy a space that may be about seven English miles in circumference, and is surrounded by a kind of gravel walk: it includes a vast range of gardens, full, as I was informed, of all those artificial beauties which decorate the gardens of China. I can only say that the entrance to the palace is by a very strong stone gateway, which supports a building of two stories; the interior court is spacious, and the range of building that fronts the gateway rises to the height of three stories, and each of them is ornamented with a balcony or projecting gallery, whose railing, palisadoes, and pillars, are enriched with gilding; the roof is covered with yellow shining tiles, and the body of the edifice is plastered and painted with various colours. This outer court is the only part of the palace which I had an opportunity of seeing, and is a fine example of Chinese architecture. The gate is guarded by a large body of soldiers, and a certain number of mandarins of the first class are always in attendance about him.

Of the magnificent and splendid apartments this palace contains for private use or public service; of its gardens appropriated to pleasure, or for the sole production of fruit and flowers, of which report said so much, I am not authorised to say any thing, as my view of the whole was very confined; but, though I am ready to acknowledge that the palace had something imposing in its appearance, when compared with the diminutive buildings of the city that surround it, I could see nothing that disposed me to believe the extraordinary accounts which I had heard and read of the wonders of the imperial residence of Pekin.

Friday 4. It cannot be supposed for a moment, that those who had no other concern in the embassy, than as a part of the retinue necessary for its exterior conduct and appearance, should be informed of any of the official circumstances of it; they could, therefore, only judge of its progress from the general arrangements which were made concerning its domestic establishment. It was, however, with particular satisfaction that the following directions were this day received from the Ambassador, relative to the future order and disposition of the tables for the different departments of the household; as an intention to domestic business seemed to announce his Excellency's opinion concerning the permanency of our residence at Pekin; and, of course, an entire diposition in the court of China to give the negotiation every advantage that might be derived from frequent conference and deliberate consultation.

The order of the tables was as follows:

The table of the Ambassador was ordered for himself alone; with two covers for gentlemen of the suite, who were to be invited in daily suceession to dine with him.

The next in precedence was that of Sir George Staunton, at which he was to be accompanied by Mr. Maxwell, one of the secretaries, Doctor Gillan, Captain Mackintosh, while he remained at Pekin, Mr. Barrow, and Master Staunton. The table of Lieutenant-colonel Benson was to be attended by the Lieutenants Parish and Crewe, Doctor Scott, Messrs. Hickey, Baring, Winder, Alexander, and Doctor Dinwiddie.

The foregoing disposition of the household commenced on this day; but it was thought proper to continue the Chinese dishes till the kitchen in the palace was completed, when a certain proportion of English cookery was to be blended with that of the country. To complete the table arrangements, the chests containing the service of plate were removed to the apartments of the Ambassador, in order to be prepared for general use.

The cabinets of British manufacture were conveyed by Chinese porters to the imperial palace.

Saturday 5. A large quantity of plated goods, hardware, and cutlery, were unpacked at Sir George Staunton's apartments, a considerable quantity of which was damaged. There were also several of Argand's lamps, with a great variety of watches, trinkets, jewellery, etc. etc. The whole of this cargo was equally divided between the Emperor and the Grand Choulaa.

The carpenters with several assistants were sent to Yeumenmanyeumen, to clean and complete the carriages, and also to set up the model of the Royal Sovereign, an English first-rate man of war.

The Emperor himself came to the palace; and, after he had taken a view of the presents, his Majesty was pleased to order eight ingots of silver to be given to each person; which were instantly received.

The account I have given of the person of the Emperor was from a partial view as he was seated in a palankin shall, therefore, repeat the more particular description of him, which was given by the six English artificers who were employed in fitting up and arranging the presents, when he came to view them, and who were the immediate objects of the imperial generosity which has just been mentioned.

The Emperor is about five feet ten inches in height, and of a slender, but elegant form; his complexion is comparatively fair, though his eyes are dark; his nose is rather aquiline, and the whole of his countenance presents a perfect regularity of features, which by no means announce the great age he is said to have attained; his person is attracting, and his deportment accompanied by affability, which, without lessening the dignity of the prince, evinces the amiable character of the man.

His dress consined of a loose robe of yellow silk, a cap of black velvet with a red ball on the top, and adorned with a peacock's feather, which is the peculiar distinction of mandarins, of the first class. He wore silk boots embroidered with gold, and a sash of blue silk girded his waist.

As to the opinion which his Imperial Majesty formed of the presents, we could not learn, as he never communicated it, at least, to any of those mandarins, by whom it would have been conveyed to the palace of the British embassy. We only knew, at this time, that the two camera obscuras were returned, foolishly enough, as more suited to the amusement of children, than the information of men of science.

A large number of bales, containing various kinds of broad and narrow cloths of English manufacture, together with a considerable quantity of camlets, two barrel organs, and the remainder of such presents as were not damaged, were removed from the palace by the Chinese employed on these occasions. Mr. Plumb, the interpreter, sometimes accompanied the presents to explain the nature and application of them, or performed that office to the mandarins, previous to their departure.

As it now was become a matter of certainty that the embassy would remain for some time at Pekin, the superb saddles which had been brought over for his Excellency, and Sir George Staunton, were unpacked and got ready, with all the elegant furniture, for immediate use.

A very large quantity of precepts were sent from the Emperor to their Britannic Majesties, accompanied with others for the Ambassador and his suite; which were, as usual, distributed among them.

Sunday 6. At noon his Excellency went, with no other attendants than two gentlemen of his retinue and one servant, to visit the Emperor; but, on his arrival at court, he very much alarmed the gentlemen with him by fainting away; he was immediately conveyed home, and continued to be very ill during the remainder of the day. The intended interview, therefore, was not effected in consequence of his sudden indisposition.

In the forenoon of this day the servants of the embassy were summoned to the apartments of Sir George Staunton, and the soldiers to those of Lieut. Col. Benson; when each person received four pieces of silk, four pieces of dongaree, (a sort of coarse nankeen) and a junk of silver, being a square solid piece of that metal, weighing sixteen ounces, as a present from his Imperial Majesty.

The gentlemen and mechanics were dismissed from their attendance at the palace of Yeumen-manyeumen; for, as all the optical, mechanical, and mathematical instruments were removed from thence, their presence was no longer necessary. Besides, several of these presents, when a trial of them was made before the mandarins, were found to fail in the operations and powers attributed to them; and others of them did not excite that surprise and admiration in the breasts of the Chinese philosophers, which Dr. Dinwiddie and Mr. Barrow expected, who immediately determined upon the ignorance that prevailed in China, and the gross obstinancy of the people.

A report was in circulation this day throughout the palace, that the embassy was to quit Pekin in the beginning of the week; a circumstance so contrary to the general expectation, that it did not at first meet with the credit which it was afterwards found to deserve.

CHAPTER XVI

Orders issued for the suite to prepare for an immediate departure from Pekin. – The Emperor refuses to allow of any delay. – Great confusion occasioned by this sudden departure. – The embassy leaves Pekin; returns to Tong-tchew. – Order of the junks which are to take the embassy to Canton. – Difficulties respecting the baggage. – The junks enter a canal; description of it. – Circumstances of the voyage. – View and cultivation of the country. – The China post described. – Pass through several large cities; a general account of them.

1793, October, Monday 7. THE carpenters were employed in strengthening the cases that contained the presents from the Emperor of China, to their Britannic Majesties.

In the afternoon the report of yesterday was confirmed by an order, issued by the Ambassador to the whole suite, to prepare for their departure from Pekin, on Wednesday. Our surprise at such unexpected intelligence may be readily conceived, but the mortification which appeared throughout the palace on the occasion, was at least equal to the astonishment: for in one moment, as it were, all the domestic arrangements which had been formed, with every attention to individual comfort and repose, were overthrown; – while our fatiguing pilgrimage was to be renewed, not only with all the humiliation that accompanies a forced submission to peremptory power, but with the painful despondency which arises from the sudden annihilation of sanguine and well-grounded hope. But, though we might, in the first moments of surprise, be disposed to feel something for ourselves, superior considerations soon succeeded, and we forgot the trifle of personal inconvenience, in the failure of a political measure which, had been pursued with so much labour, hazard, and perseverance; had been supported with such enormous expense, and to which our country looked with eager expectation, for the aggrandizement of its commercial interests. There was, however, no remedy: and nothing now could be done but to use every endeavour to prolong the period assigned to the departure of the embassy, that there might be sufficient time to make the necessary preparations for leaving Pekin with convenience; and that the Ambassador might not appear to be turned out of the metropolis of a country, where he had represented the crown of Great Britain.

For these reasons, and they were, it must be acknowledged, of some importance, the attendant mandarin was requested to state to the prime minister the impossibility of our departure at so short a notice, not only without very great inconvenience, but absolute injury; as it would be impossible to pack up and arrange the baggage, etc. of the Ambassador and his suite, in a manner to transport it with safety, in so short a time as was then allotted for that purpose,

This commission he readily undertook to execute; and, in the evening, he returned with the perinission of the Grand Choulaa, to delay the departure of the British embassy till Friday, which would have given time sufficient to make every necessary preparation.

Tuesday 8. The mandarin came with a counter-order of the permission of yesterday, from the Emperor himself, who expressly commanded the Ambassador, and all his retinue, to quit Pekin on the next day. They were thus thrown into a renewed state of confusion, which I shall not attempt to describe.

It was reported in the palace, by the Chinese, that the Emperor having considered the business as completed between the two courts, expressed his surprise that the Engish minister should wish to make an unnecessary stay at Pekin, and not be eager to return to his own conntry. His Imperial Majesty was also said to be alarmed at the number of sick persons in the retinue of the embassy, and to apprehend the communication of a contagious disorder among his subjects. It was also reported, that when the brass mortars were tried in the presence of the Emperor, his Majesty admired the skill and ingenuity of these engines of destruction, but deprecated the spirit of a people who employed them; nor could he reconcile their improvements in the system of destruction to the benign spirit which they represented as the soul, and operating principle, of their religion.

Many other reports of a similar nature were propagated; but the reason assigned by the Chinese government, for thus urging the departure of the Ambassador, was the near approach of winter, when the rivers would be frozen, and the journey to Canton, through the northern provinces, be crowded with inconvenience and impediment:

Whatever policy governed the councils of China on this occasion; whether it was an enlarged view of national interest, which it was supposed the propositions of Great Britain would not tend to advance, or any disgust or prejudice proceeding from misconduct, and mismanagement in the embassy itself, the manner in which the Ambassador was dismissed from Pekin was ungracious and mortifying in the extreme. For even if it is supposed to be a policy of the Chinese government, that no foreign minister shall be received, but on particular occasions, and that he is not suffered to remain in the country when he has finished his particular mission; it does not appear that the business was at all advanced which Lord Macartney was employed to negotiate; and he certainly would not have entered into any domestic if he had not considered himself as secure of remaining at Pekin throughout the winter. He must have been encouraged to believe that his residence would not only be permitted, but acceptable to his Imperial Majesty; and that there was a very friendly disposition in the councils of China towards the entering into a treaty with Great Britain, regarding a more enlarged system of commercial intercourse between the two countries.

The jealousy of the Chinese government had so far subsided as to express a wish for an embassy from this country, and afterwards to receive it. The power of Great Britain, its possessions in the East Indies, with the manner in which they have been acquired, and the general state of Europe, are subjects by no means unknown at the court of Pekin; nor was the English settlement at Chusan, or the manner in which it was destroyed, altogether forgotten. The Emperor himself had not only manifested a respect for the British embassy, by the great attentions which had accompanied its progress, but discovered an impatient desire to receive it, by inviting it to its residence in Tartary, when he was so soon to return to Pekin. In short, there was no apparent public reason, when the Ambassador was once received, why he should not be permitted to proceed in his negotiation; but, even if any change had taken place in the mind of the Emperor, or any prejudice arisen against the embassy, from any indiscretion. or misonduct in the management of it, which might induce the court of China to put an immediate termination to it; it is wholly irreconcileable to the common rules of political decorum and civility, as well as the principles of justice and humanity, that an Ambassador, of so much consequence as Lord Macartney, should be dismissed, under his peculiar circumstances, without the least ceremony;

and be not only ordered to depart without allowing the time necessary to make the common arrangements for his journey, but also refused a respite only of two days to his urgent felicitations. In short, we entered Pekin like paupers; we remained in it like prisoners; and we quitted it like vagrants.

This day, — — Newman, a marine, who, with three of his comrades, had been taken from on board the Lion, to fill the vacancies occasioned by the death of some of the soldiers belonging to the embassy, died of a flux; and to prevent this circumstance from being known, his corpse was conveyed away in the night.

Lord Macartney sent his own state carriage as a present to the Grand Choulaa, who refused to accept it. It was then re-demanded, to be un-slung and packed up; but no answer whatever was returned; and so short was the period allotted us to stay, and so much was to be done in it, that there was no time to make farther inquiries concerning the fate of this chariot, or the reasons of such an ungracious behaviour on the part of the minister by whom it was refused.

The hurry and confusion of this day is beyond description; and if the soldiers had not been called in to assist in packing the baggage and stores, a much greater part must have been left behind, that actually became a prey to the Chinese.

The portraits of their Majesties were taken down, but as the cases in which they had come from England, had been broke up for fixtures in the apartments, a few deals, hastily nailed together, were now their only protection. As for the state canopy, it was not taken down, but absolutely torn from the wall; as the original case that contained it had been also employed in various convenient uses, and there was not time to make a new one. The state chairs were presented to some of the mandarins; and the canopy was given to some of Lord Macartney's servants: though, in the scramble, the Chinese contrived to come in for a share. They also purloined a very large quantity of wine; nor was it possible, in such a scene of hurry and confusion, to prevent those opportunities which they were on the watch to seize. In one way or other, however, the public baggage, stores, furniture, etc. were jumbled together as well as circumstances would admit; and no pains or activity were wanting in those employed to perform that sudden and unexpected duty.

The whole of the suite was occupied, at a very early hour of this morning, in getting their packages in readiness, which were taken away by the Chinese appointed to convey them along the road. The whole of the embassy soon followed. Newman, the marine, was buried on the road to Tong-tchew, and at that town we arrived in the evening, where we found a great change in the article of our accommodations. The apartments now allotted to us, were nothing more than temporary sheds, hung with straw matting.

Thursday 10. On going to the river side we found the junks ready to receive us; and when the circumstances of the embarkation were settled, the vessels were arranged in the following order.

No. 1. The Ambassador.

2. Sir George and Matter Staunton.

3. Captain Mackintosh, Mr. Maxwell, Mr. Barrow, and Dr. Gillan.

4. Lieutenant-colonel Benson, with the Lieutenants Parish and Crewe.

5. Messrs. Winder, Barring, Huttner, and Plumb.

6. The Doctors Dinwiddie and Scott, with Messrs. Hickey and Alexander.

7. The Musicians, Mechanics.

The mandarin, Van-Tadge-In, and his attendants, were in

separate junks.

All these matters being finally adjusted, his Excellency, with Sir George Staunton, etc. went on board their junks: while the gentlemen were einployed in getting their baggage into their respective vessels, which exhibited a new and superior scene of confusion to any we had yet experienced. There was, in the first place, no small difficulty in assorting the junks, with the persons who belonged to them. Nor were there a sufficient number of coolies to transport the different effects on board the vessels. In short, those attentions which were shewn to the Ambassador on his former abode in this city, seemed to have been forgotten; and the place which was now appropriated to receive the baggage, was a small spot, on the side of the river, and protected only by a screen of matting.

I have already mentioned the strange conduct of the Grand Choulaa, respecting the chariot which he refused to accept from Lord Macartney, and then refused to return it. On our arrival, however, at Tong-tchew, the chariot appeared to have found its way thither before us; and though we were rather in the habit of being surprized, we could not help feeling a considerable degree of astonishment at seeing the carriage opposite the house appointed for the reception of the embassy, surrounded by crowds of Chinese, and many of its ornaments defaced. It was, accordingly, drawn down to the river side, and a case being made for it on the spot, to secure it from any further injury, it was re-consigned to the hold of a junk; and after having rolled a few posts in China, was finally sent to figure at Madras.

About four o'clock the whole suite were embarked, when dinner was immediately served; nor was it long before they retired to rest, after the most fatiguing day they had experienced since their arrival in China.

Friday 11. At a very early hour the junks were unmoored, and the fleet proceeded down the river: but as I have already given the best description in my power of the country through which it flows, and the local circumstances of it, I shall pass on to the day when we changed the natural for the artificial water, with one solitary observation; that though we still attracted the notice of the inhabitants who lived near the river, the respectful attentions of our former voyage were not repeated.

Wednesday 16. This morning the fleet entered a very noble canal, which communicates with the river near Tyen-sing. It is a work of great labour, and prodigious expense; and its sides are faced with masonry throughout its course. At certain distances locks are erected to give a current to the water; they are in the form of an half-moon, and confine the water to a narrow passage in the middle of the canal, which occasions a fall of about three feet. The junks acquire an accelerated motion in passing these locks, which continued for a considerable distance; and, in order to prevent their receiving any injury from striking against the walls of the lock, which, on account of the sudden ferment of the water, it is not often possible to avoid, men are always stationed there to let down large leathern pads, which effectually break the shock that would otherwise be felt from such an accident.

We passed through at least thirty of these locks in the course of this day's voyage, without being able to discover any variation in them, as to their construction, or the effects produced by them.

On each side of the canal, the country, as far as the eye can reach, is one entire flat, but smiling with fertility. Several villages, with their crowds of inhabitants, varied the scene; and at each of them the soldiers of the district appeared in military array, and saluted the fleet as it passed with three guns.

Thursday 17. We passed by several towns and villages, and at every one of them the Ambassador and mandarins were received with military honours.

It may be proper to observe in this place, that a mandarin of the second class, named Chootadzin, was on board the fleet, and was to continue with us till our arrival at Hoang-tchew, of which province he was appointed the viceroy. Van-Tadge-In, although a mandarin of the first class, was inferior to him in authority, as the office of viceroy gives precedence to the highest order of mandarins.

I observed a considerable number of rice fields, in which there were stone gutters or channels, finished with great neatness, and admirably contrived to convey water to every part of the plantations.

For some days the provisions with which we had been supplied, were not only deficient in quantity, but were sent ready dressed and cold; so that we found it necessary to dress them again, or rather heat them up as well as we could. Mr. Plumb, the vehicle of all complaints, and who, in general, contrived to procure redress, was employed on the present occasion to represent the dissatisfaction which was felt by the different departments of the embassy, respecting the deficiency and quality of the daily provisions.

Friday 18. The same flat and fertile country appeared on either side of the canal, though the view was this day varied by several gardens, in which there were plantations of that shrub which bears what is called the imperial and gunpowder teas; it grows to the size of a goosberry bush, with leaves of the same size. The former of those teas is collected from the first, and the other from the successive blossoms of that plant.

We continued to pass through a succession of locks, and to excite the curiosity of various towns and villages which poured forth their inhabitants to see the extraordinary spectacle of an European embassy.

Saturday 19. Towns and villages alternately presented

228

themselves on either side of the canal, with their prodigious population, but possessed no peculiarity, and offered no circumstances of novelty which would justify a particular description.

The representation which had been made concerning the provisions produced an immediate change in the supply of them: we this day received a large quantity of mutton and beef, with fowls and ducks; to these were added bread, flour, tea, sugar, rice, vegetables of all kinds, with soy, oil, candles, charcoal and wood; and, while the solid part of the meal, with the means of preparing it, were amply administered, the elegant addition of fruits of various kinds, and the liquors of the country, were not forgotten.

In the very unexpected situation of the embassy, it was very natural for those who cornposed the retinue of it to be continually forming conjectures, and eagerly inquiring after any information that might tend to elucidate the extraordinary circumstances of it. Thus we became acquainted with various reports on the subject, some of which we were disposed to credit, while we rejected others, as they seemed to concur with, or contradict, the events of the moment.

Thus we were not unwilling to believe, as it was propagated among us by some of the Chinese, that a Tartar mandarin had been able to prejudice the Emperor against the English people by representing them as barbarous, inhuman, and destitute of all those amiable qualities which they pretended to possess: nor were many of the suite indisposed to believe that from such an unpropitious circumstance the embassy had been treated, to use no worse expression, with such strange disrespect and peremptory dismission. It was also added, that Van-Tadge-In, the attendant mandarin, had since represented the conduct and character of the embassy in a very different point of view, in a written memorial addressed to the Emperor; which had induced his Imperial Majesty to give orders that the British Ambassador and his suite should be abundantly supplied with every thing necessary for their convenience and comfort, and that they might at all times enjoy the liberty of going on shore, and amusing themselves at their own discretion.

Sunday 20. We passed a great number of tobacco plantations. The Chinese cultivate and manufacture this plant in a very superior degree, and are supposed to possess greater varieties of it than any other country in the world.

The quantity of tobacco consumed, and, of course, grown in China, must be beyond all calculation, as smoking is universally practised, and by all ranks and ages. Children, as soon as they have sufficient strength or dexterity to hold a pipe in their hands, are taught by their parents to smoake, which they feel not only as an habitual amusement, but is considered as a preservative against all contagious diseases.

Several walled cities appeared at some distance from the canal, whose guards and garrisons were marched to its banks, in order to give the usual salute; and one in particular of very great extent and amazing population, called Tohiamsyn. The crowds of people of both sexes which came to see the junks pass, were beyond all belief.

We this day passed several stone bridges, some of them were of one, and others of two arches, which appeared to be constructed with great strength and excellent masonry. The number of locks appeared rather to increase than diminish in the course of this day's voyage.

Tuesday 22. The country offered a very fruitful scene, and, in some places, rose into hills and uplands. The water-mills, of which we saw several at work, appeared to be in a great measure the same as those used in Europe: they were corn-mills, as we were informed; and were situated in the midst of very extensive fields of that grain, which was almost ready for the sickle.

Several gentlemen of the suite went on shore to enjoy the exercise and variety of walking on the banks of the canal: but the junks were carried on with such rapidity from the quick succession of locks, that they were left behind, and the whole fleet was obliged to come to anchor till they rejoined it.

Wednesday 23. We this morning saw a very lofty pagoda situated on an eminence: it appeared to be a stone building, consisting of eight stories, each of which was encircled with a balcony, and the whole terminated in an ornamented roof that diminished to a very slender point.

Thursday 24. We this day saw the Chinese post pass along the road, on the side of the canal, with great expedition. The letters and packets are carried in a large square bamboo basket, girt with cane hoops and lined; it is locked, and the key is given to the custody of one of the attendant soldiers, whose office it is to deliver it to the post-master; the box is fastened on the courier's shoulders with straps, and is decorated at the bottom with a number of small bells, which, being shaken by the motion of the horse, make a loud gingling noise, that announces the approach of the post. The post-man is escorted by five light-horsemen to guard him from robbery or interruption. The swiftest horscs are also employed on the occasion, which are renewed at every stage; so that the posts of China may vie in expedition with the English mail.

Friday 25. The succession of populous and large towns was so continual, that it would be tedious to mention them but as a general characteristic of the country; unless some particular cireumstance, from its novely or interest, should justify description.

When I rose this morning, I was surprised to find the junk

fleet at anchor in the heart of a very large city, through the center of which the canal passes; it is here crossed by a continual succession of bridges, which are connected with a circular breast-work on each side, guarded by soldiers, who suffer no vessels to pass till they have been inspected by mandarins who preside over that department. The fleet was favoured here with the usual salute of three guns, and a very larger body of soldiers was drawn up on both sides of the canal; they were completely armed, and wore large helmets, which gave them a very military appearance, while their ranks were enlivened with several hands of colours.

At six o'clock the fleet left this city, and at ten passed through another, which, as far as we could judge from our passage, was of equal dimensions and population. Its name is Kord-cheeaung.

To the left of the canal, and in the center of the city, we saw a very magnificent and lofty pagoda: it rose to the height of ten stories, each of which is surrounded with an elegant gallery, and projecting canopies, supported by pillars.

The chief mandarin of the place has an handsome palace guarded by a fort, whose garrison came forth to salute the Ambassador, as the vessels passed by it.

In the subsequent progress of this day's voyage we passed four other cities, of equal magnitude with those which have been already mentioned; and about nine o'clock at night anchored in the city of Leeyaungoa, which was illuminated to do honour to the distinguished persons on board the fleet; nor were any of those marks of respect omitted which had been demonstrated in all the places, according to their rank, through which we had passed.

A very large body of troops, consisting at least of a thousand men, were drawn up on the banks of the canal; and each man held a pole with with a coloured paper lanthern hanging from it, which, when the troops halt, is stuck in the ground; the whole forming a very singular and pleasing spectacle.

Saturday 26. The air was this morning extremely cold; the thermometer having sunk so low as forty degrees. At seven o'clock we passed a lock, whose current bore us into the city of Kaung-hoo, which, from the great number of junks laying there, must be a place of immense trade. Indeed, the water was so entirely covered with them, that our fleet was obliged to come to anchor, in order to give time for a passage to be made between them. The canal took a winding course through this place, which is elevated above it, and its banks fall in beautiful slopes to the water.

Sunday 27. The weather was moderate and agreeable; and the prospect was varied with meadows of the richest verdure, which were covered with flocks of sheep, and herds of cattle. We passed also several large fields of paddy and millet, and the eye ranged over a vast extent of flat and fertile country.

Monday 28. The voyage of this day furnished no variety, unless a great number of flour-mills may be supposed to vary the scene.

Tuesday 29. The growing wealth of cultivation we had seen every hour as we proceeded on our voyage, and not a spot appeared which towns and villages did not occupy, but proved the skill and labour of the husbandman. This morning, however, gave us a prospect of that labour, for we passed several extensive fields, where the peasants were busy with their ploughs; these machines, so essential in agriculture, were drawn by oxen, and though of a very clumsy form when compared with those of our own country, perform their office with good effect, as the ground appeared to be got into a very promising state of tillage.

Wednesday 30. We saw a fleet of junks laden with tea for the Canton market; nor was it an unnatural, or uninteresting observation, that in the chance of commerce, some of their cargoes might ultimately be consigned to our own country, and arrive there before us.

The prospects of this day were enlivened by pagodas, and country seats; some of which were adorned with beautiful gardens, and others surrounded with the finest orchards I ever beheld.

Thursday 31. This morning the fleet passed through a walled city, named Hoongloafoo. This is another of those places where the vast number of junks which covered its canal, justify the opinion of its extensive commerce. In its neighbourhood there are large plantations of tea, extensive fields of tobacco, and a great number of flour-mills.

We had seen frequent and large plantations of rice; but the fields of cotton, which this morning presented themselves to our attention, formed a curious and pleasing novelty. I observed that the cotton was of the nankeen colour, and is plucked from the top of a short stalk.

Of cities, towns, locks, and bridges, we have seen and said so much, that the reader and the writer would be equally fatigued with the daily enumeration of them.

CHAPTER XVII

Various circumstances of the voyage. – Enter the Yellow River. – Pass several towns, lakes, etc. – Ceremonies at the city of Kiangfou. – Enter a beautiful lake; description of it. – Enter another river; circumstances of it. – Pass several cities, etc. – Dock yards for building junks. – Arrive at the city of Mee-you-mee-awng; beautiful country. – Further account of the Chinese troops. – A mandarin's palace and pagoda described.

1793, November, Saturday 2. THE canal appeared now to have assumed the form of a considerable river, and brought us to a very large city, where we came to an anchor at six o'clock in the morning, having passed a fort at the entrance, by which the fleet had been saluted.

When I mention the situation and circumstances of this city, it would be needless to describe it as a place of great trade, or speak of the inconceivable number of junks which were moored at its quays and wharfs; it will be sufficient to say, that it was washed by large canals, and that on the south side of it, there is an extensive bay which communicates with the Yellow River, to give some notion of its commercial character.

Here the fleet remained at anchor about an hour; when it unmoored, and soon entered the bay, with an alarming rapidity, through a large lock, constructed with rushes, curiously matted together, and secured with logs of wood.

This bay is of great extent, and would contain the proudest

fleets of Europe, while its shores offer an amphitheatre of landscape beauty. The hills are verdant to their very summits, which are sometirnes crowned with pagodas; and the lower parts are enriched with houses and gardens, and that variety of cultivation which distinguishes this extraordinary country.

On entering this bay, it was discovered that there were a variety of currents running with great violence, and in opposite directions, at not less than seven miles an hour; and the skill of navigating it consists in being able to get into that individual current which runs towards the place of the vessel's particular destination.

In this situation we should have been glad, if it had been consistent with the course of the voyage, to have cast anchor, and enjoyed, at leisure, the contemplation of its beauties: but the fleet immediately steered towards a large river, which it soon entered, and whose stream soon bore us, as it were, into the bosom of a rich and beautiful country.

At the mouth of this river there is a large town, with the palace of a mandarin of the first class surrounded with a strong stone wall: it is a very large edifice, crowned with turrets, richly gilt and ornamented after the fashion of the country. The front looks towards the bay, of which it commands an extensive and enchanting prospect.

Town now succeeded to town and the country offered the most beautiful views, of which no adequate idea can be given by written description. When, therefore, I mention the country as one scene of varied cultivation, divided by well-planted enclosures, peopled with farms that are surrounded by orchards, enriched with villas, and their ornamental gardens, a very inadequate picture is given of the expansive scenery on either side of the navigation which bore us through it.

At two o'clock, and as we were preparing for dinner, the

junks arrived at a very large town, through which the river took a course of at least three miles. This place is formed on a more regular plan than any which we had seen in China. The houses were uniformly built of brick, varied with an intermixture of blue stone, and seldom deviated from the height of two stories.

The usual honours of forts and military guards were received here, as through every place we passed, of whatever size or distinction it might be: the walled city, and the village, were equally attentive to this act of official civility, according to their respective capacities.

It may, indeed, be here observed, that through the whole of our travels in this country, whether by land, or by water, and not excepting Tartary, the villages, as well as the cities, have their mandarin, and his guards proportioned to the magnitude and consequence of the place where they are cantoned; and that the interior parts of the kingdom are equally secured by troops, as the frontiers, or sea coast: we may, therefore, be said to pass almost between a continued line of soldiers, on each side of the canals, or rivers; where the intervals are so so small between those villages and great towns, that they may be said to form a chain of military cantonments.

In the latter part of the afternoon we anchored, for some time, at another considetable town, where the junks stopped to take in a supply of China wine. It is situated on the side of a large lake, which, in some places, was divided only by a bank from the river on which we sailed. As I could not discover any land in the distant part of this large body of water, I was disposed to consider it as an inlet of the Yellow sea.

The country now began to wear a swampy appearance, and, of course, did not altogether retain those beautiful features, which have faintly represented it to possess, during the more recent parts of our voyage. This circumstance naturally arises from the great number of rivers, canals, and lakes, that aid the navigation of this part of the country; which being subject to occasional inundations from them, is frequently in the situation that I have described.

In the evening we saw a very fine palace belonging to the mandarin of a town, through which we afterwards passed in the night, and neither knew its form or character: nor should we have even discerned the grandeur of the mandarin's residence, if he had not illuminated it in honour of the Ambassador and his brethren on board the junks; and ordered out his guard, consisting of at least five hundred men, to enlighten with their paper lanterns the banks of the river.

Sunday 3. This morning was very keen and frosty. The fleet anchored opposite to a large lake, which appeared to communicate with several considerable rivers. The country continued its flat and swampy appearance. I was this day informed that the river whereon we were proceeding is called the Yellow river, which may probably be owing to the communications it may have with the Yellow sea. There is a considerable town situated between the lake and this river.

The junks remained at anchor no longer than was necessary to receive the usual supply of provisions and wine. In a short time we passed another lake; and, without enumerating the canals, with their stone and wooden bridges, as well as the villages and towns that claimed our transient attention, I shall come at once to another lake that appeared to be much larger than any of those which have been already mentioned. A great number of junks were sailing across it in different directions, and several hundred fishing boats were employed on it in their necessary occupations. It is said to abound in fish; those we procured were small, of the size of a sprat, but in taste and shape resembling an haddock: nor was our river deficient in its produce, as plenty of fine trout were taken in it.

At some distance from the river, on the side opposite to the lake, is a very large, and, as far as we could judge, magnificent city surrounded by a wall, named Chun-foong. The suburbs which extend towards the water, are also very considerable, and the houses of which they consist are built of a dark stone, roofed with tiles of the same colour. They are only of one story, and their windows are circular and grated with iron, which gives them a very disagreeable appearance. The wall of this town is not so high as those we have hitherto seen, and, as far as I could judge by the telescope, does not rise above fourteen or fifteen feet. The part of it that we passed could not be less than two miles in extent; which may lead us to the plausible conjecture that the city itself is at least eight miles in circumference. From its general appearance and accessory circumstances, no doubt could be entertained of its extensive commerce; and, from the dress and manners of its inhabitants, a similar opinion might be entertained of their urbanity and opulence.

At four o'clock the fleet anchored at the extremity of the wall of this city, and received a fresh supply of wine and provisions: these, indeed, were now provided in such plenty, that the poor people who navigated the junks found themselves in a state of unexpected and unexampled luxury, from the superabundance of them.

Several of the gentlemen from the other junks did us the honour to pay us a visit, which produced an evening of great mirth and festivity.

Monday 4. The weather was extremely cold. We passed two large lakes, which, by their respective branches, unite with the river. At noon we sailed through a considerable town, and beyond it, saw several small canals on either side of the river, with many boats on them employed in fishing. The country is flat and marshy, and wherever the road on the side of the river passes over swampy dips or vallies, wooden platforms are erected to preserve the level, and avoid the inconvenience of sinking into them.

A large walled city, whose name is Kiangfou, next claimed our attention. At the entrance of it a mandarin and his guards appeared on the water-side in martial figure, to give the customary salutes. At each end of the line of troops there was an elegant arch, with a connected platform, about three feet from the ground, guarded by railing, and projecting into the river. These temporary structures were covered with beautiful matting, and the rails were bound with silk of various colours, ornamented with knots and festoons. The arches were decorated in a similar taste, and the whole was erected for the convenience of the Ambassador, if it had suited his convenience to stop, and visit the mandarin.

At a small distance, and on an elevated situation, was an encampment of the mandarin's guards. The tents were pitched close to each other, in a circular form, with a small vacant space as an entrance to the mandarin's pavilion, which occupied the center. It was decorated in a very elegant manner with ribands and silken streamers: the front of it was open, and displayed its interior ornaments: it contained a table covered with a collation, and surrounded with sine chairs, with a canopy over one of them. The mandarin's attendants appeared to be in waiting; and a centinel was on duty on each side of the pavilion.

This regale was prepared with great politeness and hospitality in honour of the Ambassador and the mandarins on board the junks, if the order of the voyage would have permitted them to have delayed its progress for a short time, to have acknowledged these respectful attentions.

Each tent had a flag of green silk, ornamented with golden figures and Chinese characters flying on the top of it, so that this encampment was a very pretty and picturesque object.

At a small distance from it, there was a large town, the houses of which being built of stone gave it a very superior appearance, and the inhabitants possessed all the exterior of an opulent and polished people. Here we stopped for a short time in order to receive a supply of provisions, as well as to be furnished with a body of those men whose employment it is to tow the junks. They wore a kind of uniform, and had red caps on their heads, by which their laborious profession is known and distinguished. Our eyes were very much gratified at this place by the sight of a considerable number of women, who appeared to us not only to possess fine features, but fair complexions.

At five o'clock we came to the suburbs of a very large city, and passed at least a mile along the suburbs before we reached the wall of it. From such a view as my situation would admit, and the best information I could obtain, this place is at least nine miles in circumference. Several hundred junks were moored along its wharfs, some of which were of very large dimensions. The wall is at least forty feet in height, and has a very ancient appearance. The redoubts which support the gates are such as I had not seen in China, being in the form of an half-moon. The troops were drawn out, as in other places, on our arrival, and a very brilliant illumination, exhibited by the mandarin, did not fail to dissipate the gloom of the evening.

Tuesday 5. This morning the fleet entered a large lake, adorned with a great number of beautiful islands. The most considerable of them is on the south-west side of the lake; its length is about three quaters of a mile, but not of equal breadth. It contains a mandarin's palace, with several summer houses fancifully scattered about it; the whole shaded with the finest trees, and presenting to us as we sailed by it, a most inviting scene of rural elegance. But beauty was not the only circumstance which allured our attention to this charming island; a considerable rock, an object of comparative grandeur, also rose from the midst of its groves, and was crowned with a stately pagoda.

We had no sooner passed this delightful spot, possessing so much beauty in itself, and commanding so large a portion of fine prospect around it, than we entered another river, the mouth of which is surrounded with high lands, offering the most picturesque scenery that can be imagined: thick woods, stately edifices, lofty pagodas, and mountainous shapes, with the river and the lake, all blended together in one picture, may exercise the imagination of those who read this work, but far transcends the descriptive powers of the writer of it. It may not also be unworthy of remark, that all the houses which occupy the heights surrounding this bay, are ornamented with gilt pyramids or pinnacles, which rise from the roof, and give some of the buildings the appearance of Gothic architecture.

This river, as might be expected, soon brought us to a town, where the soldiers, which were drawn up on either side of the water to salute the fleet, were different from those we had already seen, by the variety of their dress and the colour of their standards; which were now multiplied into white, scarlet, orange, light and dark blue and green.

A mandarin's palace, very finely ornamented with painting, gilding, and silken streamers, a river crowded with junks, and a charming country on either side of it, were the only objects that presented themselves to us, till we arrived before the city of Mee-you-mee-awng. The walls are of great height, and guarded by towers; while a kind of glacis slopes down from the foot of it to a meadow, agreeably planted with trees that stretch along the side of the river, and add very much to the beauty of the place.

Here the fleet anchored for a short time to take in the usual supply of provisions; and, from the general appearance of the city, as well as of the adjacent country, they both seemed to have been formed by the hand of commerce itself for the purposes of navigation.

Beauty of situation might also be added to the abundance of its productions; for the banks of the river that passed before its walls, when they rose into height, were covered with hanging woods and gardens, which gave a charming variety to the transient scene.

To these pleasing objects succeeded one of a very different nature, and, by its contrast, acquired an additional importance. It was no less than a body of soldiers drawn up on an esplanade; the line of which, extending near a mile, divided into companies distinguished by the variety of their uniforms, and enlivened by the number, as well as colour of their standards, offered a very beautiful spectacle.

No other object for some time attracted our notice, except a small dock yard for building junks, enclosed in a fine grove, which formed a pretty picturesque scene.

The river now appeared to be proceeding boldly on into a rich, fertile country, but of more unequal surface than any we had yet seen; when, by an unexpected meander, it brought us back to the city of Mee-you-mee-awng, to astonish us with the extent of it. Here we passed through another large bridge and near a circular bastion which commanded, by its battery, every direction of the river.

On another turn of the stream, a very fine hill rose up, as it were, before us, whose summit is crowned with a magnificent pagoda, and whose declivities have all the decoration that could be conferred on them by beautiful gardens and elegant buildings. At the foot of this elevated spot are two stone arches, or gateways, which open to a walk that winds gradually up the hill to the pagoda.

The palace of the mandarin, of whose garden this hill appeared to form a part, is situated on the banks of the river, from whence a broad flight of steps ascends to the gate of the outer court. This edifice is perfectly suited, both in its size and appearance, to the dignity of its possessor. Like other buildings of the same kind and character in China, it is perfectly uniform in all its parts. The body of the house rises to three stories, and the wings are diminished to two. A paved court occupies a large space in the front; and the whole is endosed by a wall, including a large garden, that extends to the beautiful hill, of which a very inadequate sketch has been already given. The country continues to make great advances in landscape beauty; fields full of fertility, with their thick and shady enclosures; farms embosomed in orchards; villas, and their gardens, we have long continued to see: but now the mountain rises before us, not rugged and barren, but verdant to its very top; while innumerable herds of cattle, and flocks of sheep, hang down its sloping pastures.

Another town soon succeeded; and to that a lake, surrounded by hills of the same kind, and covered with the same inhabitants as those which have just been mentioned. From this enchanting spot our fleet passed through a lock, and between a drawbridge, into a canal, that divides another large commercial town. Here we saw a brick-kiln, and a great pile of bricks just made: they appear to be composed of a kind of sand, mixed up with the mud of the river. The kiln itself is built of the materials which it makes, and is in the form of a sugar loaf.

In the evening we passed a large walled city, containing all the circumstances of the various places of that description which have been already enumerated. Several pagodas were illuminated on the occasion, and had a very pretty appearance amid the gloom of night.

Chapter XVIII

The voyage continued. – A succession of various objects. – The elegant attentions of a mandarin to the embassy. – Captains of the junks punished for embezzling the provisions supplied for the use of the Ambassador and his suite. – Husbandry of the Chinese. – Preparations for sending the heavy baggage belonging to the embassy to Chusan; several persons of the suite ordered to accompany it. – Arrive at Hoang-tchew. – Captain Mackintosh, and the other gentlemen, set off for Chusan.

1793, November, Wednesday 6. A TOWN which we entered this morning, had a very dismal appearance, from the colour of the houses, which are all built of a black brick. They were, however, much more lofty than any we had yet seen in China; some of them rising to four stories; and there were very few indeed that had less than two.

We passed beneath a very handsome bridge of three arches, that appeared to be of recent erection. It was built in the manner of our bridges in England; the center arch occupying a much larger span, and rising to an higher elevation than the lateral ones. On the parapet, over the former, were six round small stones, by way of ornament, with Chinese characters engraven on them.

The mandarin's palace, a very singular structure, immediately attracts the attention on passing the bridge near which it stands.

On each side of the principal gate are two lofty walls, painted of a red colour, to prevent the building from being seen but in a front view of it. The gateway is very much encircled with sculpture; and the usual accompaniments of Chinese characters: it is of stone, and supports an apartment. The house itself is painted of different colours, with a stone gallery in front, and covered with a roof of the same material.

The mandarin who resided here had given to his hospitality the most elegant appearance. He had caused a temporary stage, or platform to be erected, from the palace to the side of the river, in case the Ambassador, and the mandarins, should find it convenient to land. The roof of this building was covered with silk of every colour; a great number of lamps were suspended from it, fancifully adorned with gauze and ribands, and the floor was covered with a fine, variegated matting. But this was not the whole of the elegant attentions which were exerted by the mandarin on the occasion as he had caused a large screen, or curtain, of this matting, to be fixed on the opposite side of the water, in order to hide some ruinous buildings that would otherwise have disgraced the gay picture he had contrived, by their deformity.

The soldiers, under the command of this mandarin, were of a different appearance from any we had seen. They wore red hats, with a very high and pointed crown; on the side of which was a brass plate, that appeared to be fastened with yellow ribands.

Towns, locks, bridges, and pagodas fill continued to appear in an hasty and astonishing succession. In the afternoon, a very large country residence was seen at some distance, with a very lofty pagoda rising, as it perspectively appeared, from the center of it. The tower terminated in a cupola, with a spiral ornament rising from the top, crowned with a ball, from each side of which a chain hung down till it touched the upper story of the building.

Soon after we had passed this structure, the banks of the river were, for a considerable distance, so high, as to obscure all view of the adjacent country.

When the fleet came so anchor, the grand mandarin visited all the junks, in consequence of a complaint that had been made against some of the captains of them for embezzling the provisions which were daily supplied for the use of the embassy. After a severe examination into this business, the mandarin was so convinced of the truth of the charge, that the persons accused were immediately sentenced to be bam-booed: they were accordingly stretched on the ground, and being held down by two soldiers, were struck in a very violent manner across the hips, till the judge gave a signal for the punishment to cease.

Thursday 7. It had been a very foggy night, and the weather continued to be hazy till ten o'clock, when. the fog cleared away, and a fine day succeeded, which unfolded to the view a charming and fertile country, bounded by hills, whose summits were crowned with pagodas.

I, this day, caught a transient view of the practical husbandry of the country; as the different operations of digging, manuring, and ploughing were observable in fields on the river's side. But though the Chinese farmers certainly produce as fine crops of grain as any I have ever seen in Europe, this circumstance must arise from the sole efforts of persevering labour, as their agricultural utensils appear to be of a very clumsy form and inconvenient mechanism.

In the course of this day we passed through a noble arch, and entered a very large town, whose houses, which are, many of them, so lofty as to reach to three stories, are covered with plaster, and universally painted black. After a course of at least two miles through this fable city, we passed beneath another arch of dimensions equal to that through which we had entered it.

Another town, of the same size and appearance, soon succeeded; where, as a part of the houses, on the side of the river, projected a small space over it, the men who towed us could be of no service, and the junks were dragged forwards very slowly by boats.

The continual intersection of canals, with the succession of lakes and rivers, may be supposed to have perplexed a more keen observation than mine; and, in the extraordinary succession of objects, I may not have always been correct as to the exact character of the water on which we sailed: the rivers may have sometimes assumed the form of canals, and the canals have sometimes expanded into the appearance of rivers; but if I should, at any time, have mistaken the one for the other, either from inaccuracy of observation, or the hurry of the moment when I wrote those remarks from whence this volume is formed, such an accidental circumstance will not operate as to the more particular and important information of it. I shall not, however, hesitate to consider it as a very noble river, which brought us beneath the walls of the city of Chaunopaung, that were crowded with its inhabitants to see us pass: and as the stream soon bore us from it, there was no opportunity to observe whether it had any circumstance of novelty worthy of record.

Friday 8. At noon the junks came to an anchor in the country; when his Excellency sent for several persons of his suite, to inform them of the regulations which would take place on their arrival at Hoang-tchew, that they might make the necessary arrangements. They were as follows:

All the heavy baggage was intended to be forwarded from Hoang-tchew to Chusan, in order to be put on board the Hindostan, and conveyed by sea to Canton. It was accordingly ordered, that no person should retain any thing but what might be necessary for present use, as the junks which would shortly receive us, were not sufficiently large to carry heavy cargoes.

It was also settled, that Lieutenant-colonel Benton, Doctor Dinwiddie, and Mr. Alexander, were to accompany Captain Mackintosh to Chusan: four servants, and two mechanics, to take care of the stores, were also to attend upon those gentlemen. The rest of the suite were to accompany his Excellency, and I was of that number,

Saturday 9. The country still continued to be as we have for some time described it. As we proceeded, the country became more unequal, the pagodas, which are almost always placed on heights, seemed to multiply; and there were few of them that did not reach to seven or eight stories. As for towns and villages there was a continual succession of them: and when they did not cover the banks of our river, they appeared at a distance, where we might suppose them to be reflected by same other water.

At three o'clock in the afternoon, the fleet was ordered to anchor in the open country, near the shore, when the mandarin, Van-Tadge-In, came round to each junk; the owners of which he ordered into his pretence, and, after a short examination, commanded every one of them to be bambooed: though I could never learn the offence which produced this example of summary justice.

Sunday 10. This morning the air was extremely cold and piercing. We passed several plantations of tallow-trees, and arrived at Hoang-tchew in the afternoon, when the whole fleet came to anchor in a principal part of the city.

The junks were now fastened together, and orders were issued to forbid any person belonging to the suite to go on shore. Indeed, as it appeared, to prevent any attempt of that kind, a body of Chinese soldiers pitched their tents in the street opposite the junks, and formed a little camp there, to do duty over the embassy.

In the same street there were also several erections like

triumphal arches, where the mandarins used to come every day, to sit in state, and, as we were informed, to consult on the affairs of the city.

Monday 11. No circumstance of any moment happened from this time, till the Thursday following, which was the day of our departure; and the business of arranging and dividing the baggage, according to the orders issued for that purpose, did not allow us much leisure for observation, if any thing had occurred worthy of attention: but the truth is, nothing did occur, except the never-ceasing uproar of the inhabitants of the city, who were continually flocking to the junks to take a view of us.

On Wednesday night the attendant mandarin passed through all the junks, and requested that the different articles of the baggage should have the respective names of Chusan, or Canton, written upon them, according to their respective destination; which was no sooner completed, than those consigned to the former place were sent off by coolies to the depot appointed to receive them.

The Ambassador ordered ten dollars to be given to the owners of each junk, for their respective crews.

Thursday 14. Lieutenant-colonel Benson, Doctor Dinwid die, Mr. Alexander, with the servants and mechanics already mentioned, set off this morning, to proceed with Captain Mackintosh, to join the Hindostan at Chusan.

CHAPTER XIX

The Ambassador, with his suite, proceed through the city of Hoang-tchew to the Green river, where they embark. – Formalities on the occasion. – Circumstances of the voyage. – Description of the country.---Respect paid to the Ambassador. – Leave the junks, and proceed by land. – Mode of conveyance. – Embark in other junks. – The voyage continued.

1793, November, Thursday 14. The Ambassador, after having received the farewell visit of the mandarin of Hoang-tchew, set off, with his whole retinue, for the Green river, where they were to embark in junks of a lesser burthen. His Excellency was carried in a Palankin, and the rest of the suite in a kind of sedan chair. The guards, commanded by Lieutenants Parish and Crewe, preceded the cavalcade.

On passing through the city gates, the embassy was saluted with three guns. The distance between the two rivers could not be less than seven miles, the whole of which was covered by the city and suburbs of Hoang-tchew. The streets were lined, on either side, with soldiers, or it would have been impossible to have passed, from the prodigious crowds of people whom curiosity had collected on the occasion.

The streets of this city are very narrow, but well paved; and the houses, which are two and three stories high, being uniformly built of brick, have a very neat appearance. The warehouses of the merchants exceed any I ever saw, both for splendour and magnitude while the shops are fitted up, both within and without, in a style of the greatest elegance. Their goods, whether inclosed in packages, or displayed to view, were disposed in the most pleasing and attracttive mode of arrangement. Hoang-tchew is a very magnificent, populous, and opulent city, maintaining by its commerce the immense number of its inhabitants; and is the capital of a province to which it gives a name.

At noon his Excellency arrived at the Green river, on whose banks a very large body of troops, all armed with helmets, and accompanied with a large corps of artillery, were drawn up in regular order: the whole consisting, as it appeared, of several thousand men; the grandeur of whole appearance was enlivened by a great number of gaudy standards and ensigns. The artillery troops were dressed in blue, and had figures of the ordnance embroidered on their cloaths by way of distinction. They consisted of several companies, which were stationed in the center, and on the flanks of the lines. Their cannon were by much the largest we had seen in China: and as the British cavalcade passed through two very elegant triumphal arches, it was saluted by a discharge of artillery.

The river being very shallow towards the shore, the junks lay at the distance of fifty yards from it, and were ranged in a line close to each other. A platform was erected from the triumphal arch to the junk appointed to receive the Ambassador, which consisted of a great number of carts fastened together, with split bamboos laid across them.

The multitudes of people assembled to see the embarkation were so great, that I should hazard credibility were I to express my opinion of them. Besides the crowds which were on foot, great numbers were mounted on buffaloes, or drawn in carts by the same animals, who were tame and docile as our oxen. Some of them had three or four persons on their backs at the same time, whom they bore with great ease, and were submissive to their riders. The buffalo is very much used in this country in every kind of draught labour, and particularly in the occupations of husbandry.

On entering these junks, they were found, though of small dimensions, to be fitted up with great neatness and peculiar accommodation. At five o'clock in the afternoon the whole fleet was unmoored, and proceeded on its voyage.

Friday 15. I went on board the store junk, where I saw the mandarin, Van-Tadge-In, examining one of the people belonging to it, concerning some misdemeanor he had committed. The poor culprit was ordered to be punished with a bastinada, and he accordingly received two dozen strokes with a bamboo across the thighs.

The greater part of this day's voyage was between ranges of mountainous country, offering a great variety of romantic and picturesque scenes. The intervening vallies were covered with the tallow and mulberry trees; from the former of which the Chinese make their candles, which are of a superior quality. This tree is here called the latchoo, and is remarkable for the beauty of its appearance: it is the size of an apple tree, having scarlet leaves edged with yellow, and blossoms of a pale purple. The mulberry tree is cultivated in China with great care, for the produce of silk, which is a principal article of Chinese commerce.

We this day passed several small villages, and a walled city, named Syountong: it is situated about three quarters of a mile from the river, and near a large forest that shades the country about it.

This part of the river, though very broad, is seldom more than two or three feet in depth, and in no place more than four. The water has a green hue, and the bottom is gravel. The beach, however, is a mixture of sand and stones.

In the evening of this day we were very much delighted with a view of the city of Zau-guoa in a state of magnificent illumination. The troops were also drawn up on the banks, as we perceived by their lanterns; and from the number of them, as well as the brilliant appearance of the place, there was every reason to consider it as in the first rank of Chinese cities. The Ambassador was saluted here as he had been by a great number of forts in the course of the day.

Saturday 16. The weather was exceedingly cold, accompanied with rain.

We passed several stone pagodas of a greater height than any we had yet seen, some of them reaching to nine stories. The environs of the river still continued to be mountainous and full of picturesque beauty, heightened by the fancy and singular genius of the inhabitants, both as to cultivation and ornament. Large plantations of the tallow and mulberry tree occasionally appeared, to vary and enliven the succession of delightful views which unfolded themselves as the stream bore us along.

The salutes of artillery were now become so frequent, that they were tiresome; as the banks of the river are, in a great measure, lined with forts, which expended their gun-powder in doing honour to the embassy. It may, indeed, be said, with a strict regard to truth, that in our long voyage through this kingdom, we had never proceeded a single mile without receiving the salute of some fort or military cantonment: nor were these honours altogether confined to the sides of the river; for this evening the fleet was an object of respect from a body of troops at a considerable distance, as we could judge from their illumination; which had a very pleasing effect.

Sunday 17. About three o'clock in the morning I was awakened by a very heavy discharge of artillery; and instantly quitting my bed, I perceived by the number of lanterns, that a very large body of men were drawn up on the shore: but this was not all; for a lighted torch was fixed to the carriage of every gun, and the bearer of each stand of colours was also distinguished by a flambeau, which gave new brilliance and effect to the military illumination.

In an early part of the afternoon the fleet anchored opposite to a small, but very pretty town; on the banks of the river; and, in a short time, the conducting mandarin visited the junks, to convey to the whole of the Ambassador's train, according to their rank, presents of perfumes, fans, imperial tea, and nankeen.

Monday 18. We now seemed to have quitted the mountainous country for an extensive plain, covered with plantations of the tallow and mulberry tree, intermixed with villages, and the ornamented habitations of mandarins; some of which were faced with a lead-coloured plaster bordered with white;—an arrangement of colours not uncommon in our own country, whether applied to the furniture of houses, or the dress of ladies.

The provisions which we now received, though by no means deficient in quantity, were far inferior in quality to those we received in the former part of our journey; which we were made to understand arose from the nature of the country, rather than from any inattention to the comfort and convenience of the embassy. Indeed, there could be no reason to suppose that the Emperor had not even been anxious to render our departure from his kingdom as agreeable as respect and exterior honour could make it. In short, from Tartary to Canton, it was a chain of salutes, which were so frequent, as I have before observed, that it might be compared almost to a train of wild-fire laid from one end of the empire to the other.

I saw a group of water-mills, consisting of ten or twelve of them, all turned by a small cut from the river, which made a circuit round a meadow where they were erected: they bore an exact resemblance to our flour-mills in England, and appeared to be worked on the same principle: they were now, however, become very common objects. Those, which I have now mentioned, were employed, as I understood, in threshing rice. Among the various circumstances common to the country, we this day saw a pagoda that rose to the height of eleven stories.

The fleet anchored at night before the gates of the city of Tooatchou.

Tuesday 19. The country in some degree returned its former appearance; the plains on each side being backed by a long range of mountains rising in the horizon.

The fleet anchored this morning before a very considerable village, to wait for the junks of Lord Macartney and Sir George Staunton, which had fallen considerably astern.

Wednesday 20. Soon after dinner the whole fleet was moored opposite to a large town, a spot which offered such a display of beautiful and contrasted objects, as I never remember to have seen. The river was, of course, the central object of the picture: on one side of it was a town with all its peculiar circumstances; and before it a military encampment with all its gay and gaudy decorations. On the other side was a range of lofty, perpendicular mountains.

The rest of this day was passed in making preparations for proceeding a short way by land; in order to embark in other junks.

Thursday 21. At an early hour the Ambassador and his whole train disembarked, and proceeded in palankins, sedans, and bamboo chairs, or on horse-back, as they severally chose: for, in all our expeditions by land the mandarin, Van-Tadge-In, always consulted the suite as to the mode of travelling they preferred, and never failed in accommodating them according to their respective inclinations.

The cavalcade proceeded but a short way, before we entered a walled city of considerable extent, and with very large suburbs, called Chanfoiyeng. It is situated in a valley formed by two large hills, and about a quarter of a mile from the river. On the summit of one of these eminences is a pagoda of a very ancient construction, and flat the top, instead of being crowned with a turret, or rising to a point, like those which every moment presented themselves to our view. On passing through the gates of this city, both as we entered and paired out of it, the Ambassador was honoured, as usual, with a discharge of artillery. The streets were very narrow and lined with shops, fitted up with that interior arrangement and display of commodities, as well as exterior decoration, which distinguished so many of the towns which we had visited.

After passing another walled city, and seven villages, which were also surrounded with walls, we arrived about one o'clock at the city of Sooeping, where dinner was already prepared. The remainder of our journey was along a good road, through a fertile country varied by hills; till, after passing, and surprising by our appearance, a succession of villages, we arrived at five o'clock at the city of Yoosaun, and were introduced to the house of a mandarin, opposite to the wharf where the junks lay at anchor, in which we were to continue our voyage. The baggage of the embassy had arrived before us, and was distributed in the several courts of the building. After being refreshed with tea, every one was busy in seeing their baggage properly stowed on board their respective junks; and, in the evening, the Ambassador and his whole retinue were safely embarked, and not only ready, but anxious to proceed on their voyage.

Friday 22. The rain was without intermission through the whole of this day, so that the junks were prevented from quitting their situation; a circumtance that did not fail to exercise the patience of the passengers of every rank, who had not yet learned to prefer the accommodations, however well contrived, on board a junk moored to a wharf, to the comforts of an housc on the shore.

CHAPTER XX

The voyage continued. – Curious circumstances of the banks of the river. – The embassy leaves the junks for vessels of a larger size. – Circumstances of the voyage. – Appearance of the country. – Presents from the mandarin of Tyaung-shi-senna. – Brief account of tombs and sepulchres. – Pass the tomb of Saunt-y-tawn, and a cluster of three cities. – Arrive at Chinga-foo.

1793, November, Sunday 24. THE fleet had sailed in the night, and anchored early in the morning before a large city called Mammenoa.

The river now flowed between a range of huge unconnected masses of stone, which, as they did not appear to be rooted in the earth, cannot be called rocks or craggs, but had all the appearance of having been disjointed and thrown about by some strange convulsion of nature. In the interstices between them there were veins of earth of different appearances, but not in regular strata; some of them were of a deep brown or black colour, others were yellow; and they were occasionally intermixed with sand and gravel. In some parts I observed people cutting the stone into the shape of bricks, and in others, there were large heaps of them, which were of a deep red. Several of these huge stones had been excavated with great labour, and formed a sort of dwelling, many of whose inhabitants came forth to see our fleet pass along before them. Some of the intervals between these stones were of sufficient extent to admit of gardens with their buildings and pagodas, which produced very picturesque, romantic, and delightful pictures. When the country, which is in the highest state of cultivation, was let in through the open spaces between these stones, it produced a curious and pleasing perspective. This very singular and stupendous scenery continued, for a length of several miles, with little change, but what arose from the lesser or greater magnitude of the objects, and the occasional decorations of art in buildings and ornamented gardens.

In the afternoon the fleet anchored before the city of Hoa-quoo, where we were agreeably surprised to receive orders for the removal of the embassy into larger junks, in which we should find a very pleasing change in our accommodations and comforts. These junks were hauled up along-side those which we then occupied, and, in a very short time, the whold of the baggage was shifted into them.

Here the grand mandarin of Hoa-quoo sent to each junk, except that which contained the soldiers, two cases of various fruits, and as many boxes of sweet cakes and confectionary.

Monday 25. The rain which had continued almost without ceasing for the last two days, abated, and the weather became moderate. The city of Quiol-shee-sheng, where the fleet anchored for some time, has nothing remarkable but its wall, which is built of the red bricks that I mentioned yesterday.

The appearance of the country was as beautiful as cultivation could make it; with a few rocks of red stone occasionally breaking the level of it. Near to some of them there appeared to be quarries where the people were hewing the large stones into smaller pieces; of the same size and figure of those already described.

The river had this day a more busy appearance than it had yet assumed, from the great number of rice mills which were at work on this part of it.

Tuesday 26. The fog of this morning so far obscured the country, as to render the distant parts altogether imperceptible. At noon, however, the atmosphere became clear, and the eye ranged over a flat, but, as usual, fertile range of country, which, as far as I could distinguish, abounded in fields of rice: but the broadest and most uninterrupted level never presented a dull or uninteresting prospect in any part of China through which we had passed; as the seats of the mandarins and their gardens, with the farm-houses embosomed in trees, and the long line of thickets that frequently forms the inclosures of fields, compose a picture which, though it may not be altogether suited to the canvass, is very pleasing to the eye in its natural appearance.

The provisions with which the junks had been for some time supplied, were of so bad a quality, that we frequently gave them to the poor people who conducted the vessels. This day, however, brought us the hope of better fare, by an improvement in the quality of the various articles which were now sent on board: but our table sunk again, on the succeeding day, to that state of mediocrity to which we had been habituated sinee our departure from Huangtchew.

Wednesday 27. The morning was very cold and hazy:—the thermometer sunk to forty-six degrees.

I saw several fields where the farmers were busy in ploughing, and in which branch of husbandry they use buffaloes. We were surprised also with a very unusual sight, which was a village of mud houses or huts, where the appearance of the inhabitants was as wretched as their dwellings. This circumstance I was not able to reconcile to the general industry of the inhabitants; and, particularly, in that abundant part of the country, where it appeared, to me at least, that industry could always find a comfortable support.

The suite this day received from the mandarin a present of

caddies of tea to every person who composed it.

Thursday 28. From the breadth of the river, the strength of the current, and boisterous wind, the waves run high, with a violent surf. Here the astonishing navigation of the river was varied by a fleet of fishing-boats, consisting of at least an hundred sail; and, during the whole of this day's voyage, we continually encountered little squadrons of them.

In the afternoon we passed the city of Tyaung-shi-sennau, which is not only one of the largest places we had yet seen, but the most commodiously situated for commerce, being near the conflux of several rivers; nor can I be accused, with justice, of the least exaggeration, when I assert, that there were not less than a thousand junks at anthor before it.

Almost opposite to this city, but situated on another branch of the river, is a large town in an elevated position, but not surrounded with a wall, which is called Tsua-seenga. Nor can I resist making the observation, that, however I might be amused with the variety of prospects, and novelty of objects which continually solicited and rewarded my attention, I never felt an interval of astonishment at the villages, towns, and cities, with which, if I may use the expression, the banks of this river were thronged; as well as the myriads of people that they poured forth as we passed by, or anchored near them.

The grand mandarin of Tyaung-shi-senna came on board the Ambassador's junk, with a numerous train of attendants, to visit his Excellency. This ceremonial was accompanied with presents of silks, pieces of fine scarlet cotton, various coloured stuffs, elegant smelling bottles, pieces of porcelain, and caddies of the finest tea.

Friday 29. A village, whose houses are all built with a blue brick, and roofed with pantiles of the same colour, was the only object in this day's voyage that possessed any circumstance of novelty. The cities, mandarins' palaces, and pagodas, did not differ, as far as we could judge, from those which the reader may think, perhaps, have been too often described. The prospect of the country was sometimes interrupted by banks of sand which continued for many miles, on each side of the river.

We passed two brick kilns, with a small villlage around them, built for the accommodation of the workmen employed in the manufactory. We could form some judgment of the trade of the place by the large quantity of bricks raised in regular piles; both of those which were burned, and such as were ready for the kiln. This place is called Yu-was, which signifies, as I was informed, a furnace for making bricks.

Saturday 30. A city, at the distance of two miles from the river, surrounded with meadows and orchards, and a very pretty small town, with several detached villages scattered about it, were the only objects which gratified our attention in the early part of this day. As we proceeded, the prospect was more delightful than the imagination can conceive; not merely from the beauty of the objects, but their contrast to each other. On one side of the river a verdant plain of vast extent, covered with herds of cattle and flocks of sheep, stretched on to a range of lofty mountains that rose boldly in the horizon; while the whole country on the opposite side of the river was shaded with forests, in whose openings we could distinguish the humble cottage of the peasant, and the painted palace of the mandarin.

Cities and towns, as usual, continually appeared on each bank of the river; and having passed a small lake, we came to a village surrounded with trees, and distinguished by the ruins of a pagoda. The part that remained consisted of three stories, and that which had fallen, lay in fragments about it.

The river, which was very unequal in its size, as well as depth, now expanded into great breadth; and as the wind blew fresh, the current swelled into what might almost be called a rough tea. The waves were so violent, that the junk in which I sailed, was in great danger of being overset.

December, Sunday 1. The thermometer was sunk so low as forty degrees, and the fields were covered with frost. The country was, for some time, bounded on either side by beautiful mountains, which sunk at length into one unvarying level; where fields of rice, and flourishing orchards, were those branches of cultivation which we could best distinguish.

I mentioned, on a former occasion, that there were no public cemeteries, or places of burial, but in the vicinity of large towns and cities; and that, at a distance from them, the spot where a person dies always affords him a grave. Hence it is that the whole country may be considered as a place of burial; and we could never turn our eyes on either bank of the river, but some trophy of death appeared, of rude construction, or more elegant form, according to the rank and opulence of the victim. Nay, it is not uncommon among the Chinese, to erect, during their lives, those sad repositories, which are to contain their remains, when they are no longer numbered among the living. A greater number than usual of these solemn objects, and of more distinguished form than are generally seen, attracted our attention in this part of our voyage, and suggested the preceding observations.

The town of Taung-fong-au, by which we now sailed, has nothing to distinguish it from those which every hour presents to us, but the pleasing circumstance, that is not common to all of them, of its being surrounded with meadows, groves, and gardens.

The town of Saunt-y-tawn, containing several elegant pagodas, which were seen above the groves that surrounded it, was a very pleasing and picturesque object. A succession of timber yards covered the banks of the river, and a large quantity of timber was soaking in the water before them, which I understood to be in a state of preparation for building junks; a principal business of the place. It must, indeed, be a principal business of the country at large; for when the internal commerce of China is considered, and that almost the whole of it is carried on in these vessels, on the numerous rivers and canals which every where intersect, and form a communication through, the greatest part of this extensive kingdom; the quantity of timber used, and the number of artificers employed, in the construction of them must render any attempt at calculation an idle presumption in a person under such confined circumstances as myself.

The quantity of gunpowder expended in paying military respect to the diplomatic fleet, has, I fear, been already repeated; but I cannot omit that the Ambassador received, this day, more than usual honour from the artillery of May-taungo, a very considerable fortress on the bank of the river.

On the other side of the water is a very stately pagoda, built on an elevated spot, with a small village scattered about it. It may be supposed to belong to the mandarin, whose country residence is at a small distance from it. Art and nature have equally combined to form the seenery of this charming place; but the most distinguishing circumstance of it is its contiguity to a cluster of three cities, which are separated by the interval of a quarter of a mile from each other. Their names are, Loo Dichean, Morrinn Dow, and Chic-a-foo. The latter is built on a large sand bank in the middle of the river, but they are, all of them, more remarkable for their situation than their extent; or, as it appeared, their commercial importance. Of brick-kilns, indeed, there were plenty about them; and at a small distance I saw vast columns of smoke, which rose, as I was informed, from the furnace of a porcelain manufactory.

In the evening we arrived at the city of Chinga-foo; where,

from the crowd of people, the bustle made by the attendants of the mandarin, with the discharge of artillery, and the firing of rockets, such a scene of noise and confusion took place, as would have alarmed the whole British embassy on its first arrival in this country.

Several temporary buildings were erected on purpose, as it appeared, to display a complimentary illumination of great magnificence, which was formed by a profusion of lamps, candles, and flambeaux.

A present of fruit and confectionary concluded the attentions which were received during our anchorage before this city.

CHAPTER XXI

The voyage continued; various circumstances of it. — Pass the ruins of an ancient building. — Peculiar modes of fishing in China. — Extraordinary custom of employing birds in catching fish. — Pass several cities, towns, etc. — Arrive at Yoo-jenn-au; its beautiful situation. — The junks anchor before Kaung-jou-foo. — The reception of the Ambassador.

1793, December. THOUGH this country abounds in a succession of never ceasing variety to the traveller, it will not, I fear; possess that pleasing appearance in the opinion of the reader; as it is impossible to convey, by words, that diverfifying character to the page of a printed book, which is seen in every leaf of the volume of nature.

The slightest bend of the river presents a new prospect, or a new view of what has been already seen. Every city differs from the last; no two villages have the same form; and a multiplicity of circumstances occur, which occasion decided differences in the landscape figure of similar objects, that are incommunicable by any art of verbal description. Thus, I fear, it will prove, that, while the writer is receiving pleasure from the variety of objects that occur to his memory, he is preparing dullness for the reader by an enumeration of them.

The weather continued to be cold. — The river, for several miles, was flanked on each side by a range of hills; but the open country again appeared with its usual accompaniments of villages, towns, and cities. These, however, were now relieved by the contrasted appearance of a magnificent wood, or forest, that spread over a great extent of country.

The season of the year was now unfavourable for rural prospects, but still the country, almost every hour, presented scenes that would appear on the canvass with great advantage, if represented there by the pencil of a master. Though the frequency of pagodas may, sometimes, produce too much uniformity in the prospects of China, there are certain situations which receive a very great addition, taken in a picturesque view, from that kind of building.

The city of Fie-cho-jennau was so obscured by the plantations of trees about it, that we could not altogether judge of its extent; though we had now been long enough in China to have other criterions, by which we could determine on the size or commerce of any place, besides personal examination of it. The number of junks which were anchored near it told the general date of its trade, while the crowd of spectators who came to gaze at us, or the number of soldiers who were drawn up to salute us, were sufficient indications of its extent and population. Of Fie-cho-jennau we had no other means to form an opinion, but they were sufficient to satisfy us that it was in the first class of Chinese cities.

Tuesday 3. We, this morning, passed by the ruins of an ancient building; but to what purpose it had been originally applied, whether as a temple, created by some great mandarin for his private worship, or a banqueting house for his private pleasure, I shall not pretend to determine; though the opinion of those I could consult was in favour of the former suggestion. It had once been a considerable edifice, and the apartments that still remained were ornamented with shell-work. The dilapidated part of that building formed a large heap of stones and rubbish. It was called by the people on board the junks, Wha-zaun.

It is altogether unnecessary when we enter upon any hilly or mountainous country, to mention the addition of pagodas, which never fail to accompany it; as that command of prospect which is possessed by elevated situation, forms the delight of these buildings, while the height of them marks the dignity of wealth of those to whom they belong.

Situation is an object of universal attention among the Chinese in erecting their places of residence, or of pleasure. Nor do I recollect seeing any house, or palace of a mandarin, which was not in the heart of a city, that had not been erected with a palpable view to the local circumstances about it. Sometimes they are seen in vallies, on the declivities of hills, and the banks of rivers; while their gardens never fail to have something of a romantic character given to them by artificial rocks, or ruins, and the introduction of grotesque forms of art or nature.

In the afternoon we saw a great number of fishermen, who had changed their nets for rods and lines, and were busily employed in their necessary business. The modes of catching fish in the lakes, rivers, and canals of China, are various, and some of them peculiar to that country.

In the lakes and large rivers they frequently use the kind of baited lines which are employed on board ships to catch fish in the sea. In other parts they use nets of the same kind, and in the same manner, as the fishermen in Europe. In some places they erect tall bamboo stalks in the water, to support a curtain of strong gauze, which they extend across certain channels of the rivers; and, where it is practicable, across the rivers themselves: this contrivance effectually intercepts the passage of the fish, which, from the baits thrown in or attached to the gauze, are brought there in shoals: great numbers of boats then resort to these places, and the fishermen are seen to employ their nets with great success.

It appeared, however, that the rights of fishery are as strenuously exerted in China, as in our own country: for we are informed, that none of these arts to get fish were employed but for the mandarin who possessed the shores of the river, or by those who paid a rent for the privilege.

The fish caught in the rivers which we have navigated, consist chiefly of a kind of whiting, and very fine trout, of an excellent quality; and they are in such abundance, that though the fishermen are so numerous, and the demand so great from the junks, the former gain a very good livelihood, and the latter are well supplied with a food, which the crews of them are said to prefer.

But the most extraordinary mode of fishing in this country, and which, I believe, is peculiar to it, is by birds trained for that purpose. Nor are hawks, when employed in the air, or hounds, when following a scent on the earth, more sagacious in the pursuit of their prey, or more certain in obtaining it, than these birds in another element. They are called Looau, and are to be found, as I am informed, in no other country than that in which we saw them. They are about the size of a goose, with grey plumage, webbed feet, and have a long and very slender bill, that is crooked at the point. This extraordinary aquatic fowl, when in its wild state, has nothing uncommon in its appearance, nor does it differ from other birds whom nature has appointed to live on the water. It makes its nest among the reeds of the shore, or in the hollows of crags, or where an island offers its shelter and protection. Its faculty of diving, or remaining under water, is not more extraordinary than many other fowls that prey upon fish: but the most wonderful circumstance, and I feel as if I were almost risquing my credibility while I relate it, is the docility of these birds in employing their natural instinctive powers, at the command of the fishermen who possess them, in the same manner as the hound, the spaniel, or the pointer, submit their respective sagacity to the huntsman, or the gunner.

The number of these birds in a boat are proportioned to the size of it. At a certain signal they rush into the water, and dive after the fish; and the moment they have seized the prey, they fly with it to their boat; and should there be an hundred of there vessels in the fleet, these sagacious birds always return to their own masters, and, amidst the throng of fishing junks which are sometimes assembled on these occasions, they never fail to distinguish that to which they belong. When the fish are in great plenty, these astonishing and industrious purveyors will soon fill a boat with them; and will sometimes be seen flying along with a fish of such size, as to make the beholder, who is unaccustomed to these sights, suspect his organs of vision; nay, it has been so repeatedly asserted to me as to prevent any doubt of the information, that, from their extraordinary docility and sagacity, when one of them happens to have taken a fish which is too bulky for the management of a single fowl, the rest will immediately afford their assistance. But while they are thus labouring for their masters, they are prevented from paying any attention to themselves, by a ring which is passed round their necks; and is so contrived as to frustrate any attempt to swallow the least morsel of what they take.

We also saw another fishing party, which, though it had more of ridicule than curiosity in it, I cannot forbear to describe. It consisted of at least thirty fishermen seated like so many taylors on a wide board, supported by props in the river, where they were angling. There was another groupe of these people near the shore, who had embanked a part of the river with sand, where, by raking the bottom with a kind of shovel, they caught large quantities of shrimps and other shell fish.

At an early hour in the afternoon we arrived before the city of Vang-on-chean, where the junks anchored for two hours, and the Ambassador received a visit from the grand mandarin. This place is of considerable extent, and covers the whole flat that lies between the river and a range of high mountains.

Wednesday 4. The river was for some distance enlivened by a succession of villages on each side of it. We then passed several considerable towns, which were succeeded by a double range of steep and craggy hills, with groves and thickets hanging down them; and wherever there was any flat or level spot, whether it was towards the bottom of these cliffs, or midway, or on their summits, an house was erected, which formed the most delightful and romantic scenery that can be conceived.

I have already observed, that, in this part of our travels through China, the villages were not only populous, but in general of a pleasing appearance, and that a clutter of cottages, whose exterior form betrayed internal wretchedness, is by no means a common object. This morning, however, presented us with one of them, where the habitations were, in a great measure, formed of logs of wood; but the eye had not leisure to give them more than a glance of commiseration, so very alluring were the charms of the surrounding country; where, not only the residences of persons of distinction, but the village and the farm house, are placed in the most romantic situations, and individually display the most pleasing pictures, or together, compose the magnificence of landscape.

Thursday 5. The weather was become moderate and pleasant; day s rant; but the river was so shoaly in some places, and had such a rocky bottom in others, that it was considered as dangerous to proceed after sunset.

The pencil of a master might here communicate same general idea of the peculiar beauties of the country through which we passed, and the continual variation of it; but it is not in the power of language to convey any correct image even of the individual objects, much less of the picture formed by the combination of them. When I mention that I have seen forests and gardens, mountains and vallies, the palace and the cottage, the city and the village, the pagoda and the mill, with a variety of subordinate, but heightening circumstances, in one view, I certainly inform my readers of the constituent parts of the prospect; but to give them the least notion of their actual arrangement and relative situation, of their proportions and contrast, of their general distance from the eye, and comparative distance from each other, is beyond any exertion of verbal description.

At a large town, called Yoo-jenn-au, which is situated at the foot of a very high mountain, the river whereon we had sailed so long communicates with another equally capacious with itself. The situation of this place may be in some measure conceived, when we consider its position at the influx of two large rivers, both pouring their streams from mountainous and rocky chasms, whole declivities are enriched with woods of various trees, and adorned, where they are capable of receiving ornament from the hand of art, with airy buildings and hanging gardens.

My curiosity led me to examine several houses which were building at this place, when I observed that the scaffolding before them was constructed according to the principles which the builders and bricklayers of our own country employ in similar erections.

We passed an island that divided the river into two equal channels, and which some mandarin had made the place of occasional retirement. It contained an elegant house, with groves and gardens, and formed a charming contrast to the shores of rock and sand, on either side of the water that surrounded it.

It will be sufficient to add, that the country never appeared in a more beautiful or romantic dress, by day, since we entered it; and the city of Kaung-joo-foo presented the most brilliant illumination we had seen by night.

A present of fruit, cakes, and confectionary, concluded the many complimentary attentions which the embassy received at this place.

CHAPTER XXII

The voyage continued. – The manner in which the Chinese water their fields. – Sepulchres. – Change in the appearance of the country. – Leave the river at the city of Naung-aum-foo to travel over land. – Circumstances of the journey. – Arrive at the city of Naung-chin-oa. – Some account of it. – The Ambassador re-embarks to continue the voyage down another river.

1793, December, Friday 6. IN this part of the river we saw a great number of the machines at work with which the Chinese water their grounds. They consist of a wheel made of bamboo, which is turned by the stream, and throws the water into large reservoirs, from whence it is let off by sluices into channels that intersect the fields.

The pretty village of Shaiboo, situated on an high bank of the river, is the only object that recalls the eye from wandering over the general beauty of the country; till, at the turn of the stream, the attention is solicited by the pagoda of Tau-ay, an ancient and very lofty building, whose upper story being fallen, gives it a more picturesque appearance, and is, on that account, emblematical of the little cemetery beneath it, which contains several sepulchres and other memorials of the dead. But whether this spot so appropriated belongs to any city or town, which we could not perceive, or is the burying place of any particular family of distinction, I could not learn. Though the ground at the foot of this pagoda is assigned to the dead, the upper part of the building is so situated as to delight the living by the view it affords of the surrounding country, and the windings of the river, for a very considerable distance.

I cannot omit mentioning the town of Whang-ting-taun, not merely because its environs are divided between woods and rice fields, but, as it is the only place of any importance which we have seen in our voyage of this day. Villages were, as usual, in frequent succession; and among many of them which wore the appearance of industry and comfort; we were dissatisfied with a collection of huts, that did not appear to be capable of preserving their inhabitants from the inclemency of winter, or the heat of summer.

Saturday 7. This was the most extraordinary day which we had yet known in China, as we neither saw city, town, or village, in the course of it. A few farm houses, with their orchards, were the only habitations that we saw in the extent of beautiful country through which we passed; nor could I, by any inquiries in my power to make, discover whether it arose from accident, or any local circumstance, that the banks of the river, which had so long teemed with cities, towns, and villages, with palaces and pagodas, would at once become so barren of them.

But though we were, for same time, deprived of the wonders of population, a very singular and curious object accompanied a considerable part of this day's voyage, to continue, to some degree, the exercise of our astonishment.

It was a very lofty, perpendicular, natural mound of red earth, that embanked one side of the river, whose naked surface was marked in a very extraordinary manner by horizontal veins or stripes of stone, in a direetion as perfectly rectilinear, as if they had been made with the line or the rule; and which continued without any apparent deviation, from this wonderful regularity, during a course of several miles.

The river was now become so shallow, that it was necessary to change several of the large junks for such as would draw less water, a circumstance which occasioned some delay; and it was not till eight o'clock that we passed the only inhabited place of this day's voyage; and which might now have escaped our notice, if the soldiers of the cantonment had not exhibited their paper lanterns, and discharged a few vollies of respect towards us.

Sunday 8. The weather has, for some time, been temperate and pleasant; the country also has gradually lost its fertile appearance, and is now become mountainous and barren; some of the mountains, indeed, are covered with wood, but the surface of the earth has here lost all that richness which had so long cloathed it. The population of the country may be supposed to have suffered a proportionate diminution; but the villages, though they are more thinly scattered than they have hitherto been, become more picturesque objects both from their form and situation.

The high grounds near the river, in many places, lose their abrupt and rugged appearance beneath the verdure of dwarf-trees of various kinds, among which the camphire tree is said to predominate.

But though the prospect was now become a mere succession of rude mountain and barren valley, it was sometimes enlivened by a pagoda in the distance, while the village still continued. to animate the banks of the river.

We now observed several sepulchres or funeral monuments that had been erected in various parts of the mountains, with excavations in the rocks beneath them to receive the dead. That an amiable superstition might wish to consign the remains of the parent or the child, the friend or the relation, to such a sepulchral retreat, elevated as it were above the world, and, as it might be thought by the Pagan mythology, nearer to that heaven, where their spirits were destined to wing, or had already taken their flight, is not inconsistent with the best feelings of nature and religion. But some of these places sacred to the dead appeared to us, at least, to be in such situations, as to render the attempt to gain access to them, a circumstance of no small hazard to the living.

About sunset we passed a large town called Syn-cham-au, which is situated on a small plain between the river and some high mountains covered with wood, nor is this romantic appearance lessened by a large pyramidical rock, with a very lofty pagoda that crowns its summit.

Monday 9. Two considerable towns and several villages, with their junks, were the principal objects of this day's voyage; till we arrived in the evening at the city of Naung-aum-foo. As the embassy was to make a journey of one day over land from this place, preparations were made accordingly under the usual directions of the attendant mandarin.

Tuesday 10. The Ambassador ordered four dollars to be given to the crews of the respective junks; and, after an hasty breakfast, the suite followed the baggage which had been previously sent on shore.

The landing-place was adorned with a grand triumphal arch, decorated with silk and streamers of various colours. Here I was presented with a ticket, the meaning of which I did not comprehend. I then proceeded along a kind of platform, covered with fine matting; its roof and railing were ornamented with ribands and silk, in the same manner as the triumphal arch and a range of lamps were suspended in a very elegant form on each side of it.

This platform led, to a circular court, surrounded by a screen of silk, which contained as well as I could calculate from the view of them, between two and three hundred horses, attended by their owners; and from which every person in the Ambassador's retinue was at liberty to chuse a beast for the journey of the day; as from the badness of the roads, and the length of the way, it was ordered that the whole suite, except the Ambassador, Sir George Staunton, and Mr. Plumb, should proceed on horseback. I accordingly chose an horse, for which I was obliged to deliver the ticket already mentioned. It was a very wild and mettlesome steed, which, on my first mounting him, was so restive and unmanageable, that I wished to make an exchange; but I had delivered my ticket, and was obliged to abide by my choice, such as it was.

When all the arrangements were settled, the horses selected, and the whole suite transformed into a body of cavalry, his Excellency, with Sir George Staunton, and Mr. Plumb, came from the junk to their palankins, and the cavalcade commenced, attended by a considerable body of Chinese soldiers.

Naung-aum-foo is a walled city of considerable extent, built on a rising ground above the river, and is commanded, both behind, and on the opposite side of the water, by lofty hills; on one of which is seen a solitary pagoda. Its suburbs are large, and, from the number of small junks, suited to the shallowness of the stream that washes its banks, it may be esteemed a place of some commercial character.

In about half an hour we got clear of the city, when every exterior object was lost in attending to the peculiarities of our own appearance. Such a troop of equestrians are not often seen in China, or any other, part of the world. The gentlemen of the suite, with the mechanics, soldiers, and servants, were on horseback; many of whom were but indifferent riders, and some of them now found themselves obliged to ride for the first time.

The horses themselves, on setting out, were also very frolicksome and ungovernable; so that the ridicule that attached itself to our general appearance, and the diversion which successively occurred from the cries of alarm, the awkwardness of attitude, and the various other circumstances, which the reader, without having been in China, may very readily conceive, served to amuse the tediousness of travelling through a mountainous and unproductive country.

At noon we came to the foot of a mountain, which was so steep as to make it necessary for us to dismount, and lead our horses over it: it was an ascent of two miles, which employed an hour in climbing. We passed several villages, and dined at the town of Lee-cou-au, where a confiderable body of soldiers, in armour, lined the road as we passed; and both on entering, as well as quitting the lines, the Ambassador was saluted with the discharge of three pieces of artillery. This military parade, with the variety of colours, which never failed to accompany the least appearance of soldiery, had a very pretty effect.

The women, in this part of our journey, were either educated with less reserve, or allowed a greater share of liberty, than in the country through which we had lately passed, as we frequently saw them indulging their curiosity in observing such a new and extraordinary sight as we must have exhibited.

I have already mentioned, that we had for some time exchanged a fertile for an unprofitable soil; and all the splendor of cultivation for the barren mountain. The eye was, however, sometimes relieved by large patches of camphire, and other medicinal trees; as I was informed by those who, I presume, were qualified to instruct me.

The sun had set when we arrived at the gates of the city of Naung-chin-oa. It stands in a plain, surrounded on three sides by mountains; on the fourth and to the south, flows the river on which we were to continue our voyage. It is a place of some extent and considerable commerce. The streets, like those of almost all the towns we have seen in China, are very narrow, but they have the advantage of being well paved, and equally maintained in the material article of cleanliness. The houses are chiefly of wood, and their general height is two stories. Though elegance, interior or exterior, is not the peculiar character of this place, some of the shops were gilt and varnished in a manner that might bring them within that denomination. At every door in the streets, after sun-set, a large paper lamp is hung up, and forms a very pretty illumination. These lamps display the name of the person who lives in the house, his trade, and the articles in which he traffics. The palaces of the mandarins are also ornamented with lamps, according to the dimensions of the building, or the rank of their inhabitants.

The streets were lined with soldiers to repress the curiosity of the people, which would, otherwise, have impeded our passage; and it was near seven o'clock when we arrived at the palace of the grand mandarin of the city. It is a very noble residence, composed of various courts, and several ranges of apartments. In spacious open galleries, on each side of the first court, tables were plentifully spread with tea, meats of various kinds, and fruits, for the refreshment of the inferior orders of the suite; while other galleries, that opened on the interior courts, were magnificently illuminated, and prepared for the higher department of it. In short, throughout the palace there was such a profusion of lamps and other lights, as, in my unexaggerated opinion, would serve the palace of an European sovereign for a month. But without this observation, which I believe to be founded in fact, it must have already appeared, in the course of this Narrative, that illumination is a very principal feature of Chinese magnificence.

The Ambassador and Sir George Staunton preferred going

to the junks instead of passing a night in the palace; and, accordingly, after having taken the refreshment prepared on their arrival, they repaired to them. The rest of the embassy remained on shore, and apartments were assigned them for their repose.

The baggage which was brought all the way from Naung-aum-foo on men's shoulders, arrived by degrees; but the whole of it had not reached its destination till nine o'clock; when all the mandarin's principal servants assisted, in depositing it in a long gallery, where it was arranged with the utmost regularity; each package having a ticket pasted on it, corresponding with the junk to which it was to be removed on the following day.

CHAPTER XXIII

The suite embarks on board the junks; the voyage renewed; circumstances of it. – A curious pagoda. – Description of sepulchres. – Vast rafts of timber. – Embark in larger junks. – Pass some curious mountains; a description of them. – Extraordinary illumination.

1793, December, Wednesday 11. AT an early hour of the morning the baggage was put on board the junks, with a regularity, as well as dispatch, that cannot well be described. There was a sufficient depth of water in this river to bring the junks close to the quay; so that the coolies, of which there were a great number, acting under the orders of the mandarin and his servants, and guarded by soldiers, soon transferred every article that belonged to the embassy on board the vessel to which it was specifically assigned.

The junks to which we were now removed were of less dimensions than those we had left; in conformity to the navigable state of the river, which only admitted vessels of small burthen About eleven o'clock the suite were all on board, and the whole fleet was ready for sailing. We accordingly renewed our voyage, and began it by passing under a wooden bridge of seven arches, or rather, if accuracy of expression should be considered as indispensable, of seven intervals. There intervals are formed by strong stone pillars, built in the water, and overlaid with planks, guarded by a double railing. This structure stretches across the river, to form a communication between those parts of the suburbs of Naung-chin-oa, which are divided by it. Forts garrisoned with troops, and well supplied with artillery, guarded either end of it; nor was the fleet unnoticed by them; as in passing the bridge it was honoured by the parade of the one, and the discharge of the other. The city itself is also well defended by walls, which are, at least, thirty feet in height towards the river, with ramparts that take the whole circuit of the place, and square towers which are not confined to the gates, but appear to rise above the walls in other advantageous situations.

At a small distance from the bridge the river divides into two branches, that take almost opposite directions: on that whose stream bore us along, we law a large quantity of small timber in rafts.

In the afternoon we passed a pagoda, situated on a bank of the river, which was of a more singular appearance than any of the great number of that kind of edifice which we had seen in our travels through the country. It consisted of five stories, which terminated in a flat roof, with trees growing on it. The body of the building, from many parts of which also shrubs appeared to sprout forth, was covered with a white plaster, and decorated with red paint in its angles and interstices.

The country still remained barren and mountainous; nor was its rude and dreary aspect enlivened by any appearance of cultivation. A considerable town called Chang-fang, was the only place we passed in the short voyage of this day.

Thursday 12. The natural face of the country was still dreary; and its artificial circumstances did not enliven it by their character. The mountains, as we passed by them, exhibited a great number of those sepulchres of which some description has been already given. These, as the former, were in situations not easily accessible, and varied in their appearance, as may be supposed, according to the wealth or dignity of the person whose remains they already contained, or were, hereafter, destined to inclose.

When we mentioned these solemn repositories in a former page, the thought suggested itself, that superstition might carry the dead to those high places, on the same principle that idolatry has raised its altars there: but, when it is considered that the dreary, uncultivated mountain is suited to the character of the sepulchre; and that there is, perhaps, something consolatory in the idea of that security which belongs to these awful, and almost inaccessible solitudes; we may probably approach nearer to the real motives of consigning the dead to these elevated tombs.

The general construction of them appears to be the same: it consists of an excavation in the mountain, chiseled out in the form of a large niche, which is then paved, and concealed by a wall with an ornamented door. Some of these places are covered with domes; from others pyramidical forms spring up, and the facades of them were, as far as I could distinguish, painted of a lead colour, with a white border.

These receptacles of the dead were succeeded by few habitations of the living that have any claim to particular notice or observation, till we came to the large and populous village of Ty-ang-koa. Here we saw a vast length of rafted timber floating down the river, with several bamboo huts erected on it, and the families belonging to them. Great numbers of people were also employed in bringing timber to the water side, either on their shoulders, or in waggons; while others were occupied in forming rafts.

The country still retains its barren aspect though a pagoda was occasionally seen to grace the summits of the mountains.

Friday 13. We this day passed a considerable town called Tya-waung, part of which was in ruins; and, a little further down the river, we came to the city of Shaw-choo; the suburbs of which extend to the water side, and where the houses are built in such a manner as to be in continual danger of falling on the heads of their inhabitants, and involving them in one common destruction. A wooden frame work, resting sometimes upon a foundation of clay or stone, with a few slender uprights, are the only supports of those habitations that ranged along the shore; where frequent ruins manifested the folly as well as the frailty of such architecture.

The fleet came to an anchor at the extremity of the city, before the palace of the grand mandarin, which was finely decorated with triurnpal arches: a platform was also erected from the banks of the river to the house, to accommodate the Ambassador, if his Excellency had found it convenient to go on shore. The soldiers belonging to the mandarin were also drawn up in due form, and gave the usual salute.

At this place large junks were prepared to receive the embassy; and, in a very short time, the whole suite and the baggage were removed on board them. Our accommodations were accordingly increased in proportion to the superior dimensions of the vessels that now contained us.

In the evening the grand mandarin sent the suite a very handsome present of china, together with a large supply of provisions; we also received, at a late hour in the evening, a large parcel of tobacco, some ducks cured in the manner of hams, of a very delicate flavour, together with a considerable quantity of dried fish.

The voyage was this day agreeably varied by an occasional, though not very frequent patch of cultivated ground, which, whatever might be its shape, size, or situation, was now become a cheering object.

Saturday 14. The weather was moderate and pleasant; and though there appeared a very small proportion of cultivated land, the mountains were some-times cloathed with wood. The village of Shoong-koank, situated on a plain, with the river before, and an amphitheatre of mountains behind it, drew our attention as a very pleasing object, and surprised us with the number of inhabitants which it poured forth to see the strangers pass.

I have already mentioned that small portions of cultivated ground now began, though very rarely, to make their appearance: this circumstance, however, had no influence on our supplies; as the provision-boats of to-day brought us the same indifferent eatables which we had, for some time, been accustomed to.

In the evening, the hills gradually approached the river, till, at length, they closed upon it, and formed a rude and lofty barrier, which, at once, confined and obscured its channel. This scenery continued for a considerable distance, as it were, on purpose to lead the eye to a mountain of such stupendous magnitude, as the description which I am about to give, will not be able to convey, I fear, to the mind of my readers. It was so late as seven o'clock at night before we arrived at the commencement of it; but the moon shone in all her splendour, and enabled the eye to trace every part of this enormous object with less distinctness, perhaps, as to minute parts, but with better effect as to its magnificent outline.

This mountain rises from the river to the perpendicular height of at least three hundred yards. The face it presents towards the water is divided between bare rock and shaggy foliage: the upper part appears, in same places, to project, over the river, and offers a most tremendous shape to the voyagers who sail beneath it: when, therefore, to such an elevation of solid rocky mountain, with its rugged base, and craggy summits, is added the extent of near two miles of lengthening precipice, some faint notion may be entertained of this stupendous object.

Its termination is equally abrupt with its beginning: and

all its parts support the savage grandeur of the whole. On the extreme point, as we passed down the river, a pyramidical rock appeared to spring up to a considerable height above the edge of the precipice, and finished in a peak.

This immense shape is separated by an intervening plain, that extends to the foot of distant mountains, from another enormous rock; which, though of different form, and less extent, possesses the same awful and majestiic character. It rises with a steep but gradual ascent from the river to a certain height; when it shoots, up, as it were, in a bold, unvarying, perpendicular elevation, to the clouds, affording another vast example of the sublime in nature.

As a range of hills may he said to conduct us along the river to these stupendous objects, a successive boundary of the same kind continued during a course of several miles after we had left them. But it was the peculiar office of this extraordinary night to awaken our astonishment by the grand exertions of art, as well as by the enormous works of nature; for, at the conclusion of this chain of hills, that had so Iong excluded any view into the country, we were surprized with a line of light that extended for several miles over mountains and vallies, at same distance from the river, and formed one uninterrupted blazing outline as they rose or sunk in the horizon.

In some parts of this brilliant, undulating line, it was varied or thickened, as it appeared by large bands or groups of torches; and, on the most conspicuous heights immense bonfires threw their flames towards the clouds. Nor was this all, for the lights did not only give the outline of the mountain, but sometimes serpentised up it, and connected, by a spiral fieram of light, a large fire blazing at the bottom, with that which reddened the summit.

The number of lanterns, lamps, or torches employed on this

occasion, are beyond all calculation, as the two extremities of the illuminated space, taken in a strait line, and without estimating the sinkings of the vallies, or the inequality of the mountain tops, could not contain a less distance from each other than three miles. Whether these lights were held by an army of soldiers, and a very large one would have been necessary on the occasion, or were fixed in the ground, I could not learn; but it was certainly the most magnificent illumination ever seen by the European traveller, and the most splendid compliment ever paid to the public dignity of an European Ambassador. Not only a vast range of country, but the course of the river, for several miles, received the light of day from this artificial blaze. Successive discharges of artillery were, at regular distances, added to the honour of this amazing and most superb spectacle.

Chapter XXIV

The voyage continued. – Description of a curious mountain. – Various circumstances of the river. – Arrive at the city of Tuyng-yan-yean. – Pass numerous villages, towns, etc. – Anchor before the city of Tyantian – Arrive at Canton. – Formalities on the occasion, etc.

1973, December, Sunday 15. AT seven o'clock this morning the whole fleet came to an anchor beneath a mountain, which is considered by the Chinese, in respect to its elevation, figure, and extent, as one of the natural wonders of their country. It is called Koan-yeng-naum.

The grand mandarin, who had the care of conducting the embassy, with that attention which distinguished every part of his official duty, had ordered the fleet to stop in this place, in order to give the Ambassador, and his retinue, an opportunity of indulging their curiosity, by taking a view of this extraordinary mountain.

It rises perpendicularly from the water to an amazing height, and terminates in a peak. Vast pieces of the rock project from the face of it in such a manner, as to have a most tremendous and threatening aspect; nor is it easy to persuade oneself, on looking up, that they will not instantly fall and fill up the channel of the river beneath them.

Several large caverns are among the curious circumstances of this mountain. The principal of them is about forty feet above the river, and the passage to it consists of a flight of fifty steps cut out of the rock, and guarded by a rail; the whole ascent being over-shadowed by a projection of the mountain. A door, prettily ornamented with painting, opens into an handsome room of about forty feet in circumference, and nine feet in height, which contains a sacred image, to whom the Chinese, on their entrance, pay their adorations. There is also a window, chiselled through the stone, with a balcony before it, from whence there is a delightful prospect of the river. From this chamber we ascended, by an artificial staircase, to two other apartments of the same size as the former, and fitted up in a manner suited to the character of the place.

These rooms were excavated at the expense of the mandarin to whom the mountain belongs, and must have been a work of incredible labour. At the foot of the steps, an arch had been erected, with the usual decoration of silk and ribands of various colours.

Though the country still continued to be rude and uncultivated; it was, occasionally, varied by large woods that hung down the steeps, or thickened in the vallies. The ranges of mountains also, that branch, off from Koan-yeng-naum, take such different directions, as to form a variety of grand, and even sublime, picttures of nature.

At noon the fleet anchored, for a short time, before the city of Shizing-ta-heng; situated on the upper part of an inclined plain, that advances with a scarce perceptible ascent from a large sandy beach of the river, to the foot of the mountains that rise behind it. This plain is also adorned with the most beautiful trees, so that the view may be supposed to consist of a river in the fore-part of it, a fine plain, covered with plantations, stretching away from the banks, and a large city beyond it, backed by a bold unequal range of mountains. When to these circumstances are added the woods on the opposite side of the river, and the magnificent pagoda which rises before them, the beauty of the landscape may be conceived without any very uncommon stretch of the imagination.

The river in a very winding course, now afforded but little variety. The same lofty barriers continued to confine its course; and where a casual opening suffered the eye to advance beyond them, it looked towards nothing more than similar objects, with no other circumstances of variation but such as might be supposed to arise from the peularities of light and shadow and the diminution of distance.

We not only observed, but also heard the labours, of large bodies of people, who were employed in blowing up certain parts of the rocks, to obtain that alone with which the Chinese form their pavements, whether for their houses, courts, or public ways.

Beneath one of these mountains was a large village, which had a very mean appearance; and, as I afterwards learned, was entirely inhabited by the people employed in blowing up rocks, and working quarries, that were in the neighbourhood of it.

Several spires of smoke ascending from the mountains, attracted our attention; when, on making inquiry concerning the fires that occasioned them, we found that it was a process preparatory to agriculture; by burning the heath on certain parts of these elevated situations, in order to commence the experiment of cultivation.

The evening of this day was also cheered by an illumination of the distant hills; and though it did not, in any degree, equal, either in extent or splendor, that which had so lately excited our astonishment, it had a very singular effect, and exhibited a very pleasing appearance.

Monday 16. Rugged and steep rocks, some of which were

covered with wood, still continued to inclose, on either side, the channel of the river. Among them arose a large mountain, shaded by an hanging forest, which was not only a very grand object in itself, but was also accompanied with circumstances that enlivened and adorned it. At the foot of it a road had been cut out of the solid rock, and to communicate with it a large arch of stone stretches across a deep chasm. In the center of the wood, there is the palace of a mandarin, surrounded with detached offices, and at some small distance a temple which belongs to it, and contains the image which is the usual object of religious worship. There are several burying places in different parts of the wood, which are the mausoleums of the mandarin's family to whom the palace belongs. It is called Tre-liod-zau.

This magnificent object, which, on a particular turn of the river, presented itself in charming perspective, is very much heightened by a contrasted succession of bare and barren mountains.

This rude and rugged scenery, at length, began to subside; when a rich, fertile level opened again upon us; and after we had been accustomed for seven days to the bleak and barren appearances of nature, the tranquil scenes of cultivation afforded a most refreshing prospect.

We now passed the city of Tsing-yan-yenn, a place of great extent and commerce. It is surrounded by a wall whose gates are flanked by strong towers, and which extends near three miles along the river; but of its breadth we were prevented from forming any accurate judgment by the intervening groves, which appear before, and rise above, the walls. The suburbs had a mean appearance; and the houses projected over the water in the same insecure and alarming manner as I have already described; a mode of building common to all towns, and lesser places, which are situated on the banks of rivers. The great number of junks which were here at anchor announced the commercial state of the city; and the succession of timber yards, all stored with great quantities of planks, and wood for every kind of construction, marked a principal article of its trade. Several regiments of soldiers were drawn up on the beach, with a train of artillery: they were accompanied with triumphal arches, decorated in the same pretty and fanciful manner which has been already repeated of other complimentary erections of the same kind.

From this place the river takes its course in a strait, undeviating direction for three miles, between a very fertile and highly cultivated country, in which rice fields appeared to abound. The mountains, which so lately rose on the banks, seemed now to have retired, as it were, into the distance, and ranged along the horizon.

In this afternoon a very serious accident happened which might have produced the most fatal consequences it was no less than a fire in one of the inferior junks; and if great exertions had not been made, the vessal would have been very soon consumed. It was supposed to have been occasioned by a spark falling unobserved from a tobacco pipe, which, trifling as it was, threatened the junk with irresistible conflagration.

The whole fleet experieneed the good effects of the rich and fertile country which we now entered, by the improvement that was experienced in every article of our daily supplies. We this day received a large quantity of excellent provisions, with a jar of a very pleasant liquor, which is extracted from the sugar cane, and resembles in flavour the rum shrub, so well known in our own country.

The ruins of a pagoda, and some of those sepulchres which I have already mentioned, gave a picturesque appearance to the spot where they had been erected, and were the concluding objects of this day's voyage.

The weather warm and pleasant, and the country in a fine state of cultivation; while the river increased in breadth, and admitted junks of a larger size than we had yet seen.

At eleven o'clock this morning we passed the large village of Ouzchouaa, with a crowd of manufactories in its neighbourhood; whether they were in the porcelain or iron service, I could not discover; but the smoke of their furnaces told us that fire was a principal operator in them.

As we proceeded, the country increased in beauty on both sides of the river, and soon became a continued chain of pretty villages, fruitful fields, and handsome houses.

In the afternoon the provision junks still improved in their cargoes, and brought us an abundant supply of excellent provisions and fruits, with a quantity of Samptchoo, a liquor which has been already mentioned.

At eight o'clock in the evening the fleet anchored before a very large and commercial city, called Sangs-wee-yenno, when the Ambassador was saluted with an amazing discharge of artillery from all quarters of it. This mark of respect was accompanied by every other demonstration of regard that could be shewn on the occasion: triumphal arches appeared with all their gaudy, decorations; temporary pagodas were erected to heighten the artificial scenery; and a platform, such as has been already described in former parts of our voyage, was prepared to accommodate his Excellency, if it should be his wish to visit the grand mandarin. To these circumstances may be added all that illumination could do, in a country where that species of splendor is so well understood and in such continual practice: so that some notion may be formed of the manner in which the fleet was received by this city.

Wednesday 18. In the course of this morning we passed several very large and commercial towns; and, if any judgment could be formed from the unceasing discharge of artillery, it may be supposed that a chain of forts lined the shore. If we are justified also in drawing a conclusion from the numbers of people on the banks of the river, and in vessels on the water, we might believe that, from the time we sailed, which was at so early an hour as two o'clock, the fleet was passing for upwards of two hours through the middle of an immense city, which had poured forth all its inhabitants to catch such an imperfect view of us, as the early part of the morning would allow.

At the dawn of day, we came to the city of Tayn-tsyn-tau, a place of great importance and immense trade. Several thousand soldiers were drawn up along the beach, with a proportionate train of artillery, which thundered out a salute as we passed.

This city, or, perhaps, to speak more correctly, the suburbs of it, are built on each side of the river; which, for many miles, was covered with junks laden with merchandise, or preparing to receive it; and some of them were of very large dimensions.

We continued sailing before, or rather through this place, till seven o'clock, and, from the rate of our passage, I have no doubt but it is eight miles in length: of its breadth, no judgment could be formed on board the fleet; but, from the general appearance of the city, and the houses of the resident merchants, with other commercial circumstances, its trade must be immense, and its opulence, in proportion: it appeared, indeed, to be inferior only to the cities of Pekin and Canton.

The river continued to be covered with a crowd of junks; so that it was with some difficulty the fleet proceeded on its voyage, which at length approached its termination; for, about noon, it came to anchor within a mile of the city of Canton, and but two miles distant from the English factory.

In consequence of an express dispatched by the conducting mandarin to Canton, to notify the arrival of the Ambassador, several mandarins in the different departments of government, came to visit his Excellency. They were soon followed by the British commissioners, the Company's supercargoes, and Colonel Benson, a very welcome visitor, for he not only brought the public dispatches for Lord Macartney, but a large packet of private letters from England, and all the newspapers which had arrived by the last ships from Europe.

Orders were issued by the Ambassador for the whole suite to disembark on the following day.

Thursday 19. The embassy was removed into larger junks, which had been previously fitted up to go down the river.

In passing down this spacious river it is impossible to describe the magnificence of its navigation; for we saw, without exaggeration, several thousands of trading junks; nor were the vessels which were crowded with people to see us pass inferior in number; while the banks on either side were covered with houses, built very much in the style of European architecture.

There are also a succession of forts well supplied with men and artillery; and their respective garrisons were drawn out in military array on the beach before them, with their colours, music, and all the ensigns of war. These forts saluted the fleet by a successive discharge of artillery, and, indeed, the air resounded for near an hour with the repeated firing of great guns from every quarter.

There were also several thousand soldiers in military junks, who added the compliment of their musquetry. It was a very large army both on land and water, and the whole of them sunk down on their knees, as a manœuvre of military respect, till the Ambassador had passed. At one o'clock we arrived opposite the English and Dutch factories; when both of them saluted his Excellency with a discharge of artillery, and instantly hoisted the standards of their respective nations.

Here we saw a great number of boats, containing all kinds

of provisions, fruits, and merchandize, for sale. They rowed backwards and forwards, announcing, at the same time, their various commodities with very violent vociferation, as is seen and heard among the owners of provision-wherries on the Thames.

It appeared very singular to us, that most of the boats which we had seen for several days, were rowed and steered by women. It is not, indeed, by any means, uncommon to see a woman, with a child tied by a linen bandage to her back, and another suckling at her breast, while she is employed in handling the oar, or guiding the helm. I have also continually observed women on shore engaged in the most laborious employments, with an infant fastened to their breast. Such unpleasing, and it may be added to the feeling mind, such an affecting spectacle, is never seen in any of those parts of Tartary through which the embassy passed; for the women there, as well as in the northern provinces of China, have their feet crippled from their infancy, so that they can never submit to such fatiguing occupations. I was permitted to take the measure of a lady's foot, who was twenty years of age, which measured no more in length than five inches and an half. Of this compression of the feet, it may, indeed, be said to be a partial practice.

Lord Macartney, with the whole suite, went ashore, and took possession of the residence which the East India Company's supercargoes had provided for the use of the embassy, during its stay at Canton. This temporary habitation was far superior, in point of accommodation, to any we had seen in our long journey through this country: nor was it among the least agreeable circumstances of our present situation, that we saw, once again, a domestic arrangement which partook of the habitual comforts of our native soil.

CHAPTER XXV

Some account of Canton; proceed from thence to Wampoa, and Macao; brief account of them. – Circumstances relative to the residence of the embassy at the latter place. – Sail for England.

1793, December, Saturday 21. CANTON, or Quanton, is situated on the south side of the river, to which it gives a name, and lies in about one hundred and twelve degrees east longitude, and twenty-four degrees south latitude. It is surrounded by a wall, near thirty feet in height, built of stone, and defended in every direction, particularly towards the river, by very strong forts, mounted with heavy artillery, and garrisoned with numerous troops. It is impossible, however, to form an accurate judgment of its extent, as it is built on a plain; the surrounding country being one continued level, except towards the south, where strangers are never permitted to go.

The streets of the city are, in general, from fifteen to twenty feet in breadth, and paved with broad stones. The houses seldom rise above one story, and are built of wood and brick. The shops have their fronts fancifully ornamented with a balcony, that rises from the pent-house roof over the door, and is adorned with gilding and colours.

The dress of the inhabitants does not differ from those which have been already described. It is, however, a very remarkable circumstance, that notwithstanding this city is so much to the southward of Pekin, the winter should be so severe as to induce the inhabitants to wear furs: and that such cloathing is not altogether considered as a matter of luxury, or confined to the higher order of the people, is evident from the great number of furriers' shops, and, as it appeared, stocked with large quantities of fur cloathing. It consisted of the skin of leopards, foxes, bears, and sheep. The skins were well dressed, made up in the form of jackets, and are worn with the hairy side towards the skin.

The Viceroy's palace at Canton, in form, dimensions, and ornaments, is the counterpart of that which the Ambassador occupied at Pekin: any description of it would, therefore, be superfluous. Of public buildings there are none, unless triumphal arches and gateways, which are very numerous, may be included under that denomination.

The population of this city is estimated at a million of inhabitants: and its large and extensive suburbs may, without exaggeration, be said to contain half that number. Indeed, if the persons are included who navigate, and live on board, the very numerous junks and sampans, or fishing boats, with which the Canton river is covered, this calculation will be considerably exceeded.

This river, as it approaches the city, is equal in breadth to the Thames in its widest part. It abounds also in various kinds of fine fish; but the water is very unwholesome for strangers, till it has stood long enough for a very considerable sediment to subside: the people, however, who live in the junks, use it, as I am informed, for every purpose and without any inconvenience, that I could learn.

When we were on the river that flows by Tong-tchew, an experiment was made respecting the water; and, in a single gallon of it, there remained, on straining it, half a pint of yellow sand; yet in this state the people of the country universally use it, and have no idea of purifying it by filtration. We had no opportunity of becoming acquainted with the common maladies of the people who live on the banks of that river—but water, so charged as this appears to be, must have some prejudicial effects on the constitutions of those who continually use it.

Though this is the only port in the empire of China where Europeans are suffered to trade, all commercial business is transacted in the suburbs, which are about a mile from the city. They are very extensive, and without any pretensions to grandeur or elegance. The streets are, in general, very narrow, and always thronged with people. The houses are of wood, consisting only of a ground floor and upper story: they all contain shops, and are fitted up within after the English manner, to which the inhabitants appear to have a decided partiality. It was not uncommon to see their names written on the signs, in English characters, and adapted to English orthography. The porcelain warehouses which I saw here, are said, and I believe with great truth, to exceed any similar repositories in the world, for extent, grandeur, and stock in trade. The warehouses of the tea merchants are all filled with extensive ranges of chests, which contain an article now become almost a necessary of life in our country, and of increasing use in every other part of Europe.

The factories of the several European companies who trade to this part of the eastern world, are formed in the style of that quarter of the globe to which they belong. The buildings are constructed of stone and brick, on a very substantial plan; but they so far conform to the architectural designs of the country, which I believe to be the best, that they inclose large courts, where there are apartments for the supercargoes and writers, as well as for the captains and mates of ships, during the time they are preparing their cargoes.

There is a range of these factories along the river, but without the least communication with each other; and their general distinction is the flag, or standard of their respective countries, which are seen flying during the day on some conspicuous part of each factory.

The several nations whose trading companies have factories here, are England, Holland, France, Sweden, Denmark, Portugal, Spain, and America. But the English, both from the extent of their buildings, and the number of their ships, appear to possess a greater share of the China trade, than the united commerce of the rest of Europe.

The residence of Lord Macartney was on the opposite side of the river; and, as a mere place of temporary accommodation, was contrived with great judgment, and arranged with uncommon attention to the convenience of the upper order of the embassy: the rest of the suite occupied come of the company's store-rooms, which were fitted up in a very neat and commodious manner for the occasion.

For several days after his Excellency's arrival at this place, he was entertained during dinner by a Chinese play, on a stage erected before the windows of his apartment; and with extraordinary feats of legerdemain, which always accompany the public entertainments of this country.

The Viceroy of Canton paid the British Abassador only one visit during his stay here, which was followed by large presents of sugar-candy, porcelain, and nankeen, to the whole retinue of the embassy.

The gentlemen of the British factory entertained Lord Macartney and the whole suite with great elegance and hospitality, on Christmas day, 1793, and the first day of January, 1794. They also made a requisition to engage the band of music that had accompanied the embassy, from whose service it was accordingly discharged, and immediately entered into that of the English factory; a very valuable acquisition in a country and situation, where so little exterior amusement of any kind is to be obtained.

1794, January. Nor can I, in this place, where I am to take leave of Canton, avoid expressing a regret, that the inhabitants of it are very different in point of honesty, from the people of every other part of China where we had been; at least, as far as my means of observation would enable me to judge. Nor is it with less concern that I attribute this local character, which is knavish in the extreme, to their being the inhabitants of the only place where there is any communication with the natives of other countries.

On the eighth of January, 1794, Lord Macartney set off with his whole retinue in boats, for the Lion man of war, then lying at Wampoa. At the same time Mr. Maxwell and Mr. Barrow, with certain attendants, were ordered to proceed to Macao, to make preparations for the reception of his Excellency at that place. They went in junks by another river, which flows from Canton to Macao, and passing by that place, empties itself into the sea.

The country on each side of the river, between Canton and Wampoa, is rich, fertile, and full of variety:—several lofty pagodas successively enlivened the distant parts of the progressive prospects.

Wampoa is the place where all ships come to an anchor, being universally prohibited to proceed further up the river.

It is a very beautiful and populous village, at the distance of about eighteen miles from Canton. The houses are built of a lead-coloured brick, with numbers of fine trees interspersed among them. The adjacent country is a continued level; but the opposite side of the river, which is not so wide here as at Canton, wears a different and more irregular appearance. At no great distance from this place there is a sand-bank or bar, passed by large vessels but at high water. There are also two necks of land that project on either side of the river, which form the passage called the Bocca Tygris. Here are strong forts on each side with batteries and troops; and as the Lion passed the received a salute of three guns from each of them.

Previous to the departure of Lord Macartney from Wampoa, he received the farewell visit of the attendant mandarin Van-Tadge-In. Of this distinguished personage and amiable man, it is impossible to use expressions beyond the merit he displayed in his care of, and attention to, every person attached to the British embassy. He was appointed by the Emperor of China to attend and conduct it; and, from the time we landed on the shore of the Yellow sea, to our arrival at Wampoa, he never quitted it for a moment. In all this long and various journey, he never neglected for an instant the duties of his office, nor omitted any opportunity of executing them in a manner the most agreeable to those who were entrusted to his care and direction: it was a talk of no common trouble and difficulty; but he was not seen on any occasion or at any time to spare himself in performing it. He was amiable in his manners, affable in his demeanor, ready in his communication, active in his arrangements, and solicitous in the extreme not only to procure all possible accommodations, but to suit them, as far as the circumstances of the country would allow, to European habits and customs. He was a mandarin of the first dais, and held a very high, if not the highest, rank in the army of China: but neither situation or dignity had elevated his mind above the discharge of duties, whatever they might be, or the suggestions of kindness, to whatever objects it might be directed. Nor was this all: in the true spirit of benevolence, he acquired a friendship for those in whose service it had been so continually employed; and his adieu to the Ambassador and the suite was accompanied with the tears of affection.

The mandarin Van-Tadge-In, we well know, is high in the confidence of his sovereign; and, from his virtues, there can be little doubt that he bears a very distinguished character in the sphere of private life, as well as of public duty. But though the testimony of respect which is recorded on this page cannot add to his fame, it will prove, at least, a sincere admiration of superior merit, and a grateful sense of condescending favour in the writer of it.

The Canton river is so well known, that it would be not only superfluous, but impertinent in me, to add another description to the many which have already been given of it.

Wednesday 14. Lord Macartney landed at Macao, and was was received to dinner at the house of the Governor. In the afternoon he went to the residence of Mr. Drummond, one of the supercargoes of the East India Company, where his Lordship resided during his stay at this place. Here the gentlemen of the several European factories have their separate houses, as they are not sufftered to remain at Canton beyond the time necessary to prepare cargoes for the ships of their respective nations.

Macao is situated in 100 degrees of east longitude, and about 22 degrees of south latitude. It is a place of some extent, and built on a rock. The houses are of stone, and constructed on the plan of European architecture, but without exterior elegance: the streets are very narrow and irregular, as they take the unequal surface of the spot on which they are erected. The public buildings consist of churches, convents, and the senate-house, which terminates the only spacious and level street in the town. The Governor's house is situated on the beach opposite the landing place, and commands a beautiful prospect, but is not remarkable for external elegance or interior accommodation. Contiguous to it is the English factory, a plain, commodious building; the other factories are in the same style, and all of them surrounded with gardens. The upper parts of Macao command very extensive views of the sea and adjacent country. The harbour is very commodious, and sheltered from the winds, but will not admit ships of great burden. The town is defended, in all directions, by strong forts mounted with heavy cannon, and garrisoned with Portuguese troops. The sea runs into the harbour, through a narrow channel between the Ladrone islands and the town, and forms a fine bay behind it, extending at least four miles, when it is bounded by a neck of land that separates it from a large river. Here the Chinese have a fort that looks towards the Portuguese territory, and it is the principal duty of the garrison to prevent strangers from passing the limits of it. No one is suffered to walk on the neck of land, nor is any boat permitted to approach that side of the shore. There is a small, pretty island, in the middle of the bay, which contains the habitation of a mandarin, who frequently resides there, but seldom visits the town.

Macao is generally supposed to be situated on an island; but the fact is otherwise; nor is there any natural barrier which separates it from the Chinese territory. The whole extent of the Portuguese possessions does not exceed four miles in length, and one mile and an half in breadth: the limits of which are accurately determined, and cannot be passed without danger.

This place is divided in its jurisdiction between the Portuguese and Chinese over their respective people. The latter, however, exact very heavy duties on all goods landed, or shipped, on account of the European factories. There is a Governor, and a Judge, appointed by the court of Lisbon, who have an arbitrary power vested in them, to the extent of their jurisdiction. There is also a Portuguese custom-house and quay, on the south side of the town, where all ships coming into the bay are obliged to pay a duty. There are not more than two hundred and fifty European soldiers for the defence of the place, who are well cloathed, and whose pay is very much advanced on their arrival there.

The residence of Lord Macartney was or of the most beautiful spots that the imagination can conceive. It was small, but built in the English manner, and surrounded with pleasure grounds of considerable extent, beautifully disposed and planted for prospect, and for shade. The view which it commands combines a most delightful picture of river and sea, of cultivated island, and mountainous shore.

The Chinese who reside in this place, retain their own customs with a rigid preference; nor has the long intercourse they have here had with Europeans of different nations, induced them to deviate in the least article from the long-established, and, as it appears, invariable usages of their country.

Macao was originally fortified by a wall, a great part of which still remains, to the east-ward of the town, where it passes between two hills, and connects itself with a fort, and a convent, that appear on their summits.

Without this wall is the common burying-ground of the place, where I saw the memorials of several of my countrymen, whose ashes repose at such a distance from their friends and native land. This cemetery, however, is exclusively occupied by the Chinese, and such Europeans who are not of the Roman Catholic persuasion; as the papists have particular places of interment for those who depart this life in the faith of their church.

1794, March. At this place Mr. Plumb quitted the service of the embassy. He was very amiable and obliging in his conduct to every one engaged in the same service with himself. He was offered a suitable provision, if he would return to England; but, though he appeared to part from his European friends with a sensible regret, he very naturally preferred to return to the bosom of his family and friends, from whom he had been so long separated, and to pass the remainder of his days in the country that gave him birth.

Lord Macartney remained at Macao till the eighth day of March, 1794, when his Lordship, and the whole retinue, embarked from the Governor's house. The troops were all drawn out on the beach on the occasion, with six brass field-pieces, from which they fired a salute of nineteen guns, which was answered by several forts.

The Lion received Lord Macartney with a salute of fifteen guns, and every other mark of respect; as did also the King Charles, from Spain, and the Bon Jesus, from Portugal, with three country ships belonging to the Engish East India Company.

Sunday 16. In the afternoon the fleet of homeward-bound East Indiamen anchored off Macao roads, to proceed under convoy of the Lion to England, when they, severally, saluted the Commodore with nineteen guns as they successively came to anchor. The companions of our outward-bound voyage, the Jackall and Clarence brigs, as the embassy was concluded, were sold; the former to Capt. Proctor, in the marine service of the East India Company, while the latter found a purchaser at Macao.

Monday 17. Early this morning the signal was made for the fleet to weigh; and at seven the Lion got under sail, in company with the following ships:

Lord Thurlow,	Lord Walsingham,
Glatton,	Triton,
Abergavenny,	Henry Dundas,
Exeter,	Ceres,
Hindostan,	Ofterley, and
Royal Charlotte,	

The Jackall, the Company's marine brig.
Hawke,
Warley,
To these homeward-bound English ships may be added,

The King Charles, Spaniard;

Bon Jesus, Portuguese;

General Washington, American.

At eleven the signal was made to form the order of sailing, and the whole fleet stood to sea.

1794, April,Tuesday 8. No occurrence happened of any kind worth relating, till three o'clock in the afternoon of this day, when the Henry Dundas made the signal for seeing six strange sail, east-south-east. A sail to the north-east proved to be the Nancy grab, of Bengal. At four, the Hindostan and Exeter received a signal to chase. At five, shewed our colours to a brig and several prows.

The brig was commanded by a Moorish captain, and well armed: the prows were also mounted with cannon, as one of them returned, with a single shot, the fire of the English ships, to bring them to. These prows had upwards of fifty Malays in each vessel, and frequently do a great deal of mischief on the coast of Sumatra, where we now were, as well as in other parts of these seas.

Friday 11. Saw two strange sail, in consequence of which all the guns were shotted, and the ship was cleared for action. They were, however, soon discovered to be English; and instead of the sharp returns of enemies, we interchanged the salutes of friendship.

Monday 14. We anchored at Angara Point; where we were employed in wooding and watering till Saturday the nineteenth; when the whole fleet set sail, and continued its course for England, except the Jackall brig, which now separated from us.

Tuesday 15. Nothing occurred between Angara Point and Saint Helena, except several very heavy gales of wind, particularly in doubling the Cape of Good Hope.

We this day anchored at Saint Helena. His Majesty's ships

the Sampson of sixty-four guns, Capt. Montague, and the Argo, Capt. Clarke, of forty-four, etc. had arrived that morning.

June Thursday 19 – July Tuesday 1. Lord Macartney and his retinue went on shore, where they remained till the first day of July, when they returned on board, and the fleet set sail for England, with the addition of the following ships which we found at anchor here on our arrival: (the two men of war excepted)

The Sampson,   64 guns,
The Argo,   44 ditto,
And the following East-Indiamen:
General Coote,
Fitzwilliam,
Belvidere,
Fort-William,
Marquis of Lansdown, with
The South Sea Whaler, Lucas of London.

Thursday 3. We parted company with the General Washington, who saluted the Commodore with nine guns, which were returned in the usual manner.

This morning the Sampson fired a gun, and made the signal for a fleet. After some hours of suspense, and having made every preparation for an engagement, it proved the outward-bound fleet of East-Indiamen, under convoy of his Majesty's ship Assistance, Capt. Brunton; which now parted company with his convoy, and joined our fleet.

Nothing occurred during the remainder of our passage, that would justify my adding a line to this page, till the third of September, when at three A.M. we were seriously alarmed with running foul of a fleet off Portland Roads; which was soon discovered to be the grand fleet, under the command of Earl Howe, coming up the Channel. This strange accident was attended, however, with no other inconvenience than the damage which was received by the Royal Charlotte, Triton, and Osterley Indiamen.

At five o'clock P.M. we anchored safe, after a long and curious voyage, at Spithead; and soon felt the inexpressible satisfaction of once more treading the terra firma of our native country.

CHAPTER XXVI

Brief account of the passage from Hoang-tchew to Chusan, by Captain Mackintosh, etc. – Various customs of the Chinese, etc. – Miscellaneous articles, etc.

Of this short account of the passage of Hoang-tchew to Chusan, by Captain Mackintosh, and the gentlemen who separated from the embassy at the former place, to join the ships at the latter, I speak on the authority of others; and, therefore, give it a place among the miscellaneous matter which I could not introduce elsewhere, without breaking the chain of narration which the nature of the work appears to require.

The river which took this detachment of the suite to Chusan, differed very little, as I was informed, in exterior appearance from those that have been already described. A succession of mountains and rocks, and cultivated plains, formed the natural scenery of its banks, while the pagoda and the palace, the village and the city, were the artificial objects that enlivened or ennobled the prospect which the stream offered to the voyagers on it.

But this river met with interruptions that we never experienced in those on which we passed and its course was occasionally broken by cataracts of a deep fall and formidable appearance. Such circumstanccs would necessarily impede the navigation of the rivers where they present themselves, if the unparalleled industry, perseverance, and I may surely add, the ingenuity of the Chinese, had not surmounted this obstacle; and in a manner, which it requires some confidence in those who informed me of it, to relate.

To accelerate the passage of vessels at those places where the difference of levels forbids any further progress on the surface of the water, the powers of mechanism are applied to let the vessel down into a lower stream, or lift it up into an higher one, in the following manner. In the first place, two strong stentions are fixed in the center of the river, from which two large beams are made to project in a state of suspension over the water: to these, strong blocks are attached, with ropes of sufficient strength; so that when a junk arrives at the place, she is well secured afore and aft, to preserve an equilibrium; when the persons, who are always stationed at these places for the purpose, and are accustomed to the business, hoist the junk, with its passengers and cargo, from one part of the river into the other, over every intermediate obstruction. So certain is this extraordinary operation, that it occupies but a few minutes in its execution, and is not considered by those who navigate these rivers as attended with greater danger, or more liable to accident, than many other frequent contingencies which are inseparable from the voyages on them.

Captain Mackintosh and his party were treated by the mandarins of the different cities and towns through which they passed, with a degree of attention and hospitality equal to that which the embassy itself received. They were ten days in their passage from Hoang-tchew to Chusan.

I shall now proceed to give some detached accounts of the manners and customs of the Chinese, as they were offered to my observation.

To give an accurate description of the marriage ceremony in China, is to do little more than to reply to the Abbé Grolier, whose account of the Chinese nuptials, as well as of many other of their cuiloms,- is altogether erroneous. The Abbé says, "On the day appointed for the ceremony, the bride is first placed in an inclosed chair, or palankin, when all the articles that compose her portion are borne before and behind her by different persons of both sexes, while others surround the lady herself, carrying flambeaux, even in the middle of the day." The marriage ceremony which I saw at Macao, had little in common with this description, but the palankin. The bride, seated in that machine, was preceded by music, and ensigns of various colours were borne by men both before and in the rear of the procession, which consisted principally of the relatives of the bride and bridegroom, who escort her to the house of her husband, where a feast is prepared, and the day is passed in mirth and festivity. Nor is the evening concluded with those absurd ceremonies with which the Abbé Grolier, and other authors, have ridiculously encumbered the consummation of a Chinese wedding.

The idea which he and others have propagated of the rigid confinement of the Chinese women, is equally void of truth. In different parts of that extensive country different customs may prevail; and the power of husbands over their wives may be such as to render them masters of their liberty, which they may exercise with severity, if circumstances should at any time suggest the necessity of such a measure, or caprice fancy it; but I do not hesitate to assert, that women, in general, have a reasonable liberty in China; and that there is the same communication and social intercourse with women, in Europe, is considered as a predominant charm of social life.

The Abbé has also alerted, with equal ignorance of the country whose historian he pretends to be, that masters are desirous of promoting marriage among their slaves, in order to increase the number of them, as the children are born to inherit the lot

314

of their parents. This is a mere fable, as there are no such class of people as slaves in the Chinese empire. They cannot import slaves in their own vessels, which are never employed but in their domestic commerce; and he must be afflicted with the most credulous ignorance, who believes that they import them in foreign bottoms. If, therefore, there are any slaves in China, they must be natives of the country; and among them, it is well known, that there is no class of people who are in that degrading situation.

Certain classes of criminals are punished with servitude for a stated period, or for life, according to the nature of their offences; and they are employed in the more laborious parts of public works. But if this is slavery, the unhappy convicts, who heave ballast on the Thames, are slaves. There is a custom, indeed, in China, respecting this class of criminals, that does not prevail in England, which is, their being hired for any service they are capable of performing: and this frequently happens, as these convicts may be had at a cheaper rate than ordinary labourers. This regulation, however, has one good effect, that it exonerates government from the expense of maintaining such unhappy persons without lessening the rigor or disgrace of the punishment. But I re-assert that slavery, by which I mean the power which one man obtains over another, by purchase, or inheritance, as in our West India islands, is not known in China. Indeed, some of the Chinese in the interior parts of the country were, with difficulty, made to comprehend the nature of such a character as a slave; and when I illustrated the matter, by explaining the situation of a negro boy, called Benjamin, whom Sir George Staunton had purchased at Batavia, they expressed the strongest marks of disgust and abhorrence. The conversation to which I allude took place at Jehol, in Tartary; but at Canton, where the communication with Europeans gives the merchants a knowledge of what is passing in our quarter of the globe, poor Benjamin was the cause of some observations on his condition, that astonished me when I heard, and will, I believe, surprise the reader when he peruses them. The boy being in a shop with me in the suburbs of Canton, some people who had never before seen a black, were very curious in making inquiries concerning him; when the merchant, to whom the warehouse belonged, expressed his surprise, in broken English, that the British nation should suffer a traffic so disgraceful to that humanity which they were so ready to prosess: and on my informing him that our parliament intended to abolish it, he surprised me with the following extraordinary answer, which I give in his own words: — "Aye, aye, black man, in English country, have got one first chop, good mandarin Willforce, that have done much good for allau blackie man, much long time: allau man makie chin, chin, hee, because he have got more first chop tink, than much English merchant-men; because he merchant-man tinkee for catch money, no tinker for poor blackie man: Josh, no like so fashion." The meaning of these expressions is as follows: "Aye, in England, the black men have got an advocate and friend, (Mr. Wilberforce) who has, for a considerable time, been doing them service; and all good people, as well as the blacks, adore the character of a gentleman, whose thoughts have been directed to meliorate the condition of those men; and not like our West India planters, or merchants, who, for the love of gain, would would prolong the misery of so large a portion of his fellow-creatures as the African slaves. But God does not approve of such a practice."

That some general knowledge of the politics of Europe may be obtained by the mandarins and merchants in the port of Canton, might be naturally expected, from their continual communication with the natives of almost every European country; and as many of them understand the languages of Europe, they may, perhaps, sometimes read the Gazettes that are published in our quarter of the globe. But that the question of the slave trade, as agitated in the British Parliament, should be known in the suburbs of Canton, may surprise some of my readers as it astonished me. Nor will it be unpleasing to Mr. Wilberforce to be informed, that, for the active zeal which he displayed in behalf of the nations of Africa, in the senate of the first city of Europe, he received the eulogium of a Chinese merchant beneath the walls of an Asiatic city.

There are frequent festivals in China, and we saw at Macao the principal of them, which celebrates the beginning of the New Year. According to the Chinese calendar, it commences on the second day of our month of February, and is observed with great joy and gladness throughout the whole empire, and by an entire suspension of all business. Of any religious ceremonies, that usher in the dawn of the year, I cannot speak, as all the distinctions of the season which appeared to us, consisted of feasting by day, and fireworks by night. This festival is prolonged, by those who can afford it, for several days: and they, whose circumstances confine their joy to one day, take so much of it, that they generally feel its effects on the next.

Of the manner in which they keep or observe their ordinary holidays, I shall give the following account:

In the first place they purchase provisions according to their situation and capacity, which are dressed, and placed before a small idol, fixed on an altar, with a curtain before it: and such an altar, in some form or other, every Chinese has in his habitation, whether it be on the land, or on the water, in an house, or a junk. This repast, with bread and fruit, and three small cups of wine, spirits, and vinegar, are, after a threefold obeisance from the people of the house to the idol, carried to the front of their dwelling: they there kneel and pray, with great fervour, for several minutes; and, after frequently beating their heads on the ground, they rise, and throw the contents of the three cups to the right and left of them. They then take a bundle of small pieces of gilt paper, which they set on fire, and hold over the meat. This ceremonial is succeeded by lighting firings of small crackers, which hang from the end of a cane, and are made to crack over the meat. The repast is then placed before the idol or Josh, as it is called (a term which means a deity) and after a repetition of obeisances, they conclude with a joyous dinner, exhilarated by plenty of spirits, which are always boiled in pewter or copper vessels before they are taken.

On the first of March it is usual, according to ancient custom, for dramatic pieces to be performed on stages in the principal street of the different towns throughout the empire, for the amusement of the poor people, who are not able to purchase those pleasures. This beneficent act continues for a succession of several days; at the expense of the Emperor; so that every morning and evening, during this period, the lower classes of the subjects enjoy a favourite pleasure without cost, and bless the hand that bestows it on them.

Of the knowledge of medicine among the Chinese I can say no more, than that I was witness, in one instance, to a skilful application of it, in the case of John Stewart, a servant of Capt. Mackintosh; who, on our return from Jehol, had been seized with the dysentery, which increased so much on the road, that at Waunchoyeng, there were no hopes entertained of his being able to leave that place. Whether it arose from the desire of the patient, or was suggested by any person in the suite, I know not, but a Chinese physician was called to his assistance; when the man's case was explained to him by Mr. Plumb, in the presence of Sir George Staunton. The physician remained a considerable time with his patient, and sent him a medicine, which removed the complaint, and restored him to health.

The people are, in general, of an healthy appearance: it is very rare, indeed, to see persons marked with the small pox; and, except in the sea-ports of Macao and Canton, several of the disorders unfortunately so frequent in Europe are not known in China.

The caxee is the only current coin in China: any other species of money is absolutely forbidden. It is made of a white metal, and is about the size of our farthing, with a small square hole driven through the middle, for the purpose of running them on a string to be composed into candareens and maces: but although the terms candareen and mace are employed to certify a certain quantity of caxees, there are no coins in the country which bear that specific value; so that, in fact, they are only imaginary denominations, like our pounds, etc.

The comparative estimation of the caxee with British money cannot be ascertained with any degree of accuracy, as it bears no sterling value even in that country; every province having its particular caxee, which is not current in any other. In the province of Pekin a Spanish dollar will produce, in exchange, from five hundred to five hundred and eighty caxees, according to the weight of the dollar, which the Chinese prove by a small steel-yard like ours in England, though they sometimes employ scales. In the province of Hoang-tchew the dollar obtains from seven hundred to seven hundred and fifty caxees; in other places it will find a still more various exchange.

I cannot conclude this volume without paying a tribute of respectful veneration to the great and illustrious, the wise and beneficent Sovereign of China; who, in a long reign of near sixty years, has, according to the general voice of his people, never ceased to watch over and increasc their happiness and prosperity. Of the manner in which he administers justice, and gives protection to the meanest of his subjects, the following anecdote, which I frequently heard in the country, is an affecting example.

A merchant of the city of Nankin had, with equal industry and integrity, acquired a considerable fortune, which awakened the rapacious spirit of the Viceroy of that province: on the preternce, therefore, of its being too rapidly accumulated, he gave some intimations of his design to make a seisure of it. The merchant, who had a numerous family, hoped to baffle the oppressive avarice that menaced him, by dividing his possessions among his sons, and depending upon them for support.

But the spirit of injustice, when strengthened by power, is not easily thwarted in its designs; the Viceroy, therefore, sent the young men to the army, seized on their property, and left the father to beg his bread. His tears and humble petitions were fruitless; the tyrannical officer, this vile vicegerent of a beneficent sovereign, disdained to bestow the smallest relief on the man he had reduced to ruin; so that, exasperated by the oppression of the minister, the merchant, at length, determined to throw himself at the feet of the sovereign, to obtain redress, or die in his pretence.

With this design he begged his way to Pekin; and, having surmounted all the difficulties of a long and painful journey, he at length arrived at the imperial residence; and, having prepared a petition that contained a faithful statement of his injuries, he waited with patience in an outer court till the Emperor should pass to attend the council. But the poverty of his appearance had almost frustrated his hopes; and the attendant mandarins were about to chastise his intrusion, when the attention of the Emperor was attracted by the bustle which the poor man's resistance occasioned: at this moment he held forth a paper, which his Imperial Majesty ordered to be brought to his palankin; and, having perused its contents, commanded the petitioner to follow him.

It so happened, that the Viceroy of Nankin was attending his annual duty in the council: the Emperor, therefore, charged him with the crime stated in the poor man's petition, and commanded him to make his defence: but, conscious of his guilt, and amazed at the unexpected discovery, his agitations, his looks, and his silence, condemned him. The Emperor then addressed the assembled council on the subject of the Viceroy's crime, and concluded his harangue with ordering the head of his tyrannical officer to be instantly brought him on the toint or a sabre. The command was obeyed; and while the poor old man was wondering on his knees at the extraordinary event of the moment, the Emperor addressed him in the following manner: Look, said he, on the awful and bleeding example before you, and as I now appoint you his successor, and name you Viceroy of the province of Nankin, let his fate instruct you to fulfil the duties of your high and important office with justice and moderation.

APPENDIX:
CONTAINING AN
ACCOUNTS OF THE TRANSACTIONS
OF THE
SQUADRON
DURING THE ABSENCE OF THE
EMBASSY,

Till their Return on Board his Majesty's Ship, the Lion, at Wampoa.

APPENDIX

Remarks on Board his Majesty's Ship the Lion, in the Yellow Sea.

August 1793 Monday 5. Moderate and cloudy. A.M. killed a bullock, weight 341lbs. got all the baggage into the junks, with soldiers, mechanics, servants, botanists, etc. At half past eight the Ambassador went on board the brigantine Clarence, manned the ship, and saluted him with 19 guns and three cheers, as did the Hindostan.

Tuesday 6. Ditto weather. Adam Bradshaw, a light dragoon, departed this life, and his body committed to the deep. A.M. washed the lower and orlop decks, fumigated the ship with devils, washed the sides and beams with vinegar.

Wednesday 7. Light breezes and cloudy. People employed occasionally. A.M. killed a bullock, weight 282lbs. sail-makers repairing main-top-sail.

Thursday 8. Ditto weather. At 9 P.M. the Clarence anchored, and brought the Jackall's men on board. At half-part four weighed and made sail, sounded in 7 and 9 fathoms water. At noon killed a bullock, weight 301lbs. Hindostan and Clarence in company.

Friday 9. Moderate and cloudy. P.M. served tobacco, sounded from 15 to 17 fathoms water, observed several small meteors in the air. At 6 A.M. saw a junk steering S. E. Killed a bullock, weight 323lbs. saw the land bearing south-east.

Saturday 10. At anchor off the high land of Tangangfoe.

Light breezes and clear. P.M. at sun-set extremes of Mettow islands from S.E. to E. by N. 5 or 6 leagues distant. A.M. killed 2 bullocks, weighed 400lbs. At 8 the high land of Tangangfoe N.E. by E. 3 or 4 leagues. At noon came to with the coasting anchor in io fathoms water — soft mud.

Sunday 11. Moderate and hazy. At half-past noon the Hindostan came to. At 6 weighed; at 9 made the anchoring signal with a gun, and came to with the coasting anchor in 9 fathoms water, Mettow islands from N.E. by E. to east: killed a bullock, weight 290lbs. At 5 A.M. weighed and made sail. At 7 shoaled our water from 9 to ½ 7. ¼ 7 and ½ 4 fathoms water. At 8 came to in 7 fathoms water, Mettow island from N. by W. to E. by N. At half-past 9 weighed.

Monday 12. Light airs and squally. At half-past 3 P.M. came to with the coasting anchor in 21 fathoms water, Tangangfoe town, S. by W. ½ W. killed a bullock, weight 287lbs. A.M. received a present of provisions and vegetables. Sailed the Clarence.

Tuesday 13. Light breezes and cloudy. P.M. received several hogs, sheep, etc. At 7 weighed, sounded from 21 to 16 fathoms water, tacked occasionally, washed the lower and orlop decks, and the sick birth with vinegar. At noon the Hindostan in company.

Wednesday 14. Light airs, inclinable to calm. P.M. 5 made Sail. At 7 shortened sail. and came to in 11 fathoms water with the coasting anchor, eastermost of Mettow islands. North, a low rocky point S. S. E. 3 or 4 miles. At 7 weighed and made sail. At noon the Clarence joined us.

Thursday 15. Light breezes and cloudy. P.M. tacked occasionally. At half-past 6 shortened sail and came to with the coasting anchor in 9 fathoms, cape Cheatow E. by S. Departed this life Philip Payne, seaman. At 5 A.M. committed his body to the deep, weighed and tacked occasionally.

Friday 16. Moderate and cloudy. P.M. at 2 came to with the coasting anchor in 7 fathoms water, cape Cheatow N. ½ E. A.M. at 7 the Clarence weighed and made sail to found. At 9 we weighed, foundings from ¼ 4 to ½ 5 fathoms water, cape Chcatow N. by W. Employed occasionally.

Saturday 17. Coon Coon Island 37°3'3 N. Light airs. P.M. tacked occasionally. At half-past 6 the westermost point of the land E.N.E. – the eastermost of Coon Coon Sheen islands N.W. by N. tacked every 2 hours. A.M. hove to and hoisted in the launch, killed a bullock, weight 289lbs. Hindostan and Clarence in company.

Sunday 18. Light airs. At 4 P.M. in 1st reef top-sails extremes of the land to the easterward S.E. by E. A.M. sounded from ½ 13 to 16 fathoms water. At 7 tacked, sounded in 16 fathoms water. Hindostan and Clarence in company.

Monday 19. The Continent S. S. W. distant 7 leagues. Light breezes and cloudy. P.M. sent the yawl to sound to what appeared to us a shoal, but proved to be the reflections of the clouds. At 6 extremes of the land from S. E. by E. to W. by S. distant 3 leagues, tacked occasionally, and sounded in 30 fathoms water. A.M. killed a bullock, weight 280lbs. washed lower and orlop decks. Hindostan and Clarence in company.

Tuesday 20. Mandarin's Cap. N.W. by N. 37° 19' N. Ditto weather with a south-east swell. P.M. at 3 squally. At 5 light airs, saw the land from S. by W. to S.W. by W. 6 or 7 leagues. At midnight calm. At 4 A.M. light airs, with a S. E. swell. At 6 cape Chanton, S.S.W. 19 fathoms water. Employed occasionally.

Wednesday 21. Light airs with a south-east swell. P.M. at 3 squally. At 4 cape Chanton N.W. ½ N. Sounded in 16t fathoms water. At midnight clear. A.M. employed occasionally.

Thursday 22. Moderate and clear, P.M. saw a whale, and at half-past 9 an eclipse of the moon, which continued to half-past

12, never being more than two thirds eclipsed, by which we calculated our longitude to be 122 deg. 41 min. east of Greenwich.

*It appears evident from this observation, that those histirians who have treated of China were very imperfect in their geographical estimates; as Pekin, which is considerably to the eastward of that coast where the observation was taken, is only stated at 116 degrees of east longitude; so that the difference is almost 7 degrees; a cogent proof of their ignorance relative to the interior history of this empire.

Friday 23. Light breezes and clear. P.M. at 2 sounded in 22 fathoms water. At midnight sounded in 20 fathoms water. At 4 A.M. sounded in 19 fathoms water. At 6 made sail, and at 8 sounded in 20 fathoms water.

Saturday 24. Light breezes and clear. Tried the current and found it set N. ½ E. 2 miles; at 8 cloudy, at midnight no bottom; at 3 A.M. made sail, washed the lower and orlop decks, Hindostan and Clarence in Company.

Sunday 25. Moderate and clear. P.M. made sail; at midnight departed this life Robert Chambers, cooper; at 2 A.M. committed the body to the deep; at 6 saw the land bearing from S. by E. to S.S.W. at 7 squally, at 9 Clarence island 6 or 7 miles bearing S. by E. at noon sounded in 20 fathoms.

Monday 26. Whelps S.S.W. Buffalo's Nose N W. Moderate and cloudy. At 5 P.M. extremes of Jackall's island from west to W.N.W. At 6 departed this life Wm. Bell, seaman; at 9, committed the body to the deep. Lion island W. Blunt Peak island W. by S. in 7 fathoms water.

Tuesday 27. Off Tree-a-top island. Fresh breezes with rain. At 1 P.M. came to with the coasting anchor in 5½ fathoms. Buffalos Nose S.S.E. Truman's island S. ½ E. At 5 out launch, at 6 the cutter with Mr. Whitman went on an embassy to Chusan. A.M. frequent gusts of wind.

Wednesday 28. Fresh breezes and squally, with rain. People employed occasionally.

Thursday 29. Squally, with rain. Departed this life Mr. Wm. Cox, 4th Lieutenant, sent the body on shore to be buried. A.M. arrived the Clarence.

Friday 30. *At anchor off Kitto's Point.* Squally, with rain. At 2 P.M. weighed, turning through Goff's Passage; at 7 anchored in 11 fathoms, Kitto N. E. ½ N. At 5 A: M. weighed, at half past 7 anchored in 10 fathoms, Kitto Point N. 1/2 E. Read Mr. Omanny's commission as 4th Lieutenant, and Mr. Warren's as acting to the ship's company.

Saturday 31. Squally, with rain. Employed occasionally; sent the cutter to sound and washed the decks.

Sunday, September 1. Moderate and cloudy. A.M. half-past 4 weighed, working into Chusan harbour, at 11 came to with the coasting anchor in 9 fathoms; carried out a kedge with 4 hawsers to warp the ship into the anchoring place; at half past 11 weighed. Employed, warping.

Monday 2. Fresh breezes and squally, with rain at times. Employed warping to the kedge; at 2, came to with the best bower in 6 fathoms, moored ship a cable each way, best bower to the N.N.E. small bower S.S.W. center of the hill at the east end of Chusan town N.E. by E. ¾ mile. A.M. light breezes and fair; loosed sails to dry. Employed rounding the small bower cable.

Tuesday 3. *At anchor in Chusan harbour.* Light breezes and cloudy. P.M. sent down royal masts and rigging, unbent the sails, and unrove the running rigging. A.M. sent down top-gallant masts. Received water.

Wednesday 4. Light breezes and fair. Employed overhauling day the rigging; at 6 A.M. sent the sick on shore, struck yards and top-masts, shipped fore and main top-masts.

Thursday 5. Light breezes and cloudy. Employed overhauling the top-mast rigging; received a bullock on board.

Friday 6. Light breezes and cloudy, with lightning in the S.W. People fitting the rigging afresh. A.M. launch watering, killed a bullock, 201 lbs. Departed this life Richard Welsh, seaman; committed his body to the deep.

Saturday 7. Moderate and cloudy. Employed about the top-mast rigging, received 2 bullocks and 105 pumpkins. A.M. employed as before, killed a bullock, 204lbs. washed lower or orlop decks.

Sunday 8. Moderate and fair. Employed about the rigging, killed a bullock, 286lbs. A.M. yawl watering, received a bullock and 4 goats. Punished a seaman with 12 lashes, for theft.

Monday 9. Light breezes and cloudy. A.M. received water per launch, rigged the top-mast, killed a bullock and 4 goats, 291lbs. received water per launch and 2 bullocks.

Tuesday 10. Moderate and cloudy, with heavy rain. A.M. light winds and fair. People about the rigging and blacking the yards, caulking over the side, launch watering, killed 2 bullocks, 395lbs.

Wednesday 11. Light airs and cloudy. Employed overhauling the rigging. A.M. roused up the best bower cable and stowed staves under it. Departed this life Stephen Pounce, seaman; interred the body. Moderate and cloudy, with heavy rain.

Thursday 12. Moderate and cloudy, with heavy rain. Employed as necessary. A.M. launch and yawls watering.

Friday 13. Moderate breezes with rain. Employed as before, launch and yawls watering. A.M. employed clearing the after-hold and rattling the top-mast rigging. Saluted a mandarin with 3 guns.

Saturday 14. Moderate breezes with rain. P.M. employed in the after-hold, saluted a mandarin with 3 guns, and a superior one with 7. A.M. punished a seaman with 12 lashes, for drunkenness.

Sunday 15. Light breezes and cloudy. Arrived the Endeavour brig. A.M. the Endeavour saluted with 7 guns, returned 5; received water, employed starting it; swayed up the lower yards, fidded top-gallant and royal masts, rattled the lower rigging, received bread from the Hindostan.

Monday 16. Moderate breezes. Employed watering.

Tuesday 17. Light winds and cloudy. P.M. received bread from the Hindostan. A.M. sent the launch to the Jackall's assistance, she being on shore without the harbour. Employed shifting the coals and rattling the rigging. Fired 21 lower deck guns, being the Emperor of China's birthday; killed a bullock and 4 goats.

Wednesday 18. Moderate and cloudy. Launch assisting the Jackall; at midnight fresh breezes and squally, with violent peals of thunder and fierce flashes of lightning; struck the royal masts, secured the pumps and magazines. A.M. yawls watering.

Thursday 19. Moderate and cloudy. Yawls watering, got royal masts upon deck, struck yards, top-masts and top-gallant-sails. A.M. people employed occasionally; received from the Hindostan beef and pork.

Friday 20. Light breezes and clear. Employed in the after-hold, caulkers on the larboard side, received on board beef from the Hindostan, and water per launch.

Saturday 21. Light breezes and clear. Employed stowing the after-hold; launch and yawls watering, received from the Hindostan beef and pork. A.M. received from ditto beef, oatmeal, and flour; cooper repairing the heads of the casks. Scraped the larboard side.

Sunday 22. Light breezes and cloudy. Employed stowing away provisions, coopers as before. A.M. cleared hause, launch watering.

Monday 23. Light breezes and cloudy. Caulkers as before. A.M. punished a seaman with 12 lashes, for insolence. Coopers and caulkers as before, launch and yawls watering. Received bread from the Hindostan.

Tuesday 24. Light breezes and cloudy. Caulkers on the larboard side, received peas from the Hindostan, received water. Painters about the stern. A.M. received pork, beef, oatmeal, and flour, from the Hindostan.

Wednesday 25. Fresh gales and squally. People and painters as before. A.M. employed scraping the sides, received 4 bullocks, killed 2, weight 426lbs.

Thursday 26. Fresh gales and squally. People and painters as before. A, M. received rum from the Hindostan, received water on board.

Friday 27. Moderate and fair. Received beef and pork from the Hindostan, painters about the sides, caulkers, and sail-makers employed, people in the hold, received a bullock, killed 2, weight 432lbs. A.M. received from the Hindostan beef, pork, suet, and vinegar. Launch and yawls watering.

Saturday 28. Moderate and fair. Painters as before, sail-makers repairing the Clarence sails, received pease, oatmeal, and flour from the Hindostan. A. M, received vinegar, beef, and pork, from the Hindoflan, and water per yawls.

Sunday 29. Fresh breezes and cloudy. P.M. completed the holds, received 3 bullocks, killed 2, weight 371lbs. received from the Hindoflan beef, pork, suet, and vinegar. A.M. yawls watering.

Monday 30. Fresh breezes and cloudy. Gunners painting the guns. A.M. carpenters repairing the launch on shore, people pointing the ends of the cables, received bread from the Hindostan, served vinegar to the people.

Tuesday October 1. Moderate and fair. Gunners as before, carpentcrs repairing the launch, killed two bullocks, 311lbs. set up the fore and main rigging. A.M. sail-makers as before.

Wednesday 2. Moderate and cloudy, with rain. Received 8 bullocks, 16 goats, and 700 bundles of wood, saluted a mandarin with 7 guns, received wood from the Hindostan. A.M. coopers shaking empty casks; yawls watering, killed 2 bullocks, 367lbs.

Thursday 3. Moderate and cloudy with rain. Carpenters repairing the launch, killed 2 bullocks, 305lbs. coopers as before. A.M. received 2 bullocks, scraped lower gun-deck, yawls watering.

Friday 4. Fresh breezes and cloudy. Carpenters lining the lower deck ports and repairing the launch, cleared hause, received water, killed 2 bullocks, weight 307lbs.

Saturday 5. Fresh breezes and cloudy. Employed working up junk, carpenters as before, caulkers caulking the launch's bottom. A.M. rain. Employed working up junk, killed 2 bullocks, 300lbs. received water per yawls.

Sunday 6. Fresh breezes and cloudy. Carpenters, caulkers, and sail-makers as before; received water per yawls, killed a bullock, 241lbs. A.M. received on board a bullock, cleared hause.

Monday 7. Moderate and fair. Caulkers on lower-gun deck, received 4 bullocks. A.M. received water per yawl, washed and smoked lower gun deck, carpenters repairing the launch, sail-makers repairing the foresail, caulkers on board the Clarence, killed 2 bullocks, 431lbs.

Tuesday 8. Moderate and fair. Caulkers and sail-makers as before, received 2 bullocks, killed 1, weight 273lbs. A.M. employed watering, surveyed the gunner's stores, the sick returned on board.

Wednesday 9. Light breezes and fair. Carpenters lining lower deck ports. A.M. swayed up top-masts, lower yards, and top-gallant-mails. Sail-makers as before, killed a bullock, 228lbs.

Thursday 10. Light breezes and fair. Employed sctting up the top-mast rigging, coopers repairing banacoes, received water per yawls. A.M. cleared hause, killed 2 bullocks, 240lbs.

Friday 11. Light breezes and fair. P.M. sent a party to bring off the launch. A.M. rove the running rigging and bent the sails, sail-makers making hammocks, received wood, killed a bullock, 215lbs. yawls watering.

Saturday 12. Moderate and fair. P.M. received 2 bullocks and 4 goats, killed 2 bullocks, 479lbs. The grand mandarin paid us a visit, saluted him with 7 guns on his coming on board and leaving the ship, manned ship at his passing. A.M. employed getting ready for sea.

Sunday 13. Moderate and fair. Received 4 bullocks and 8 goats. A.M. unmoored ship, employed watering; at 11 weighed the small bower, and shifted 2 cables length further down, and came to in 6 fathoms, received 2 bullocks, and killed one of them, weight 228lbs. Sailed the Endeavour and Jackall.

Monday 14. Light breezes and cloudy. Received wood and 2 bullocks, killed 1, weight 293lbs. sail-makers as before: departed this life Thomas Addison, seaman; interred the body.

Tuesday 15. Moderate and cloudy. Caulkers on the main deck. A.M. killed a bullock, weight 234lbs.

Wednesday 16. Light breezes and fair. Sent 10 invalids on board the Hindostan. A.M. punished a seaman with 12 lashes, for riotous behaviour.

Thursday 17. Moderate and clear. Saluted a mandarin with 7 guns, returned the Hindostan's salute with 9: at 5 weighed, found the anchor stock gone; half-past five came to with the coasting anchor in 19 fathoms, Deer Island N. by W. A.M. half-past 9 weighed, turning towards Kitto Point, carpenters employed making an anchor stock.

Friday 18. Moderate and clear. P.M. at 3 running through Goff's Passage; at 4 saluted a mandarin with 4 guns on his leaving the ship; half-past 5 came to with the coasting anchor in 7 fathoms, Buffalo's Nose S.W. by W, hoisted in the launch, killed 2 bullocks 462lbs. A.M. at half-past 6 weighed and made sail, Clarence in company; at noon Patchacock island N. W. ½ N. 7 or 8 miles.

Saturday 19. Fresh breezes and cloudy. Half-past noon extremes of Hefan islands from S.W. by W. to S. W. by S. at 6 in 2d reefs, at 10 in 3d reefs: at noon the Clarence in company.

Sunday 20. Fresh breezes and cloudy. P.M. at 2 out 3d and 2d reefs; strong breezes, at nine in 3d reefs. A.M. killed a bullock, 224lbs. at 9 lowered the top-sails to keep the Clarence a-head; sail-makers making a covering for the pinnace: at noon Clarence in company.

Monday 21. Fresh breezes. P.M. at 2 hoisted the top-sails, at 6 spoke the Clarence, at 5 A.M. out 3d reefs, at 10 saw 6 junks, at noon several junks in sight; carpenters stocking the best bower anchor, Clarence in company.

Tuesday 22. Fresh breezes and cloudy. P.M. at 5 out 2d, reefs. A.M. at 6 saw Pedro Blanco N. by E. ½ E. at noon the west end of the great Lama N. by. W. east end N.E. by N. armourers at the forge.

Wednesday 23. At anchor off Macao, among the Ladrones. Ditto weather. P.M. at 4 the body of the island of Tarlow Chow N.N.W. shortened sail and came to with the coasting anchor in 6¾; sent the Clarence to Macao. A.M. at 9 weighed and made sail; at noon came to with the coasting anchor in 8 fathoms, Tarlow Chow N. By E. ½ E. Macao town W.N.W. 7 or 8 miles.

Thursday 24. Ditto weather. Yawls watering. A.M. gunners stretching breeching stuff, coopers repairing banacoes.

Friday 25. Ditto weather. Yawls watering. A.M. squally; coopers as before.

Saturday 26. Fresh breezes and cloudy. Yawls watering, sail-makers making coats for the masts. A M. yawls as before, shewed our colours to a ship in the offing, cleared the boatswain's store-room.

Sunday 27. Fresh breezes and fair: Yawls watering. A.M. employed occasionally.

Monday 28. Light breezes and pleasant weather. P.M. the Clarence anchored close to us; passed us the Washington, American ship: A.M. sail-makers covering man-ropes, and other jobs.

Tuesday 29. Ditto weather. Yawls watering; at 8 sailed the Clarence for Macao. A.M. at 6 weighed, found the stock of the coasting anchor gone, made sail, half-past 9 shortened sail and came to with the best bower in 10 fathoms, Tarlow Chow N.W. by W. ½ W. Sam Coke N.W. ½ N. carpenters fitting a new anchor stock, a swell E.S.E. At noon weighed and made sail, sail-makers as before.

Wednesday 30. Off Macao, among the Ladrones. Light breezes and pleasant weather. Half-past 12 found the fore-top-mast sprung, down top-gallant-yard and mast upon deck, shortened sail. At 4 came to with the best bower in 10 fathoms water, Tarlow Chow E.N.E. down fore-top-mast, sent the pinnace and yawl on service, carpenters fishing the foretop-mast, and cutting another fid hole, washed lower gun-deck.

Thursday 31. Fresh breezes and foggy. Carpenters as before, swayed the fore-top-mast and end, and slatted the top-mast rigging. A.M. fidded the top-mast, and set up the rigging; carpenters making a coasting anchor stock, the boats returned on board, anchored a schooner with hands for us.

Friday November 1. Ditto weather. Swayed up the fore-yard. A.M. swayed up top-gallant-masts, carpenters as before, sail-makers repairing the main-sail.

Saturday 2. Moderate and fair. P.M. at 4 arrived a ship from the N.N.E. which chewed French colours, sent the boats after her, cut the best bower cable and made sail, fired a shot to bring her to. At 6 the run into the Typer, hauled our wind to port, tacked occasionally: at half-past 7 came to with the coasting anchor in 5 fathoms water, Macao town W. by N. 3 miles, Tarlow Chow 7 or 8 miles: at 9 the boats returned. A.M. at 5 sent an officer to Macao. Departed this life Stephen Smart, quarter-master: at 8 committed his body to the deep: half-past 9 weighed and made sail, turning towards the buoy of the best bower, coopers packing empty staves.

Sunday 3. Moderate and fair. P.M. at half-past noon shortened sail and came to with the coasting anchor in our old birth; employed creeping for the end of the best bower cable, and getting it entered hove short on it. A.M. hove up the best bower. Half-past 8 weighed the coasting anchor and made sail; washed lower and orlop decks. At noon the body of Tarlow Chow, E. by S. 6 miles.

Monday 4. Light airs and cloudy. At 5 Affes Ears S. ¼ W. 6 miles. A.M. at 9 fresh breezes and cloudy: split the fore-sail, clewed it up to repair, rove double sheets and proper tacks.

Tuesday 5. Ditto weather. At 6 Pedro Blanco N.N.E. A.M. at 3 in 2d reefs. At 7 split the main-top-sail, clewed it up to repair. Half-past 7 tacked down top-gallant-yards, carried away the mizen-top-sail-yards, unbent the sail, sheeted home main-top-sail. At noon got up a jury mizen-top-sail-yard, and set the sail. Carpenters making a mizen-top-sail-yard.

Wednesday 6. Moderate and cloudy. P.M. unbent the fore-sail and bent another; sounded in 23 fathoms water. At midnight in 3d reefs, and furled mizen-top-sail. At 3 A.M. set the mizen-top-sail; sail-makers making a new main-top-sail out of two sprit-sail courses. Half-past 10 tacked out 3d reefs. At noon got up a proper mizen-top-sail-yard. Pedro Blanco, E.S.E. 7 miles.

Thursday 7. Ditto weather. P.M. unbent the mizen to repair, sail-makers as before, and repairing the fore-sail. A.M. tacked occasionally.

Friday 8. Fresh breezes and cloudy. P.M. at 8 more moderate, out 2d reefs. At midnight tacked. A.M. carried away the jib-stay and haul-yards, spliced them: carpenters making a machine to make rope with.

Saturday 9. Ditto weather. P.M. at 4 unbent the new fore-fail, and bent the old one. At 2 A.M. carried away the jib-tack, repaired ditto. At 5 carried away the main-top-gallant-sheet, spliced ditto, employed making a rope.

Sunday 10. Ditto weather. P.M. at 5 in 2d reefs; at 7 found the foretop-mast sprung 5 feet above the cap, in 3d reef fore-top-sail, down foretop-gallant-yard and mast. A.M. strong gales, clown main and mizen-top-gallant-yards: at 4 in 4th reef fore-top-sail: at noon squally, furled the mizen-top-sail.

Monday 11. Fresh gales and cloudy. P.M. at 4 wore ship: at 6 strong gales and hazy, with a heavy sea, handed fore-top-sail: at 8 heavy gales, handed main-top-sail, split the main-sail, set main-stay-fail, and handed part of the main-sail, set main-stay-sail, and handed part of the main-sail, the remainder having blown from the yard: at 9 set main-top-sail: at half-past 9 set mizen-top-sail: at A.M. split main-top-sail, furled it, balanced and set rnizen: at 3 set storm, fore and mizen-stay-sail: at 6 split main-stay-sail, hauled it down to repair: at half-past 8 set fore-top-sail, close reefed, unbent main-tap-sail, and sent it down: at noon a heavy sea.

Tuesday 12. Fresh gales and cloudy. P.M. at 2 unbent the remainder of the main-sail, bent another main-top-sail, and set it close reefed. At 6 furled the fore-sail, bent another and furled it. A.M. at 5 out 4th and 3d reefs fore-top-sail, and 3d reef main-top-sail, set mizen-top-sail, saw the land N.W, by W loosed courses. At 8 found the main top-mast sprung in the cap, out 2d reef mizen-top-sail, At noon the mst end of the Great Lama, E.N.E. Affes Ears W.S.W. swayed up fore-top-gallant-mast.

Wednesday 13. Light breezes and fair. P.M. at 4 out all reefs: at 7 shortened sail and came to with the coasting anchor in 16 fathoms water, Cockerpow N.W. by W. A.M. at 9 weighed and made sail: at 11 in 2d reefs, tacked ship. At noon the Grand Ladrone, W. by E. a heavy swell.

Thursday 14. Fresh breezes and clear. At 1 came to with the coasting anchor in 13 fathoms water, the Grand Lama, W.S.W. A.M. at 6 weighed and made sail: at 10 shortenel sail and came to with the coasting anchor in 7¼ fathoms water, Tarlow Chow, N.N.E.

Friday 15. Ditto weather. P.M. at 4 weighed and made sail; at half-past 4 came to with the coasting anchor in 7 fathoms water, Sam Coke, E. ½ S. A.M. half-past 6 weighed and stood into Sam Coke. At 7 came to with the coasting anchor in 6 ¼ fathoms water, Sam Coke, E.S.E. 1 mile, got fore and main-top-gallant-masts upon decks: yawls watering.

Saturday 16. Fresh breezes and hazy with rain. Sent the main-top-mast down, and another up; carpenters making a fore-top-mast out of the old main one, sent down the fore-top-mast, and cut it up, it being unserviceable in its proper use. A.M. fidded main-top-mast, and swayed up the yard: employed making rope.

Sunday 17. Fresh breezes with rain. Carpenters converting the main-top-mast into a fore one. A.M. arrived the Clarence.

Monday 18. Moderate and cloudy. Dried sails, yawls watering, swayed up top-gallant-masts, and set up the rigging: yawls watering.

Tuesday 19. Moderate and hazy. P.M. yawls as before, carpenters repairing the Clarence boat, sail-makers repairing the fore-sail, people making rope, sailed the Clarence. A.M. rove new fore and main-top-sail-braces: yawls watering.

Wednesday 20. Fresh breezes and fair. P.M. at 5 loosed and hoisted top-sails, fired 4 shot to bring to a vessel in shore, she shewed English colours, sent a boat on board her. A.M. mustered at quarters, found the ship driving, dropt the best bower, carpenters repairing the yawl.

Thursday 21. Fresh breezes and cloudy. P.M. at 1 fired a shot and brought to a brig under American colours, sent an officer to examine her papers, and found she belonged to the isle of France, named the Emilla, Dumist and Roufell, merchants on the said island, last from the N.W. coast of America, with 271 fur skins on board; detained her as a prize, sent a petty officer and 7 men to take charge of her. At half-past 1 weighed the best bower. A.M. at 5 the prize fired 3 musquets, sent a boat on board her, found her driving, secured her with hawsers, etc. At 8 found our ship driving, dropt our hest bower; the yawl that was astern of the prize was lost, the officer brought her stern on board.

Friday 22. Fresh breezes. P.M. at 4 hove up the best bower, employed making rope. A.M. found the ship driving, dropt the bell bower. Half-past 7 struck top-gallant-masts, made the hawser, the prize was riding by fast to the ship through the gun-room port forward.

Saturday 23. Fresh gales and cloudy. P.M. employed working up junk: at 5 anchored the Clarence. A.M. the Clarence drove, with 3 anchors, a head; sail-makers repairing the fore-sail.

Sunday 24. Fresh breezes and clear. Sail-makers repairing the main-sail, the Clarence weighed her anchors, sent her under the lee of Tarlow Chow for shelter. A.M. mustered at quarters.

Monday 25. Fresh breezes and clear. People employed occasionally. A.M. weighed the best bower, and parted the coasting cable, let go the small bower, yawl, and pinnace creeping for the end of the cable. Cast off the prize.

Tuesday 26. Moderate and clear. Received 9 seamen and a boy from the Clarence, yawl and pinnace as before, sail-makers repairing courses. Departed this life Thomas Steward, seaman.

A.M. committed the body of the deceased to the deep.

Wednesday 27. Moderate and clear. P.M. yawls and pinnace as before, creeping for the end of the cable, which they got; employed securing it. A.M. sailed the prize brig for the Typer, to land the prisoners at Macao.

Thursday 28. Light breezes and fair. P.M. at 5 hove up the best bower and warped the ship to the coasting anchor, got the end of the cable on board, and weighed the anchor, made sail. At half-past 5 came to with the best bower in 7¼ fathoms water, Sam Coke, E. by S. 2 miles. A.M. yawls watering, bent the coasting cable, the inner end to the anchor, washed below. Arrived the Emilla.

Friday 29. Moderate and cloudy. P.M. at 3 weighed and stood in for the watering island, but falling little wind came to again with the best bower in 5 fathoms water, Sam Coke, E. by S. sail-makers repairing the courses. A.M. yawls watering.

Saturday 30. Fresh breezes and cloudy. P.M. at 3 weighed and stood nearer to Sam Coke. At 4 came to with the hest bower in 6 fathoms water, body of Sam Coke, E. by S. 1 mile. A.M. Stayed the masts, and set up the rigging.

Sunday December 1. Fresh breezes and cloudy. Small boats watering, sail-makers repairing courses. A.M. caulkers about the water ways.

Monday 2. Fresh breezes and cloudy. Employed occasionally. A.M. employed knotting yarns and making rope, sail-makers repairing maintop-sail. People employed occasionally.

Tuesday 3. Fresh breezes and cloudy. Small boats watering the Clarence. A.M. hoisted out the launch, sent a kedge anchor and hawser on board the prize; carpenters repairing the pinnace.

Wedneday 4. Moderate breezes. Employed making rope, sailed the prize from the Typer. A.M. fresh gales and hazy. Sail-makers repairing the main-top-sail. Sailed the Clarence.

Thursday 5. Moderate and hazy. Employed as before. A.M. small rain, swayed up top-gallant-mast. At 11 the Clarence arrived from the Typer, with some Engish seamen from the Emilla prize, sent the boat on board and took them out.

Friday 6. Light breezes and thick foggy weather. Launch watering, carpenters repairing the boats. A.M. half-past 8 weighed and made sail, tacked oceasionally; passed by 3 Dutch ships.

Saturday 7. Moderate breezes and pleasant weather. P.M. at 2 tacked, half-past 3 came to with the best bower in 14 fathoms water, the north end of Linton island, N. by W. south end E. N. E. anchored the Clarence. A.M. washed decks, sailed the Clarence.

Sunday 8. Light airs and clear. Launch watering, received 3 bullocks. A.M. killed them, weight 513lbs. launch watering.

Monday 9. Light airs and cloudy. P.M. received 11 bullocks, killed 4, weight 689lbs. A.M. struck main-top-gallant-mast, and lowered the main-yard, listed the main rigging, to splice one of the shrouds, it being stranded in the wake of the service; sent the yawl on board the Warley Indiaman in the offing.

Tuesday 10. Moderate and hazy. Employed fitting the main shrouds. A.M. passed by the Warley for Canton, employed staying the main-sail and setting up the rigging, anchored the Clarence. A.M. Swayed up the mainyard and rattled the rigging.

Wednesday 11. Light breezes and clear. P.M. sail-makers making skreens for the fore hatchway, sailed the Clarence. A.M. received water per launch, carpenters repairing the cutter.

Thursday 12. Light breezes and clear. P.M. received wood and 6 bullocks. A.M. launch watering, swayed up royal masts, people making nippers and rope, painters employed painting the cabin and cutter; arrived the Clarence.

Friday 13. Light airs and fine. P.M. received water. A.M. at 6 weighed and made sail, as did the Clarence, running towards the Bocca Tigris. Half-past 9 inclinable to be calm, shortened sail, and came to with the best bower in 6 fathoms water, veered ½ a cable the entrance of Bocca Tigris, N.N.W.

Saturday 14. Fine weather. At 3 P.M. weighed and made sail, tacked occasionally. At 7 in tacking touched the ground, run the after guns forward, hoisted out the boats to tow, sent a boat to sound round the ship. Half-past 7 the Clarence anchored on our larboard bow, carried out a hawser to her, and hove on it, but finding her anchors came home, sent down royal and top-gallant-yards and royal masts on decks, struck top-gallant-masts, furled the sails, barred the ports in fore and aft, stocked the coasting anchor, and bent the stream cable to it, when a-ground the body of Langute, S.W. ¾ west, the north eastermost of Sama Chow islands, N. by W. the south westermost W.S.W. at dead low water having 15 feet the ship heeled to port. A.M. employed starting water, carried out the coasting anchor to the S.E. and hove a strain, but could not move her, started more water. Half part 11 the Clarence weighed and anchored on our larboard, killed 5 bullocks, weight 640lbs.

Sunday 15. Light breezes and pleasant weather. P.M. the Clarence hauled along-side and received our small bower anchor and 2 cables, slipt the end from the hawse, and took it in at the larboard stern port. Half-past 3 the Clarence hauled off and laid the anchor to the eastward, hove taut: at ¾ flood slipt the stream, and hove off to the eastward in 6 fathoms water. A.M. fidded top-gallant and royal masts, swayed up the yards, Clarence weighing the coasting anchor.

Monday 16. Light breezes and fine weather. Hauled the Clarence alongside and took the coasting anchor from her. A.M. at 7 weighed and made sail, half-past came to with the best bower in 5 fathoms water, moored ship, the north fort at the entrance of Bocca Tigris, N. south fort N.W. by N. a small rocky island at the entrance, N.N.W. received 1733lbs of beef.

Tuesday 17. Light breezes and fine weather. Punished a searnan with 12 lashes, for theft, exercised great guns, sail-makers making a quarter-deck awning.

Wednesday 18. Light breezes. Received water. A.M. sail-makers as before, gunners thumming a screen for the magazine, saluted a mandarin of the first order with 3 guns on his coming on board.

Thursday 19. Weather as yesterday. Saluted a mandarin with 3 guns on his leaving the ship, passed by a ship under English colours. A.M. arrived 4 ships bound to Canton, viz. Ceres, Abergavenny, Osterly, and Lord Thurlow; sent a boat on board them.

Friday 20. Light breezes and clear. People making stoppers, sail-makers repairing the Clarence's fore-top-sail, exercised the guns.

Saturday 21. Moderate and cloudy. Got the guns out of the cabbin, completed 6 on the quarter deck and 2 on the fore-castle. A.M. half-past 9 weighed with a pilot on board to take us up the river, received 103lbs. fresh beef.

Sunday 22. Light breezes and cloudy. Employed working through the Bocca Tigris, 2 forts saluted us with 3 guns each, we returned equal number, they likewise displayed the colours over the guns and drew themselves up in ranks: at 5 shortened sail, and came to with the small bower in 5 fathoms water, veered ¾ of a cable the north point of Sketop island N.N.W. a pagoda on the said island N.W. A.M. sail-makers making a poop awning, people making stoppers.

Monday 23. Light breezes and clear. P.M. weighed and made sail, half-past past 2 anchored with the small bower in 6½ fathoms, veered ¾ of a cable, the north point of Sketop island N.N.W.½W. A.M. at 3 weighed, out all boats to tow, which were assisted by

19 Chinese boats with another tow-rope; half-past 3 crossed the bar between 2 lines of boats full of lights; half past 7 came to with the small bower in 6 fathoms, veered away and moored ship S.W. by S. and N.E. by N. a cable on the small bower to the ebb and ½ a cable to the flood, a square pagoda S.E. offshore 1 ½ cable, Wampoa town W.S.W. 2 miles, found here the Hindostan, Royal Charlotte, Osterley, Ceres, Earl of Abergavenny, and Lord Thurlow, English Indiamen; Jackall, Company's marines and 2 Americans; received on board wood.

Tuesday 24. Light breezes and clear. P.M. employed occasionally. A.M. read Mr. Omanney's commission from the Lords of the Admiralty as 5th Lieutenant, but as Lieut. Cox's commission was vacant, Captain Gower ordered him to act as 4th; read the order, and Mr. Tippet's acting order as 5th, likewise Mr. Warren's as 6th; also the articles of war, and Capt. Gower's orders to the ship's company; washed decks, arrived the Glatton.

Wednesday 25. Light breezes and clear. People employed occasionally. A.M. received 715lbs. of fresh beef: at noon part of the soldiers that attended the Ambassador to Pekin returned on board.

Thursday 26. Light breezes and clear. P.M. and A.M. carpenters fixing spare cabbins under the half deck.

Friday 27. Light breezes and hazy. P.M. employed occasionally. A.M. people making rope, came along-side several country boats with the Ambassador's baggage, and 13 chests of presents for the company from the Emperor of China.

Saturday 28. Moderate and cloudy. P.M. received water, employed stowing the Ambassador's wine, punished 2 seamen with 12 lashes each, for disobedience of orders; and 4 ditto with 12 lashes each, for disobedience and drunkenness.

Sunday 29. Light breezes and hazy. Employed stowing the after-hold. A.M. received. 595lbs. fresh beef.

Monday 30. Light breezes and hazy. P.M. manned ship for his Excellency Viscount Macartney, as did the Hindostan and Clarence; his Excellency was cheered by all the ships as he passed; at 2 he came on board, at 5 he left the ship. A.M. employed fleeting the rigging, punished 2 seamen with 12 lashes each, for disobedience of orders.

Tuesday 31. Light breezes and fair. Employed letting up rigging, and in the after-hold, cleared hause, sent 13 casks of beef and 7 of pork on board the Hindostan. A.M. arrived the Lord Walsingham from England, sent 30 casks of beef and 25 of pork on board the Warley, employed in the hold.

1794, January, Wednesday 1. Light breezes and fair. Employed in the hold, sent 13 casks of beef and 7 of pork on board the Hindostan.

Thursday 2. Moderate and cloudy. P.M. employed as before. A.M. carpenters nailing battin in the hold to stow staves over, coopers setting up casks.

Friday 3. Fresh breezes and fair. P.M. employed in the holds, fell overboard and was drowned Alexander Ramsay, seaman. A.M. employed in the hold.

Saturday 4. Light airs and clear. Arrived the Hawke and Exeter from England. A.M. people employed occasionally, arrived the Henry Dundas from England.

Sunday 5. Light airs and clear. People as necessary, received a boat load of water, arrived a Spanish ship, received a top-mast from the Ceres Indiaman. A.M. employed in the after-hold, washed lower gun decks.

Monday 6. Light breezes and fair. Employed in the afterhold, coopers repairing banacoes, punished a dragoon with 12 lashes, for disobedience of orders, riotous behaviour, and drunkenness.

Tuesday 7. Moderate and cloudy. Received 3064lbs. of bread and some of the Ambassador's baggage. A.M. bent sails, punished 2 seamen with 12 lashes each, for theft, and a marine with 12 lashes, for insolence.

Wednesday 8. Moderate and cloudy. Employed as necessary. A.M. employed getting the baggage belonging to the Ambassador and suite on board, received on board wood.

Thursday 9. Light breezes and fair. Manned ship and saluted Lord Macartney with 15 guns on his coming on board, his suite likewise embarked, employed getting in the baggage. A.M. cleared hause, and unmoored ship; at 11 weighed the small bower, and dropt a little lower down the river, and came to with the small bower, received 1600lbs. of fresh beef.

GLOSSARY
OF
CHINESE WORDS.

CHINESE.	ENGLISH.
Tongau	Sugar.
Pytong	Ditto, moist.
Pyntong	Sugar-candy.
Swee	Water.
Lyangswee	Ditto, cold.
Kieswee	Ditto, hot.
Pynswee	Ditto, ice.
Man-toa	Bread.
Tchau	Tea
Ttchau-woo	Tea-pot.
Tchee-tanna *(in the northern provinces)*	Eggs.
Kee-tanna *(in the southern provinces)*	Ditto.
Yien.	Tobacco.
Yien-die	Tobacco-pipe.
Jee-au	Fowls.
Yaut-zau	Ducks.
Ly-fau *(in the northern provinces)*	Rice.
Faun-na *(in those about Hontchew provinces)*	Rice.
Mee *(southern provinces)*	Ditto.
Joo-au	Wine.
Samtchoo, or Sowtchoo.	Spirits.
Yeu-oa	Fish.
Loa-boo	Turnips.
Ghutz-yau	Pepper.
Jishimau	To ask the name of a thing or place.
Chou-au	Good.
Boo-chou	Bad.

Yinna . . . . Salt.

Poit-zie . . . . General term for greens.

Tannau . . . . .Coals.

Yoong . . . . A hawk.

Pyeng . . . . .Soldier.

Pyng . . . . Ice.

Quoitzao. . . . . Chop-sticks for eating with.

Laatchoo . . . . Candle.

Tchooa . . . . Light.

Tzou-shia . . . . Shoes, *in general*.

Chow-chow . . . . Visuals *or* meat.

Chee-fanna . . . . To eat meats.

Kowaa . . . . To broil.

Mann, Mann . . . . Stop *or* wait.

Lobb, Lobb . . . . Joining *or* coition.

Tziu . . . . Paper.

Josh . . . . God, *or* Deity.

Chinchin . . . . To supplicate *or* pray.

Youwass . . . . Furnace.

Too-paa . . . . A pagoda.

Tong-joo . . . . A sweet spirit like rum-shrub.

Chop-chop . . . . . . To make haste.

Foockee . . . . Man.

Foockee-lou . . . . . Good-morrow, Sir.

Niodzaa . . . . Milk.

Hoong . . . . Cheese.

Toudzaa . . . . Knife.

Ickoochop . . . . . . Very best.

Icko . . . . One.

Liaungko . . . . . . Two.

Suangko . . . . Three.

Soocko . . . . Four.

Oocko .... Five.
Leowcko .... Six.
Shicko .... Seven.
Packo .... Eight.
Jowcko .... Nine.
Sheego .... Ten.
Sooee .... Sleep.
Hongjoo ...... Red-wine.
Tchau-wanna .. A tea-cup. s
Jeebau .... 2 ¼ cubits *or* 1 yard.
Tyshausuee .... Bed.
Meeoulaa ..... Have not *or* cannot.
Kamshaa ...... gift or present.

About The Author

Frances Wood was Curator of the Chinese collections at the British Library for nearly 30 years. She was responsible for the joint British Museum-British Library exhibition on the Macartney Embassy in 1992. Her work on the collections includes books and essays on the Silk Road and the Stein collection, a survey of Sir Hans Sloane's Chinese books and an essay on William Alexander's sketches made on the Embassy. A graduate of both Cambridge and Peking universities, she has published many books, including "Did Marco Polo Go To China?" and "No Dogs and not Many Chinese".